Mediating Modernism

Mediating Modernism considers the history of modern architecture in Britain; however it is not primarily about the building of architecture itself but about influential architectural ideas and debates. This book brings to light the role of the publications, language and images which, in the act of 'describing', 'interpreting' or 'illustrating' it, in fact create the architecture by articulating and framing it.

Focusing on the crucial role played by the architectural media in creating architectural discourse, Andrew Higgott analyses the key books and architectural journals that have shaped thinking about architecture from the 1920s to today. This review seeks to examine and clarify why British architecture is now a world leader; as well as looking at those ideas that are seen to have negative results.

Seven chapters reflect a succession of discourses, including Brutalism, Archigram and AA School work, over the past eighty years. First, the transformation of architecture to a new style relevant to modern life, then the campaign to reconstruct Britain's cities; later the rejection of the universal approach of modernism in favour of the local and specific in the 1950s. The emphasis on technology in the 1960s proposed the making of architecture that enables rather than exists. More recently, architecture has been re-imagined as closer to art, finally reaching the analysis that architecture is primarily a cultural practice. Over this period, British architecture has adopted more forms, and taken more directions than could have been imagined.

Thus *Mediating Modernism* documents the journey from Blomfield's 1920s conservatism to radical current projects by such practices as Plasma Studio. The chapters identify the process of change, where ideas in architecture shift and modify; at the same time arguing that, in Britain, the history of modern architecture can best be understood through the history of its published media.

Andrew Higgott is Principal Lecturer in the School of Architecture and Visual Arts, University of East London. An architectural historian, he has previously contributed to a number of books including *Travels in Modern Architecture* (Architectural Association, 1989), *Architecture and the Sites of History* (Butterworth, 1995) *The Modern City Revisited* (Routledge, 2000) and *Peter Salter: 4+1* (Black Dog, 2000).

Mediating Modernism

Architectural cultures in Britain

For Flora

best wishes

Andrew Higgott

Andrew Higgott

Routledge
Taylor & Francis Group
LONDON AND NEW YORK

First published 2007
by Routledge
2 Park Square, Milton Park, Abingdon, Oxon OX14 4RN

Simultaneously published in the USA and Canada
by Routledge
270 Madison Ave, New York, NY 10016

Routledge is an imprint of the Taylor & Francis Group, an informa business

© 2007 Andrew Higgott

Typeset in Lucida by Wearset Ltd, Boldon, Tyne and Wear
Printed and bound in Great Britain by TJ International Ltd, Padstow, Cornwall

All rights reserved. No part of this book may be reprinted or reproduced or utilised in any form or by any electronic, mechanical, or other means, now known or hereafter invented, including photocopying and recording, or in any information storage or retrieval system, without permission in writing from the publishers.

British Library Cataloguing in Publication Data
A catalogue record for this book is available from the British Library

Library of Congress Cataloging in Publication Data
A catalog record has been requested for this book

ISBN10: 0-415-40178-X (hbk)
ISBN10: 0-415-40177-1 (pbk)

ISBN13: 978-0-415-40178-4 (hbk)
ISBN13: 978-0-415-40177-7 (pbk)

Contents

	Illustration credits	vi
	Acknowledgements	vii
	Introduction	1
1	Making it new: the discourses of architecture and modernism in Britain	3
2	The mission of modernism: James Richards and the *Architectural Review*	33
3	The forgetting of art: the Abercrombie Plan for post-war London	57
4	The shift to the specific: the new interpretation of materiality in Brutalism and the Functional Tradition	85
5	The opposite of architecture: *Archigram* and *Architectural Design* in the 1960s	117
6	Searching for the subject: Alvin Boyarsky and the Architectural Association School	153
7	Architecture *as* discourse: rethinking the culture of architecture	189
	Select bibliography	205
	Index	212

Illustration credits

The author and publishers would like to thank the following individuals and institutions for giving pemission to reproduce illustrations. Every effort has been made to ensure that material in copyright has been cleared, but in the case of any error or omissions we would be happy to correct them at a later printing. Other photographs are by the author.

Archigram Archive 1.3, 5.1, 5.2, 5.3, 5.4, 5.5
Architectural Association 6.2, 6.6, 6,10, 6,11
Architectural Design 5.7, 5.10, 5.11, 6.1
Architectural Review 2.2, 2.3, 2.4, 2.5, 4.6, 4.10
Valerie Bennett/Architectural Association 6.14
Blueprint Magazine 1.7
Iain Borden 7.2
Eric de Maré/Architectural Association 4.8, 4.9
Elsevier 2.7
Zaha Hadid/Architectural Association 6.7
Nigel Henderson 4.2
E.R. Jarrett/Architectural Association 1.13
Cornel Naf/Architectural Association 6.8
Penguin Books 2.1
Plasma Studio/Peter Guenzel 7.7
Cedric Price/Architectural Association 5.8, 5.9
Mark Prizeman/Architectural Association 6.4
Derek Revington/Architectural Association 6.3
RIBA/Dell and Wainwright 2.6
RIBA/John Havinden 2.8
RIBA/William Toomey 4.4
RIBA Library 4.3b
Routledge 7.1, 7.3
Peter Salter 6.13
Peter St John/Architectural Association 6.9
Mark Smout 7.4
Ada Wilson/Architectural Association 6.5
F.R. Yerbury/Architectural Association 1.8, 1.9, 1.10, 1.12

Acknowledgements

Thanks to individuals who have helped with ideas and discussion in interviews on the subject of the book, particularly Paul Finch, Peter Murray, Ellis Woodman, Fred Scott and Ros Diamond, and Brett Steele and Mark Cousins at the AA. Thanks also for interviews done in the past towards work which became part of this book, particularly the late James Richards, William Firebrace, Nicholas Boyarsky, Nigel Coates and Peter Salter. Thanks to Cliff Nicholls, Head of the School of Architecture and the Visual Arts at the University of East London, and Signy Svalastoga and other colleagues for support in particular of two short periods of sabbatical, in 2001 to formulate the project and in 2005 to write a substantial proportion of it. Thanks to the former Heads of the School of Architecture at UEL, Christine Hawley, the much-missed Ron Herron and for the inspiration of Peter Salter's Headship from 1995 to 2002. Particular thanks to Nick Weaver for his long-term encouragement and support, and for being the first person to invite me to teach architectural history and theory.

The Architectural Association provided a second and more fulfilling education for me after English at Cambridge, and continues to be an important influence, particularly with seminars I have taught there in recent years, including a version of this book in 2002. Teaching at the East London School over two decades has enabled me to develop my ideas and knowledge on a daily basis in a remarkable (and underrated) architectural school: this has been a huge opportunity even if sometimes in the past an overload. Excellent students have provided stimulation, especially on the Masters' programme (now MA Architecture: Interpretation and Theories) since 1995: it would be invidious to pick out individuals in the strong and inventive group of its graduates.

Colleagues at the School who have contributed to this work include James Heesom, Katie Lloyd-Thomas, Nigel Butcher and Tim Wray. In the wider group of teachers of history and theory in schools

ACKNOWLEDGEMENTS

of architecture, including colleagues in AHRA (Architectural Humanities Research Association), I appreciate in particular conversation over the years with Robert Harbison, Brian Hatton, Diana Periton, Iain Borden, Adrian Forty, Jonathan Hill and Sandy McCreery.

The extraordinarily stimulating atmosphere of the AA led by Alvin Boyarsky made it far more than an academic institution and without which, however distant a memory, this book would undoubtedly not have happened.

And thanks finally to members of my family, to Slobodan who introduced me to architecture and friends including Alan, Simon, William and Jonathan and most of all to Ciro.

Introduction

This is a book about the history of British modern architecture, and it is not about buildings but about publications. It takes as its subject certain influential ideas and debates taking place within architectural culture, expressed in key journals as well as books. It takes for granted that buildings do not speak for themselves, but rather through the interpretations that are made of them; and presumes that architectural projects are invariably created within the context of believing in specific ideas.

Each period of the recent past has been characterised by a dominant set of ideas which have then set up a process of action and reaction. The history of modern architecture in Britain is characterised by a series of prevailing theories, each represented in publications that embody as well as recount those ideas. The visual form and design of these publications, the language with which they create their discourse, help to make concrete this new thought. Particularly significant are the *Architectural Review* in the 1930s and 1950s, *Architectural Design* in the 1960s, *Archigram* and recent Architectural Association (AA) publications, as well as official plans and a number of key books all having had a wide influence.

These themes reflect a succession of discourses over the past seven decades. First, the transformation of architecture to a new relevance to modern life, then the necessity of rebuilding the city: later the rejection of the universality of modernism, succeeded by the making of architecture that enables rather than exists. More recently, architecture has been re-imagined as closer to art, repudiating the rational positivism of modern architecture, and finally reaching the analysis that architecture is primarily a cultural practice.

At a fundamental level, the book charts the mediation of modernism in Britain through this extensive period, with the evidence of built work as corroboration. Thus it documents the journey from Blomfield's Regent Street (p. 4) to Plasma Studio's Madrid Hotel

INTRODUCTION

(p. 201). Over this period of eighty years, architecture has adopted more forms and taken more directions than could have been imagined. A walk down a British city street will show the evidence of these key ideas, as disparate buildings created to reflect these positions stand cheek by jowl.

It would be possible to write a longer book with the false trails, the big ideas that never went anywhere, the journals that lasted for one issue. But *Mediating Modernism* refers to the process of change, when ideas in architecture shift and modify: at the same time it asserts that architecture exists through and in the media. As Beatriz Colomina has written, the history of modern architecture and the history of the published media are exceptionally close.

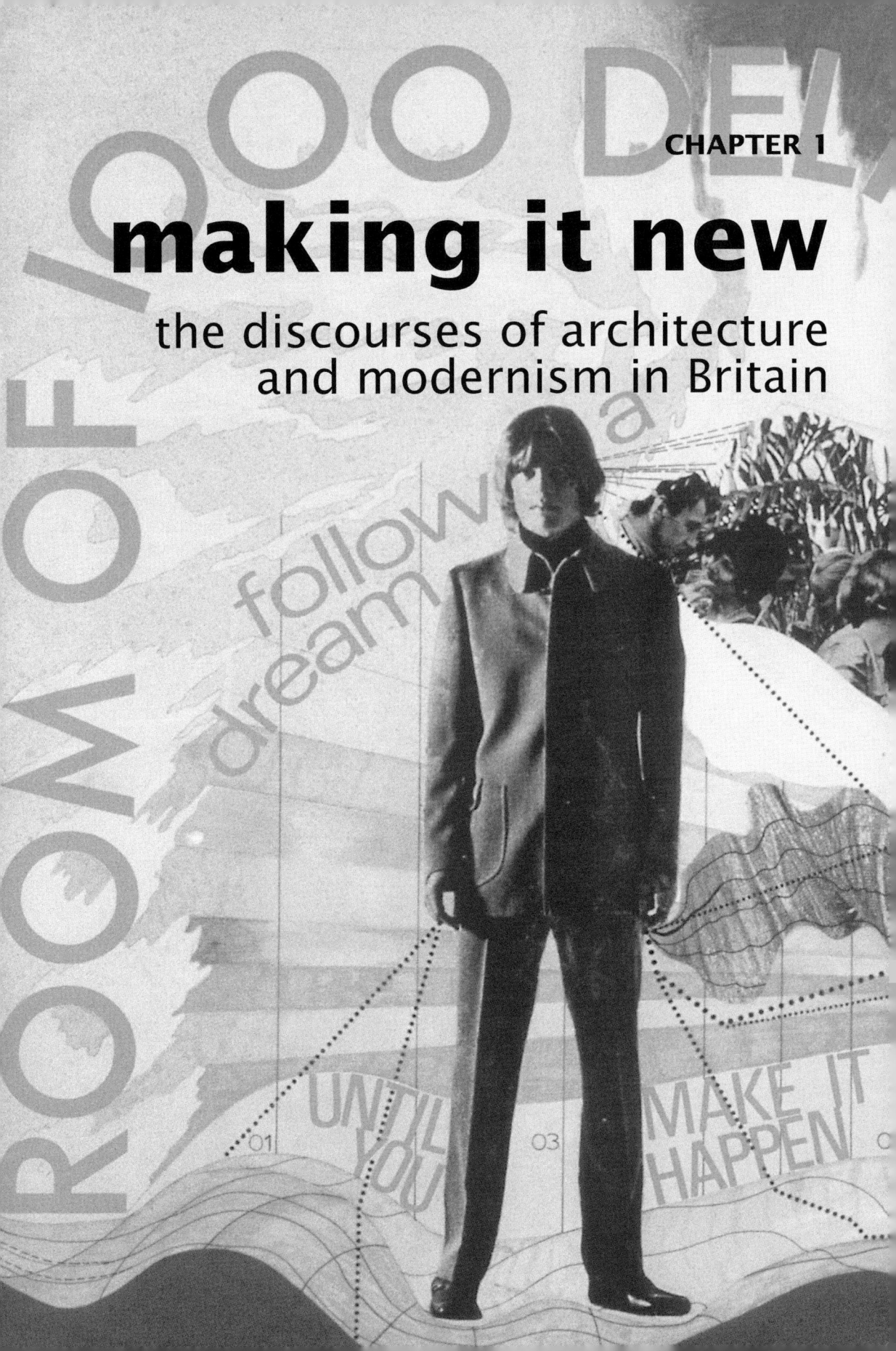

CHAPTER 1

making it new

the discourses of architecture and modernism in Britain

MAKING IT NEW

> Modernism or *Modernismus* as it should be called on the German precedent, has invaded this country like an epidemic, and though there are signs of reaction, its attack is insidious and far-reaching, with the wholly fallacious prospect of a new heaven and a new earth which it dangles before the younger generation.
> (Reginald Blomfield, *Modernismus*, 1934)[1]

The younger generation of Blomfield's[2] time, and the generations that came later, have largely not followed his advice. Instead, the thought of 'a new heaven and a new earth' has generated the process of making and re-making the practice of modern architecture over the intervening seven decades. A series of critical shifts within overlapping and discontinuous discourses aimed to address the question of what, after all, modern architecture should be: the primary purpose of this book is to recount these narratives which were so compelling in their time. Blomfield's book[3] spoke for his own generation of established architects, and was published at exactly the time when modern architecture first emerged to be a convincing force in Britain. He is aware that he is entering into contention with those holding opposite beliefs: in the years after him, a series of influential journals and books continued this dialectic. Modernism, given that it is by definition a culture of resistance, has been manifestly the propagator of polemic which defines the territory it demands to occupy.

Much of the most innovative architecture of the second half of the twentieth century came from Great Britain: the Smithsons, Archigram, Rogers, Foster, Koolhaas and Hadid are among many others whose work gained international significance. Having played no part in the early formulation of modernism, Britain found itself, to much surprise, to be the home of the most significant architectural work. It has been central in the formulation of new polemic and practice more than any other single country, whether in the post-war field of city rebuilding and later the expressions of Brutalism, the technological imperative of Archigram, or the new modernities generated at the Architectural Association (AA) School. But behind the achievements of specific architects and their built and unbuilt work lies a rich architectural culture which can be seen most acutely through key books and journals in their formulation of ideas, and these are examined in the chapters that follow.

It would be possible to write a history of modern architecture in Britain through a series of critical buildings which seem to represent the spirit of their particular time: buildings which have become famous, and form a narrative of the changes and development in the way architecture has been practised. Or it would be possible to take

1.1
Regent Street quadrant, London rebuilt 1923–8 by Reginald Blomfield, author of the anti-modernist text *Modernismus*, 1934.

another line, which would connect those buildings to a series of individuals who seem to have shifted the ground on which architecture stands. But the approach of this book takes a different course, and instead looks at what underlies these phenomena; the debates, issues, questions and assumptions which have been behind these individual projects and individual actions. The idea is, then, of developing a history of British architectural culture, a narrative of the main shifts in architectural thinking: of articulating the different ideas of how architecture should be practised, of what it should be for. And if one does that, it appears that each period had its common ground, a set of assumptions, or perhaps more accurately contained a dialectic of opposing forces. What most forward-thinking people believed to be true in the period of the 1950s was different from what were the background assumptions in the 1960s, and far more dissimilar 'truths' existed in more distant periods. The unspoken assumptions of such positions contrast with each other over time, that for example architecture was obliged to be a social practice, to make the world a better place; or that architecture was above all compelled to relate to new technologies and build new forms emerging from them; or that architecture was essentially a cultural practice which emerged from the specifics of a place and its qualities.

After all, architecture is never in reality about the functional, never simply the fulfilment of a brief: and functional justification is a pretext for the architect's more complex intentions which relate to the cultural context in which he or she participates. Architectural discussion generally focuses on buildings: but many if not most buildings are not *architecture* in the sense of truly forming part of its

1.2
National Theatre, London: Denys Lasdun and Partners, representing an interpretation of pre-war modernism but completed in 1977.

discourse. The speculatively built estate, the industrial installation, or the developers' office block have at best liminal references to the 'art' of architecture. The world is full of such *facsimiles* of architecture in this exacting sense: thus the discourse of architecture as a specific practice and as an art that expresses and interrogates cultural values misses its target if it concentrates on buildings and projects that lack any original aspiration.

The position of this book locates architecture firmly in the wider realm of culture, beyond that of the accustomed dialectic of architecture alternatively being a science or an art. Architectural ideas contain traces of ideologies derived from a far wider range of reference than generally acknowledged: and the making of architecture has been seen on the one hand as the realisation of a political aim, on the other as an expression of the subversion of established structures. In its articulation both of the fundamental values of a culture and the attributes of inhabited space, it relates both on the largest and smallest scale to basic human questions. In the period of modernism, architecture has been seen as the expression of new forms in art, based on abstraction and anti-historical expression. Furthermore, it emerged from and was determined by the new technologies that were available increasingly through the nineteenth and twentieth centuries. But a cultural reading asserts that beyond this, architecture is always the fulfilment of particular ideologies, the making of building projects taking place very much in the context of what is assumed to be appropriate. A cultural interpretation makes little distinction between what is built and what is not: after all, what comes to be built is largely a matter of good fortune, and the availability of finance. Equally, those architects who build extensively are not always those with the most critical ideas, and for the most part are not those who debated and generated the inventive thinking which informs their work.

The particular importance of publications must be emphasised. While discourse – a synonym of discourse is *dialogue* – exists perhaps most of all in conversations, by their nature inevitably unrecorded, those ideas also appear in the form of journal articles, in the editorship of journals, in books which may develop a standing and influence. Texts may define discourses at the same time as not being their sole component. Government reports and the making of strategies by various authorities also express highly specific points of view: the individuals who shape and control institutions are aware of the publication as an embodied expression of their values. Thus the methodology of this book is to analyse specific publications – books, journals and articles – which have been instrumental in transforming the culture of architecture in Britain.

MAKING IT NEW

1.3
***Room of 1000 Delights**,
Peter Cook: Image and
text from the magazine
self-published by the
members of the
Archigram group,
Archigram 9, 1970.*

A second fundamental issue is the great significance in these publications of how they are designed, how their illustrations are used, and what graphic layout employed. Layout and graphics give weight and meaning to their subject and effectively manufacture its importance. The language that is used embodies a particular meaning rather than the simple communication of fact, and certain words are made to focus that interpretation. The published photograph has been one of the most important communicators of architectural ideas, even if, for the most part, it bears little relation to the experience one might have of the built reality it represents. Pictures have a visceral immediacy as the assumed embodiment of truth, despite their many limitations in the representation of architecture; in particular that they can scarcely illustrate space. The reality of architecture portrayed in professional journals and books does not come unfiltered, but is edited, framed and presented in such a way that it is transformed. It *becomes* the architecture: the book or journal constructs a reality rather than representing it. Thus books and articles create architecture; rather than simply talking about it, or simply representing it, they reify an individual and specific set of assumptions and from that point of view make clear what architecture is, and should be. The media provide an alibi, presenting arbitrary architectural intentions as naturally occurring fact. The role of the architectural publication is to provide a correlative to the fortuitous wishes and desires of those designing architecture as well as those interpreting it. Publications furnish the conditions for the transformation and establishment of the values of architectural culture.

Books can thus be powerful things, and in the history of modern architecture in particular, have become highly polemical texts. Le Corbusier's *Vers une architecture*, mistranslated into English by Frederick Etchells as *Towards a New Architecture*,[4] without doubt had the greatest single influence, in its field as revolutionary as Karl Marx's political treatises of the previous century. As a publication it leaves much to be desired, with frequent repetition and lack of structure, in fact disclosing its origin as a series of articles. It declaims rather than argues its position, and this perversely is its strength: there is an effectiveness in hearing and rehearing such phrases as 'a great epoch has begun, there exists a new spirit'. Its reiteration of such axioms, which become calls to battle, cuts through contemporary, more genteel debates. But even more effective are its visual attributes, which set up a new mode of presenting ideas that took account, for the first time in an architectural publication, of the possibilities of layout and photography in the printed media. While none of these qualities is quite so strongly represented in a British publication, it underlines how a publication might work, and each of the publications chosen for discussion here uses the possibilities of layout and image in distinct ways.

Theories of modern life

The approach of this book, as a cultural history of British architecture which has chosen to concentrate on what underlies the production of architecture, is shaped by a reading of theories that interpret the conditions of modern life. Modernism claimed to be objective, the 'making it new' which would deliver the world from the deleterious effects of centuries of stifling tradition that had long ago lost any connection with the actual circumstances of life. Instead of the narratives of myth, religion and history itself, the modern world would face *reality*: as Le Corbusier and Ozenfant wrote in the first edition of *L'Esprit nouveau*: 'Nothing is worthwhile which is not general, nothing is worthwhile which is not transmittable. We have attempted to establish an aesthetic which is rational, and therefore human.'[5] Existing frameworks of meaning were then to be overturned, in favour of the visceral immediacy of authentic life. Thus the long-standing fixed picture of the world was turned around: but the new science of psychoanalysis made the experiencing subject itself a changing and complex entity. The world of the subject and object was a condition of instability.

The Structuralist view, initiated by Ferdinand de Saussure,[6] is that nothing can exist by itself, only by its relationship to other things within a structure. For him, language consists of arbitrarily determined signs, and a word may only be understood in its relation to the structure of language as a whole: thus individual speech is not 'original' but exists on a plane beyond the individual's will and creation as part of an abstracted system. The extension of this into any field of human activity is to undermine the traditional view of the autonomy of the individual act: the individual always operates in relation to a pre-existing system. As the modernist poet T.S. Eliot wrote in relationship to poetry:

> the existing order is complete before the new work arrives, [but] the whole existing order must be, if ever so slightly, altered . . . the past should be altered by the present as much as the present is directed by the past.[7]

In relationship to history, this certainly put in doubt the idea of the 'genius' who as an individual changes the world, an autonomous

1.4
Barbican Estate in the City of London by Chamberlin Powell and Bon, begun 1958: looking towards Mountjoy House, completed 1971: the most successful post-war reconstructed area in Britain, including public buildings and housing for over 4,000.

actor in charge of their medium, and instead sees the individual forming a part of a defined practice.

Roland Barthes developed a very particular and ahistorical practice of criticism, which saw all the products of a culture as equivalent. In his *Mythologies*[8] he talked about the Eiffel Tower, but also gladiator films and steak and chips. Apart from being the unwitting generator of countless later articles which take the products of popular culture very seriously, Barthes' work is important in making clear how meaning is created; the Eiffel Tower 'attracts meaning the way a lightning rod attracts thunderbolts.'[9] Whatever the intention of its 'author', the engineer Gustave Eiffel, the Tower's shifting significance is something for which he is not responsible. As Barthes argued elsewhere,[10] the intentions of the author are meaningless in the development of an interpretation. Any text consists not of one authorial voice but is a montage of unconscious influences and existing texts, as well as the interpretation which the reader brings to it. In relation to architecture, Barthes' position opens up the possibility of a radical clarification of the architect's role in relation to their production: far from being able to control the meaning of a building and the reaction of its users, any work stands as part of a far wider culture, open to interpretation and misinterpretation.

But it is Michel Foucault, with his term '*discourse*', who in *The Archaeology of Knowledge*[11] really set up the framework for a new kind of history and a new basis for criticism. His rendering of De Saussure's Structuralism is that everything exists within a discourse: it is contingent on it and part of it. What he terms 'statements' within a discourse could be a book, an article, an utterance, a client or a building: a *discursive formation* brings these together in their diversity, but can never be definitive, is always provisional, and should not be seen as equivalent to the kind of history which unifies diversity into a singular narrative. As he wrote:

> discourse [is] a group of statements in so far as they belong to the same discursive formation; it does not form a rhetorical or formal unity, endlessly repeatable, whose appearance or use in history might be indicated (and, if necessary, explained); it is made up of a limited number of statements for which a group of conditions of existence can be defined.[12]

Thus it is in Foucault's *archaeology*, a term that does not imply the search for a beginning, that the evaluation of the products of culture can take place, conditioned by an enquiry of rediscovery and free from absolute judgement.

Royston Landau in his essay 'Notes on the Concept of an Architectural Position'[13] is among those who have applied Foucault's thought to architecture. It is his key idea that the *production* of an architect includes their writing, discussion and set of beliefs, quite separate from what his or her buildings might look like, which underlies his study. But Landau also speaks of significant individuals' work apart from those key architects who build what are seen as the most important buildings. This includes authors, editors of journals, those who put on exhibitions, those who run schools of architecture and professional bodies. Landau's position does not privilege the architect who builds over the architect who does not build: but equally would see government policy, the individual significant client and their decisions as equally important, as well as positions taken by those who edit magazines and who head schools and institutions. As Foucault pointed out, the sum knowledge of any subject is a construction that is far more inclusive than a conventional structure of analysis.

Foucault's own position has been a contributing influence on a number of recent books of architectural theory and history. Particularly groundbreaking is Beatriz Colomina's *Privacy and Publicity: Modern Architecture as Mass Media*.[14] For Colomina, maybe the true site of 'modern architecture' as it has been developed is not the suburban location of a series of inconveniently located villas, but the pages of the far more accessible publications that document and present this work. Le Corbusier, for her, is the first architect, and certainly not the last, to understand this and develop his work with reference to its relationship to the media. His *Complete Works*[15] (which are nothing of the kind) carefully present and illustrate his work as a continuum. Presentation is far from straightforward; pictures are manipulated, and unbuilt projects given an equal significance to those that are built. The 'new photography' and the architecture of what came to be called the International Style were both products of a modernism created in response to the machine. While her concern is rather wider in scope, for Colomina modernism's transformation of the house created a public role for private space. But her emphasis on the role of the media in creating rather than simply representing architectural ideologies is the substantial innovation of her book.

Adrian Forty also presents in *Words and Buildings*[16] an important and radical new idea, and sets up a new subject for architectural study – the language that is used by modern architects and by those interpreting it. Words create meaning – and are influential in doing so. 'Structure', the 'user', even 'form', are among the specific terms seen by Forty as decisive in relation to modern architecture. At the outset, he quotes Barthes in his essay 'The Fashion System' who, in relation to the social practice of fashion, writes: 'Why does it interpose, between the object and the user, such a luxury of words (not to mention images), such a network of meaning[?]'[17] The same could be said, Forty argues, for the system of language that runs parallel to the system of the making of buildings: the new words which modernism required were effective in bringing it into being. Each of the eighteen 'key words' whose etymology he analyses as crucial to the making of modernism, have become invisible as their meaning is so widely assumed: 'space', many readers would be surprised to hear, only came into importance in architecture relatively recently with the writing of Semper, while 'flexibility', which might be assumed to be a good thing, had a very specific time span from the 1950s to the 1970s. More fundamentally, Forty, like Colomina, discovered and investigated a new theme within architectural historical analysis which served to deconstruct its meaning and assumptions.

The question of architecture's representation in the published media is one that has far more importance than it has yet been given. Kester Rattenbury's edited collection of critical essays and influential images, *This Is Not Architecture* is one of a small number of publications that have recently appeared.[18] The writing of books which become influential, and even more the editing of magazines – what they choose to include, and very importantly how this material is framed – can be seen to create architectural discourse as much as anything does. The resulting emphasis on the visual as the means to comprehend modern architecture has meant that the architectural photograph can be interpreted as a misrepresentation of a more purposive modernism. The history of modernism has been shaped by the development of the visual media in parallel with the practice of modern architecture: the new architecture, new media and new photography worked together to mutual advantage. Had they not done so, the *forms* of modernism rather than any deeper level of its meaning or realisation, might not have become so pervasive.

The media have a history as a subject, and the work of 'media studies' originated with Marshall McLuhan. A Canadian Professor of English, McLuhan published three books in the 1960s which were highly influential for a new understanding of the media. They developed his radical position, exposing how the printed or electronic medium had a transformative role on all social interaction, even at that time with computers scarcely invented. *The Gutenberg Galaxy* (1962) examined the historical importance of the shift to printing and beyond. *Understanding Media* (1964)[19] introduced the memorable phrase 'the medium *is* the message' and described how

MAKING IT NEW

1.5
Trelawney Estate, Hackney, London, begun 1957: a relatively early example of a social housing estate on modernist principles built by a local authority in the inner city.

man was becoming the extension of the various transformed modern media, rather than the media being dependent on man. The 1967 book *The Medium is the Massage*,[20] with its punning title, took on a new synthesis of form and content: pages without text, huge sometimes shocking images, text which was repeated, text printed backwards. Its form underlined what the 1960s had already begun to demonstrate, that knowledge, art, and what is described as culture, had been irrevocably changed. And, more than that, any carefully constructed argument was no match for the powerful impact of the modern media. Showing both extraordinary foresight and imagination to create a book which could participate in the condition it interrogated, McLuhan made it clear that the world had been transformed, even if to a great extent this transformation had not been noticed.

This lack of awareness was equally true of architects, with notable exceptions. The architects who formed Archigram in 1961 became world famous through exactly that device, of creating a medium of their own, *Archigram* magazine (see p. 121), which communicated their work, even without the physical existence of a single building. It could be said that they, almost alone, invented a new way of becoming an architect, solely validated by the media which they themselves had generated.

Architectural discourses

The narrative of architecture in the twentieth century was, for the most part, located between several polarities: social engagement, cultural representation, technological incorporation and formal innovation. There was rarely a balance within this dialectic; rather, the emphasis on one to the exclusion of others has been the primary cause of modern architecture's numerous failures. Architecture cannot solely be determined by its technological means, but neither can it solely be expressed by innovation in its form. This book is selective of what seem to be the most significant dominant themes in the history of British modernism: there are at any time overlapping discourses, and in fact each period, which in Britain approximates to the sequence of decades, contains a dialectic of opposing positions. The 1930s saw the fundamental battle of establishing modernism: initially this contrasted with the position of questioning and denial of its necessity, and later with the development of a local identity. The period of wartime and after was really expressed by contrasting positions on just how modern cities should be rebuilt. The 1950s differentiated the large-scale fulfilment of the modernism defined in earlier decades with what is called here 'the shift to the specific' in terms of materiality and site. The 1960s saw the development of a massive modernist building programme now inflected by a Brutalist aesthetic with its opposite, an architecture that was provisional and expendable. The 1970s and 1980s, seen here in the explosion of new ideas at the Architectural Association, developed its complexity against a redundant modernism, and later stood against the simplicities of the postmodern position. In the 1990s, the dominance of so-called high-tech architecture elicited several responses that questioned but also reiterated more fundamental architectural values.

A word means something different after a decade has passed: meaning is a shifting rather than a fixed thing. 'Architecture' is no exception; its properties and values moving almost imperceptibly until they may mean the opposite of what was formerly the case. A retrospective view is no doubt misleading: the discourses celebrated here as the key ideas of a period did not, in large part, seem to be that at the time. Its authors were perhaps ignored, sometimes ridiculed: they certainly, and by definition, stood outside what were the commonly accepted ideas of the day. They were not taken seriously; they were seen as irrelevant to the real business of architecture or they were even seen as dangerous. Just as the ideas of modernism were dismissed by Blomfield in 1934 as an 'extreme of crude and unabashed brutality',[21] so Archigram in the 1960s or NATO

MAKING IT NEW

in the 1980s were seen as self-indulgent irrelevancies. Both, as well as many other positions, were to be important as new realisations of architectural possibilities, which in their turn would become established and perhaps later repudiated.

Despite popular belief, history does not speak for itself. It is, rather, a series of accepted judgements which shift sometimes almost imperceptibly, sometimes swiftly. In Britain in the 1960s, it was generally believed that the nineteenth century had produced bad art and bad architecture. As a result, most of Victorian Whitehall as well as St Pancras Station were seriously threatened with demolition. It was believed that, in terms of absolute quality, these buildings were bad. In the end, with British hesitancy, most survived: Euston Station Arch (which was defended by the young progressive architects Alison and Peter Smithson) was one of a few major casualties. This situation is not exceptional; similarly, once disdained modern buildings such as the housing tower blocks by Goldfinger[22] are now valued, not as curiosities, but as *good* architecture. The reverse is true of Cumbernauld town centre designed by Geoffrey Copcutt and completed in 1966, widely praised by Banham[23] and many other critics on its completion. A 2005 television programme *Demolition*[24] saw it awarded the highest number of votes, in favour of its destruction, of any British building.

1.6
Office blocks, Snow Hill Birmingham, 1964–6: urban redevelopment associated with new road building in a city which was to adopt and realise a larger-scale programme of modern reconstruction than any other British city.

Perhaps the most successful British buildings emerging from the material discourse of the 1950s, while not strictly Brutalist, were not completed until the mid-1970s, when there was remarkably little notice taken of one, the Barbican development and general hostility to the other, the National Theatre. Lasdun's National Theatre was completed in 1977, located on the London South Bank which had been designated in Abercrombie's 1943 plan for London as a culture zone. It could though be seen as embodying a reading of Le Corbusier's pre-war work, as well as reflecting the new materiality of the early 1950s. Lasdun thus produced a building which participated in several discourses in British architecture, but the timing was inauspicious. The year of its completion was close to the lowest ebb of appreciation of the architectural qualities it had. If (hypothetically) the Barbican and National Theatre had been completed a decade earlier, not only their immediate, but also their lasting reputation would surely have been higher.

The Millennium Dome, a lightweight tent structure provided as an enclosure for the built exhibition installations within, was designed by Mike Davies of Richard Rogers and Partners at the end of the 1990s but represents a long-nurtured idea with clear roots in the designs of Archigram in the 1960s. It is almost inevitable that architectural theory, which takes a while to become acceptable, and another long period to become realised, means that built buildings are frequently an expression of a past discourse and judgements on their worth have already moved on. Chronology is in any case a tricky thing, and one of the problems involved in conventional historical narrative. Adolf Loos, one of the first architects to develop a cultural reading of architecture, pointed out in *Ornament and Crime* (1908), that while he might be 'up to date', his neighbour was living in the 1880s, and his enemies in an earlier century.

This is not to say that buildings are simply the embodiment of prevailing ideas. But, rather, that the context of ideology provides the field from which the building emerges, and publications may determine just how architecture is understood and also shape architects' actions as designers. Far from belittling the achievement of building, this assumption leaves ample space for the uncovering of the qualities of the physical, of the here-and-now, which every building has. Theory, as active applied theory, is a way of understanding what gets built – and not just the 'famous buildings' by celebrated architects, but the diffusion of ideas affecting the whole urban fabric. The results of an architectural discourse, the common assumptions of a given period, create the context for practice by those who have no ambition to create originality: thus the spread of architectural ideas creates a shift into a kind of vernacular of practice, as can be seen in any city and town. However, there is an unfortunate corollary, illustrated by the example of the discourse of the 1950s: the Smithsons' polemic assures them of a significant role, and like Le Corbusier they were highly conscious of the role of the media. The irony may be that an undoubtedly original architect such as James Stirling definitively eschewed the architectural manifesto and for that reason does not appear as the significant figure he was in the discourse of the period.

The discourses this book primarily deals with are seven, placed in sequence. First, the stage of the discovery and proselytising of modernism as established in continental Europe, seen more as an appropriate new style rather than a movement, and exemplified by the editorial work of James Richards at the *Architectural Review* from the mid-1930s. Second, the discourse of reconstruction which examines texts published during the Second World War, with its programme of comprehensive city rebuilding, a utopian mission to create model communities and focusing on Patrick Abercrombie's officially commissioned 1943 County of London Plan. The third theme is the new interpretation of materiality seen both in the writing of Alison and Peter Smithson and the campaigns of the *Archi-*

tectural Review, primarily in the early 1950s: effectively a shift from the universal to the specific solution, and encompassing what came to be called Brutalism. The work of *Archigram* magazine, an approach later taken up by a revived *Architectural Design*, provides the fourth chronological discourse, a technological imperative transposing the practice of architecture from the making of an object to servicing the human subject: with this challenge to convention, British architectural culture earned wide acclaim. The field of architecture within the highly international Architectural Association School, under the chairmanship of Alvin Boyarsky, sought and created radical alternatives to the hegemony of modernism, which provides the theme of the chapter concentrating on the 1970s and 1980s. The final subject is recent rethinking of the basis of architectural practice in the 1990s, manifested by the great increase in the volume of publication of architectural books and journals and which has served to reinforce a split between the pragmatics of practice and rigour of theory.

These themes, it can be argued, provide not only the most resonant ideas in the history of British architecture since the 1930s, but also form a thread of action and reaction, of development and repudiation, if read as a sequence. It would be reasonable however to read each chapter as a self-contained subject, rather than the dialectic of the succession of discourses, and the book would make no claim to be a complete historical overview. A number of significant discourses have not been included. The immediate post-war years, for example, saw the surprising adoption of Rudolf Wittkower's book *Architectural Principles in the Age of Humanism*[25]: first published as an academic paper in 1949, it became influential for a generation of architects, not least the young Smithsons. Renaissance systems of proportion would seem an unlikely subject for their generation, although a connection can be made with certain of Le Corbusier's preoccupations.[26] Opposite, but occurring at the same time, was a resurgence of Swedish influence as a model of socially committed and humanist architectural practice, influencing the design of housing developments and new towns. This link with Sweden and a softer version of 'modern' began in the mid-1920s, as described below (see p. 23) and, arguably, has never gone away: Colin St John Wilson's 'Other' tradition[27] is the most consummate extension and realisation of this discourse.

Among others that had influence in Britain was the representation of the position of science as the basis for thought and design in architecture. This can be seen in particular in the work of Richard Llewelyn Davies,[28] both in his practice and his leadership of the

Bartlett School through the 1960s, which he transformed from a *Beaux-Arts* school to one based on environmental research. One outcome was the development of design for the mass production of industrialised building, and the account of the widespread adoption of commercial building systems (Camus and Larsen Nielsen being the first for housing), alongside local authorities' own CLASP system, is a significant and perhaps entirely negative history.[29] Also in the same period the massive programme of social housing was planned according to the principles of the 1961 Parker Morris Report *Homes for Today and Tomorrow*.[30] The history of the British social housing programme is comprehensively researched, documented and discussed in Glendinning and Muthesius's 1994 book *Tower Block*,[31] while the post-war building of schools is covered in Andrew Saint's excellent 1987 study *Towards a Social Architecture*.[32]

The anti-modernist movement, beginning with Blomfield and his contemporaries, merits a book by itself and can scarcely be included in the current study. The writing of the Cambridge historian David Watkin, particularly in *Architecture and Morality* (1977)[33] is one recent manifestation: the survival and revival of historical forms in the later twentieth century gained much from the growth of the conservation movement which becomes a discourse in itself.[34] Developing over perhaps a ten-year period, 1975 saw the foundation of SAVE Britain's heritage and the publication of *The Rape of Britain*,[35] which catalogued current and prospective urban destruction by what seemed to be the alliance of architects, planners and ignorant local authorities. A wider view would indicate that the practice of modern architecture itself was in crisis: the drive to redevelop British cities ground to a halt, not only for economic reasons; those economic reasons also led to the collapse of the public commission, non-existent after the accession of the Conservative government four years later. The year 1975 also saw the first publication of the term 'postmodernism' in the writing of Charles Jencks, and much of his essay was also a plea for conservation, as well as presenting the argument that the visual language of modern architecture was one that simply didn't communicate and had negative social consequences.[36] The term was a major influence for over a decade, and developed into the practice of applying historical references to otherwise 'modern' buildings, prefigured in Jencks's 1977 book *The Language of Post-Modern Architecture*.[37]

Andreas Papadakis's editorship of *Architectural Design*[38] through the 1980s began, as far as Britain is concerned, the making of a wide and inclusive forum for architectural publication. Rather than reflecting a highly specific agenda, the contributions and guest-

MAKING IT NEW

1.7
Blueprint **magazine published from 1983, edited by Deyan Sujdic: issue 44 featuring Rem Koolhaas 1988.**

editorships of a wide variety of architects, writers and academics provided opportunities for the airing of a bewildering variety of themes; most of these (outside, and to some extent opposed to, the AA's contemporary culture) would effectively have had no outlet through then existing publications. The process was to enliven British architectural discourse, even if the publications (more books than periodicals) sometimes had shortcomings as either magazines or books. The other publication which typifies the 1980s is *Blueprint*,[39] founded by Peter Murray and edited by Deyan Sujdic.

While very much reflecting practice rather than more discursive issues, the journal took a highly specific and in effect prophetic position, and one that was specifically modern rather than postmodern. It relocated architecture into the wider sphere of design and reiterated the autonomy of the designer, no longer cowed as in the 1970s by the widespread rejection of the public, and turned their work into something to celebrate. Its covers emphasised the architect or designer as a 'personality', but overall its popularising tendency led gradually to a wider acceptance of modern design as something accessible and eventually popular, prefiguring the role in the mass media that architecture developed in the 1990s, which had never previously been the case in Britain.

Discovering modern architecture

The relation of Britain (as the then leading industrial nation) to the development of modernism is a complex one. Advances in technology (exemplified by the building of the great railway structures and the Crystal Palace) did not generate a culture that, some historians retrospectively felt, should have spontaneously created a new architecture. But the development in Britain of the anti-industrial Arts and Crafts movement, which Nikolaus Pevsner saw as the harbinger of modernism, made an entirely different synthesis of what the modern world needed as a representative architecture.[40] Writers other than Pevsner did not follow the same line, and a more commonly held view is that of the pre-history of modernism through French rationality and through neoclassical austerity: the early twentieth century in Britain saw very little new thinking, and even the years after the First World War were dominated by varying versions of historicism. Developments were taking place elsewhere in Europe that were leading to the revolutionising of architecture as a practice, but from which Britain was excluded.

A precursor to the main themes of enquiry of this book is the work of Howard Robertson and Frank Yerbury.[41] In some two hundred articles, the vast majority published in the *Architect and Building News* from 1925–31,[42] Robertson and Yerbury introduced Le Corbusier, Perret, Asplund and Oud to British architectural culture. Ahead of other traveller-critics of the English-speaking world, Robertson and Yerbury visited, photographed and criticised whatever buildings were new in Europe, certainly not limited to those that came to be defined as modernist. They provided the first, often highly naïve accounts of the most significant modern buildings before there was any understanding, let alone polemic, about a 'modern movement'.

Their work thus forms a pre-canonical sense of modern architecture, before what was established by consensus as 'important'. In terms of the historiography of modernism, their work is valuable, preceding Hitchcock and Johnson's travels which led to the Museum of Modern Art's 'International Style' exhibition of 1932.[43] Yerbury's role was initially that of photographer, although at a later stage he developed into the co-writer and later sole author of certain of these articles. Robertson on the other hand was Principal of the Architectural Association School and the author of two books in the period: *The Principles of Architectural Composition* (1924) and *Modern Architectural Design* (1932).[44] While the former reflects, even in its title, the influence of the *Beaux-Arts*, that influence is modified in the second book with much new material introduced emerging from his European travels. Robertson was also briefly the only British delegate to CIAM (the Congrès Internationaux d'Architecture Moderne). Reyner Banham, in a rare recognition of the importance and impact of their work, described in 1953 how

> these two [Robertson and Yerbury], journeying around the world, found architecture in a ferment of which England knew nothing, and combated this ignorance in a famous series of weekly articles, spread over the late 1920s and early 1930s in *The Architect and Building News*, with occasional deviations into the *Architectural Review*.[45]

The most notable British buildings of the 1920s included Reginald Blomfield's rebuilt Regent Street, while banks, offices, town halls and other public buildings continued to be built almost exclusively in some interpretation of Michelangelo, Mansart or Wren. Robertson, despite the influence of his own architectural education at the Paris *Beaux-Arts* School, had doubts about this historicism. In response to Blomfield's contention that 'the deliberate search for originality is futile',[46] he asserted:

> Is not an original thought in a mechanical age like ours more valuable, even if it is imperfect, than the same old repetition? What is the meaning, in the facades of the great departmental stores, of friezes or sacrificial ox-skulls or garlands? And what defence can there be, in these or any other days, for building huge fake Orders supported on steel points?[47]

Frank Yerbury, the Secretary of the Architectural Association, first travelled in Europe in 1922 when he led an AA excursion to Holland. There the party visited buildings that were representative of

MAKING IT NEW

1.8
City Hall, Stockholm, Ragnar Ostberg 1923: photographed by F.R. Yerbury and described by him as 'the finest modern building in the world'.

modern Dutch work, such as the Amsterdam Bourse by Berlage and housing by De Klerk. These became the subject of the first article on contemporary architecture written by Robertson and illustrated by Yerbury's photographs.[48] The following year Robertson and Yerbury visited the Jubilee Exhibition in Gothenburg in Sweden. The centrepiece was Arvid Bjerke's Congress Hall, a design of timber arches supporting a row of clerestories. Robertson's own design for the London Royal Horticultural Hall, the subject of a successful competition entry soon afterwards, reproduced similar forms in concrete. At least as influential was the other high point of this Swedish excursion, the new Stockholm Town Hall. Ragnar Ostberg's building, beautifully sited on the waterfront and inspired by National Romantic forms, made an immediate and lasting impression – Yerbury called it 'the finest modern building in the world'.[49]

Yerbury decided to make this work better known and on his return arranged an exhibition of drawings and models which opened in London in May 1924. This exhibition originated the influence of Sweden on British architecture, developing particularly in the 1930s and re-emerging in the post-war years: Swedish architecture was seen as a humane and evolutionary version of the modern, rooted in tradition but not traditional. To British architects it seemed highly appropriate, and, at least for a while, the answer to the quest for a new and appropriate style. For Yerbury himself, the acknowledgement which came with the exhibition and publication served to establish him as an influence within a sphere far larger than the AA. He was awarded an honorary ARIBA, and the book on Sweden[50] became the first in a long series, largely published by Ernest Benn and including volumes on Dutch, Danish and French architecture, which brought a collection of unfamiliar modern architecture to Britain.[51] Thus by 1925 the insularity of British architectural culture had been challenged.

Buildings such as Le Corbusier's villas at Garches and Passy, Mendelsohn's Einstein Tower and Schocken shops, schools by Dudok, Oud's housing in Rotterdam and May's in Frankfurt, Asplund's Stockholm Library and Woodland Chapel, churches by Perret and Art Deco shopfronts in Paris all had their first exposure in Britain in the *Architect and Building News*. But this was not an exclusive history: along with the now celebrated names and buildings were such forgotten examples as the YWCA building in Amsterdam and the First Church of Christ Scientist in Berne, as well as such apparent anachronisms as

1.9
Schocken Shop, Stuttgart, Erich Mendelsohn, 1926: photographed by F.R. Yerbury and published by him and Howard Robertson in the *Architect and Building News*, 1929.

the Sacré Coeur in Paris. In early 1927 there appeared the first article on houses by Le Corbusier, 'Architecture of the Modernist School'. Fair-mindedly, it starts by reminding us of the controversial nature of the work: 'There are many people who refuse to regard as architecture the buildings which are being put up in France by a group of men who are attempting to express design in the very difficult terms of modern life.' But Robertson, with his eminently rational nature, considers the various innovations of the modernist vocabulary, and sees a logic at work, not least in the apparent reduction of costs. He concludes: 'These houses show whatever virtue lies in a clean simplicity, the shapes being entirely reasonable. Details such as the doorhoods, window boxes, balcony rails, etc., could obviously be enriched were the means forthcoming.'[52] Later in that year an article on the Weissenhof Siedlung in Stuttgart gave a somewhat harsher judgement, while at the same time reminding the reader that other European countries were without the highly developed English tradition of small and comfortable houses and cottages. Talking of verandahs, white walls and flat roofs, Robertson and Yerbury comment with a degree of accuracy, if not approval:

> These characteristics are the most obviously salient ones, but behind them lies something very much more fundamental which is responsible for the effect of strangeness which is produced by buildings of Mallet-Stevens, or Van der Rohe, or Le Corbusier. It is a something which derives from the idea behind these conceptions, an idea which presupposes not only a change in architectural standards, but a change in the human personality of the sort of tenant for whom these houses are destined.[53]

Thus the idea was identified that this architecture was not simply intending to be a new style, but brought with it the new idea of the transformation of domestic life.

The architecture of Germany, whether by Höger, Poelzig or Mendelsohn, was however perceived as being more likely to form the basis of a new tradition than modern French work by Le Corbusier or Mallet-Stevens. Robertson and Yerbury wrote in 1928:

> In a survey of the executed work of the modern school, it is to Germany that falls the premier position ... Always those architects who were part of the modern movement have attempted to express the idea and function behind the building: an interest in the expression of construction has taken only a very secondary place.[54]

While this argument could be used to justify a very different kind of architecture, in which expression is subordinate to the resolution of structure, the authors were here defending the streamlined forms of a building by Mendelsohn or Poelzig as having a representative quality, or, as they would have put it, 'character': a distinctly unmodernist term used by Robertson in his *Principles of Architectural Composition*.[55]

In terms of housing, Robertson and Yerbury often reiterate their satisfaction with traditional English house forms and assert that the new architecture of Europe would not appeal to the English, since there already existed a perfectly good tradition of building small, comfortable houses and cottages: 'In all its major essentials, the English traditional type of small house can remain unchanged without the reproach of unsuitability to modern needs.'[56] New materials and techniques should be used with caution: for example, they admired the work of Perret in evolving new forms for the architecture of concrete, although traditional craftsmanship and the judicious use of crafts in decoration still seemed preferable. Principally, they wanted a sensible building, rationally planned and conceived; for architecture, after all, was a practical art.

1.10
Garage Marbeuf, Paris, Bazin and Laprade 1929: photographed by F.R. Yerbury and published by him and Howard Robertson in the *Architect and Building News*, 1930.

While mild in tone and hesitant in the face of theory, Robertson and Yerbury's views, when placed in relation to those of other key contemporary figures in the British architectural world, were radical and revolutionary. Blomfield accused them of misleading the young; William Davidson wrote, in the correspondence columns of the *Architect and Building News*, that their praise for foreign work was misplaced.[57] Strong disapproval of the new was also expressed by AA President Gilbert Jenkins, who, after a visit led by Yerbury to the Weissenhof Siedlung in 1927, accused its architects of deliberate sensationalism: 'A French exponent of modernism has built a concrete and plate glass box to form one of these new abodes: one could not conceive it as a home for anyone save a vegetarian biologist.'[58] British disapproval of Le Corbusier's work extended also to his writings: 'The Dead City' was Trystan Edwards' title for his review in the *Architectural Review* of Le Corbusier's *The City of Tomorrow*.[59]

Yerbury and Robertson presented their work as reportage rather than polemic, as in the introduction to *Examples of Modern French Architecture*, where they describe themselves as the 'compilers' rather than the 'authors' of a 'modest collection of plates'.[60] However, in certain quarters, any receptivity to new ideas from abroad was enough to make them appear extreme, and the loneliness of their roles as radicals in the British architectural scene is demonstrated by a survey of the rest of the architectural press at this period. With the exception of the *Architect and Building News*, to which they were major contributors, British periodicals dealt with very little contemporary architecture, and what they did cover was mostly British. The buildings documented in *The Builder* of 11 January 1929, for example, are Sir Edwin Cooper's National Provincial Bank in the City, Elcock and Sutcliffe's Daily Telegraph building, a house in Sevenoaks by Baillie Scott, and Giles Gilbert Scott's Salvation Army College in south London. Buildings such as these, with the exception of the Daily Telegraph building, which showed the influence of the 1925 Paris Exhibition, were all developments of long-standing British traditions.

A new and less cautious attitude to the modern idiom begins to appear in Robertson and Yerbury's writings during this period. The Van Nelle Factory in Rotterdam by Brinkmann and Van der Vlught is described by them as a fulfilment of the possibilities of the new aesthetic: 'the sense of light and space, of organised grouping, of colour beautifully disposed ... are all things which are as good to live with in a house as in a factory.'[61] In May 1929 they published an article on Le Corbusier's villa at Garches, incorporating an examination of his work – material that would have been far from familiar to their readers. Comparing the house with nearby work that is based on English Arts and Crafts models, they are startled by the contrast, almost as if a conversion has occurred:

> One suddenly realises that the 'English' houses are wrong, and that Le Corbusier's house is right. A motor-car stands before its door. One sees that the motor-car and the house are in tune, that the design of house and car are in the natural harmony which has always obtained between man-made objects of any period which is truly an epoch. The coach has gone, the garb of its occupants, the house which filled them. Today, another vehicle, another dress, another architecture.[62]

The following decade saw the building of houses by Connell, Ward and Lucas completed in 1930 and Emberton's Royal Corinthian Yacht Club in 1931, among the first in Britain in the new aesthetic. But the decade also saw the survival of Blomfield and Cooper, and thriving practices with a traditional view of architecture continued beyond it. However, the 1930s saw the realisation of ideas introduced in the mid-1920s, the most significant examples being Swedish-influenced buildings such as the competition successes of Grey Wornum[63] with the Royal Institute of British Architects

MAKING IT NEW

1.11
The Quest of the Ideal: article on Le Corbusier's Villa at Garches by Howard Robertson and F.R. Yerbury with distinctly un-modernist layout, in the *Architect and Building News*, 1929.

(RIBA) headquarters in London and James and Pierce with Norwich City Hall. According to one assessor, the latter was a competition for which 'every damned Swedish architect has gone in'; he was referring to the obvious influences at work in the British architects' submissions.[64] Work by Holden for London Transport such as Arnos Grove

1.12
Villa Stein, Garches, Le Corbusier; completed 1928: photographed by F.R. Yerbury, 1929.

underground station had a clear Swedish source; in 1930 he and Frank Pick had toured northern Europe, specifically in the footsteps of Robertson and Yerbury. There was also work influenced by Dudok, such as Hornsey and Greenwich town halls and numerous pithead baths; at a slightly later date there were many versions of Mendelsohn's Schocken shop and Universum cinema, notably the Peter Jones store in Sloane Square, London, by Crabtree.

These are some of the direct progeny of Robertson and Yerbury through their communication of the ideas of European architecture to Britain. Reyner Banham may be right in his judgement that the variety of their examples confused the issue, 'sending the younger generation dashing off madly in several directions at once'.[65] But the generation who passed through the AA in Robertson's time included those who would later be the most committed to the ideal of the functional, to the use of new technology, and to the adoption of a socially committed role for architecture. Evidence of their influence can be found in the years immediately following the Second World War, when a softer version of the modern was embraced: an architecture of social concern, lacking in modernist rigour what it made up for in humanity. They opened the possibility of a specific form of modern architecture to be realised by a later generation.

It would be a mistake, however, to view Robertson and Yerbury as being implacably opposed to the traditional work being produced

MAKING IT NEW

1.13
Norwich City Hall, James and Pierce, 1938: evidence of the Swedish influence in British architecture of the 1930s, and the subject of a special *Architectural Review* issue; photograph E.R. Jarrett.

in England, or as wholehearted supporters of the more radical architecture they introduced to their readers. They were far too cautious for that. As late as 1931, towards the end of their prodigious joint effort, their ambivalence towards the architecture of their time was still apparent, and they are referring to the exact period when for most later historians, the significant work of the modern movement was achieved: the Bauhaus building, housing at Stuttgart and

Frankfurt, the Purist villas of Le Corbusier and Mies's Barcelona Pavilion among much else:

> When the history of the present phase of architectural development is written, it may be that the achievement of the years in which we are living will be summed up as mediocre. Emphasis will be laid on the lack of uniform tendencies, on the amount of individual experiment which has no sequence ... Astonishment, perhaps contempt, may be levelled at this seeming chaos, at these twentieth-century decades in which crystallised no style, in which all architects seemed agreed only to differ.[66]

It was in the following eight years, in particular through the very different attitude of the *Architectural Review*, that modernism would become the dominant discourse in British architecture.

Notes

1. R. Blomfield, *Modernismus*, London: Macmillan, 1934, p. v.
2. Reginald Blomfield (1856–1942) was a leading member of the architectural profession in Britain, awarded the RIBA Gold Medal in 1913: among his last works was the reconstruction of the Regent Street Quadrant (1923–8).
3. Blomfield argued that architecture in such countries as Britain did not need a 'new architecture', as it gathers 'all that may be learnt from the changing conditions of modern life, yet not losing touch with the splendid heritage of the past' (*Modernismus*, p. 61).
4. Le Corbusier, *Vers une architecture*, Paris: Cres et Cie, 1923; *Towards a New Architecture*, trans. F. Etchells, London: Rodker, 1927.
5. Le Corbusier and Amedee Ozenfant, 'Sur la plastique' in *L'Esprit Nouveau*, I, 15 October 1920. Quoted in T. Benton, C. Benton and D. Sharp, *Form and Function*, London: Granada, 1975, p. 89.
6. Ferdinand de Saussure: Linguist and author of *Course in General Linguistics* (1916). On de Saussure see F. Gadet, *Saussure and Contemporary Culture*, London: Hutchinson, 1989.
7. T.S. Eliot 'Tradition and the Individual Talent' in *Selected Essays*, London: Faber, 1951, p. 15.
8. *Mythologies* was published in French in 1957. An English edition was published in 1972 (London: Cape). See also *The Eiffel Tower and Other Mythologies*, New York: Hill & Wang, 1979.
9. See Susan Sontag (ed.), *A Barthes Reader*, London: Vintage, 1993, p. 238.
10. 'The Death of the Author' in Roland Barthes, *Image Music Text*, London: Fontana, 1977.
11. Michel Foucault, *Archaeology of Knowledge*, London: Tavistock, 1972.
12. Ibid., pp. 116–17.
13. Royston Landau, 'Notes on the Concept of an Architectural Position', *AA Files* 1, Winter 1981–2, pp. 111–14.
14. B. Colomina, *Privacy and Publicity: Modern Architecture as Mass Media*, Cambridge, MA: MIT Press, 1994. Her contrasting counterpart to Le Corbusier is the work of Loos, who refused engagement with the media and destroyed records of his work.

15 Le Corbusier, *Oeuvre Complete* [Complete Works], London: Thames & Hudson, 1964–70.
16 Adrian Forty, *Words and Buildings: a Vocabulary of Modern Architecture*, London: Thames & Hudson, 2000.
17 Forty, op. cit., p. 13.
18 Kester Rattenbury (ed.), *This Is Not Architecture: Media Constructions*, London: Routledge, 2002.
19 Marshall McLuhan, *The Gutenberg Galaxy*, London: Routledge, 1962; *Understanding Media*, London: Routledge, 1964.
20 Marshall McLuhan and Quentin Fiore, *The Medium is the Massage*, Harmondsworth: Penguin, 1967.
21 Blomfield, op. cit., p. 64.
22 Ernö Goldfinger's Balfron Tower in the Brownfield Estate, Poplar, London designed in 1963 and the Trellick Tower, Cheltenham Estate, North Kensington, London, designed in 1967.
23 See R. Banham, *Megastructure*, London: Thames & Hudson, 1976, p. 168ff. for a discussion of its qualities.
24 *Demolition*, Channel 4, 20 December 2005, presented by Kevin McCloud, with George Ferguson RIBA President and Janet Street-Porter.
25 R. Wittkower, *Architectural Principles in the Age of Humanism*, London: Warburg Institute, 1949.
26 See Le Corbusier, *Le Modulor*, London: Faber and Faber, 1954.
27 See Colin St John Wilson, *The Other Tradition of Modern Architecture: the Uncompleted Project*, London: Academy, 1995.
28 Richard Llewelyn Davies had trained in the immediately pre-war AA, and later set up a practice with John Weeks, responsible for the London Stock Exchange and the plan for Milton Keynes.
29 See Barry Russell, *Building Systems, Industrialisation and Architecture*, London: John Wiley, 1981.
30 Central Housing Advisory Committee's Sub Committee on housing standards, chaired by Sir Parker Morris, *Homes for Today and Tomorrow*, London: HMSO, 1961.
31 M. Glendinning and S. Muthesius, *Tower Block: Modern Public Housing in England, Scotland, Wales, and Northern Ireland*, New Haven: Yale University Press, 1994.
32 Andrew Saint, *Towards a Social Architecture: the Role of School Building in Post-war England*, New Haven: Yale University Press, 1987.
33 David Watkin, *Architecture and Morality*, Oxford: Clarendon, 1977.
34 See Elain Harwood and Alan Powers (eds) *The Heroic Period of Conservation*, London: The Twentieth Century Society, 2004.
35 Colin Amery and Dan Cruickshank, *The Rape of Britain*, London: Paul Elek, 1975.
36 Charles Jencks, 'The Rise of Post-Modern Architecture', *AA Quarterly* October/December 1975, pp. 3–14.
37 Charles Jencks, *The Language of Post-Modern Architecture*, London: Academy, 1977.
38 Papadakis took over the magazine, then in financial trouble, in late 1976, and became Editor in 1979.
39 *Blueprint* was first published in October 1983 by Peter Murray with Sujdic as Editor and Simon Esterson as Art Editor.
40 As in Pevsner's text, *Pioneers of the Modern Movement*, London: Faber and Faber, 1936.
41 Robertson and Yerbury's publication of articles on modern architecture is the subject of Andrew Higgott (ed.), *Travels in Modern Architecture*, London: Architectural Association, 1989. As well as an extended version of this essay, this book has extracts from twenty of the *Architect and Building News* articles. Yerbury's architectural photography is illustrated and commented on by Andrew Higgott and Ian Jeffrey in *F.R. Yerbury: Itinerant Cameraman*, London: Architectural Association, 1987.
42 See A. Higgott, *Travels in Modern Architecture*, pp. 122–8 for a full bibliography of these articles.

43 The International Style exhibition at the New York Museum of Modern Art in 1932, curated by Henry-Russell Hitchcock and Philip Johnson, may be seen as responsible for establishing modernist architecture as an international practice. Hitchcock commented positively on the modern coverage of the *Architect and Building News* in an article in *Architectural Record*, February 1929.

44 Howard Robertson, *The Principles of Architectural Composition*, London: Architectural Press, 1924; *Modern Architectural Design*, London: Architectural Press, 1932. Robertson's career as an architect included the building of the British Pavilion for several international exhibitions, including Paris (1925), Brussels (1935) and New York (1939). His role as representing British architect can also be seen in his membership of the UN building committee in New York, and he was awarded the RIBA Gold Medal in 1949.

45 *Architectural Review*, September 1953, pp. 161–8.

46 Quoted by Howard Robertson in 'Post-war Glimpses of Architectural Vitality', *Architect and Building News*, 19 March 1926, p. 223.

47 Ibid.

48 'Modern Dutch Architecture', *Architectural Review*, August 1922, pp. 46–50.

49 *Swedish Architecture of the Twentieth Century*, edited by Hakon Ahlberg, London: Ernest Benn, 1924, p. 3.

50 Ibid.

51 *Dutch Architecture of the Twentieth Century*, London: Ernest Benn, 1926; *Modern Danish Architecture*, London: Ernest Benn, 1927; *Examples of Modern French Architecture*, London: Ernest Benn, 1928; *Modern European Buildings*, London: Gollancz, 1928; *Modern Dutch Buildings*, London: Ernest Benn, 1931.

52 'Architecture of the Modernist School', *Architect and Building News*, 29 April 1927, pp. 745–8.

53 'The Housing Exhibition in Stuttgart', *Architect and Building News*, 11 November 1927, pp. 763–6.

54 'Some Modern German Buildings', *Architect and Building News*, 9 March 1928, pp. 354–8.

55 Robertson, *Principles of Architectural Composition*, pp. 65–76.

56 'The Housing Exhibition in Stuttgart', *Architect and Building News*, 11 November 1927, pp. 763–6.

57 Correspondence, *Architect and Building News*, 25 April 1930, p. 546.

58 President's Address, given by Gilbert Jenkins at the Architectural Association, 24 October 1927, reported in *Architectural Association Journal*, November 1927, p. 155.

59 *Architectural Review*, September 1929, pp. 35–8.

60 H.M. Robertson and F.R. Yerbury, *Examples of Modern French Architecture*, London: Ernst Benn, 1928.

61 'A Poem in Glass and Steel', *Architect and Building News*, 30 May 1930, pp. 687–90.

62 'The Quest of the Ideal', *Architect and Building News*, 10 May 1929, pp. 621–5.

63 Wornum, late President of the AA, had accompanied Yerbury on a trip to Sweden in 1930.

64 James Bone in the foreword to Yerbury's *One Hundred Photographs*, London: Jordan Gaskell, 1935.

65 *Architectural Review*, September 1953, pp. 161–8.

66 'Poverty and Promise: Examples of Dutch Detail', *Architect and Building News*, 23 October 1931, pp. 92–5.

CHAPTER 2

the mission of modernism

James Richards and the *Architectural Review*

THE MISSION OF MODERNISM

> The words 'modern architecture' are used here to mean something more particular than contemporary architecture. They are used to mean the new kind of architecture that is growing up with this century as this century's own contribution to the art of architecture; the work of those people, whose number is happily increasing, who understand that architecture is a social art related to the life of the people it serves, not an academic exercise in applied ornament [and] that the new architecture that we are calling 'modern' . . . is something that is needed in the world today. They believe also that in developing and perfecting it so as to answer this century's problems and to be in tune with its outlook, they are helping in the revival of architecture as a live art.
>
> James Richards, *An Introduction to Modern Architecture*, 1940[1]

Richards would have been the obvious choice for Penguin Editor Allen Lane in searching for an author for one of the first series of Pelican books, number 61, introducing modern architecture. Written in 1938, it appeared only in the different circumstances of early wartime years; Richards' wartime experiences were, as for the majority of his generation, to change his thinking. But the book is the expression of his highly effective and powerful position in the later 1930s as Editor of the *Architectural Review*, member of the MARS (Modern Architectural Research) group, and a figure well connected with the principal modern architects in Britain and Europe.[2] Colin Rowe has written of Richards' book as being the embodiment of a particular view of history in its calling for 'true' progress after architecture's domination by wrong-headed issues of style in the nineteenth century and beyond.[3] For Richards, the modern building was to be the reification of progress and the manifestation of an ideal world. As the language of Richards' *Introduction* shows, certain qualities are seen as necessary, such as technical advances, the solution to problems and social needs; others can be disregarded, such as aesthetic intentions, custom or conventional appearance. As such, Richards' position represents a second stage of the modernist project: from the avant-garde project towards the mainstream of practice; from its origination to its dissemination.

Those in the 1930s who were convinced of the mission of modernism could not construct utopia – first, a battle had to be won – but they could produce it by writing it. So their publications embodied rather than simply represented the new order. They were the manifestation of a world that could come into being. As Arata Isozaki has recently written: 'Architectural writings *as projects* were focused on constructing architecture as utilitarian entities and accelerating

2.1
James Richards, *An Introduction to Modern Architecture*, published in 1940 as part of the first series of Pelican Books: the cover design shows Kensal House (see 2.11).

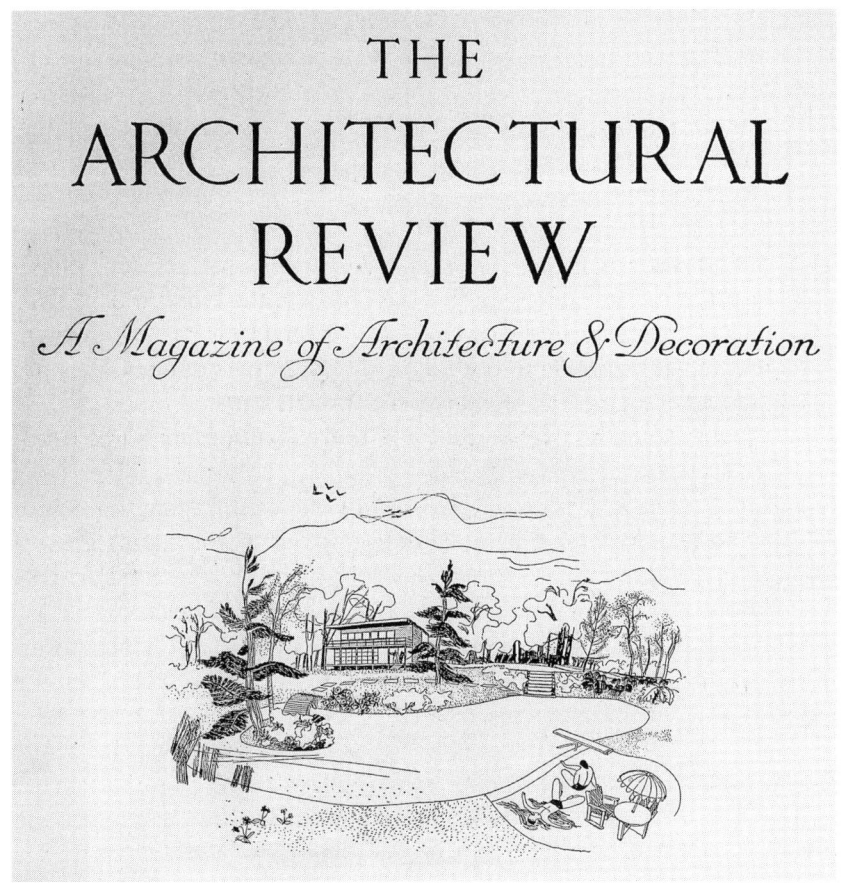

2.2
Architectural Review, April 1938: cover drawing by Gordon Cullen, showing house at Cobham by Raymond McGrath with garden by Christopher Tunnard.

the progressive movement towards utopia ... In the 1960s utopia was, ironically, realised.'[4] In the early modernist period, the book or text became of particular importance as a kind of realisation: this signified also that the texts themselves bore no ambiguity, they were indeed expressions of utopia. The qualities of these texts were those of the world they attempted to bring into being: clarity, order, technical advancement, a new kind of beauty, not to mention the utopian dream of social harmony. The qualities of architecture which Richards expounded in his *Introduction to Modern Architecture* were its common purpose within the mass of people; architecture was a social art matching the concerns and needs of the century. And what underlay it? A response to the industrial revolution, and the consequent growth of new urban life: what was needed was an eminently rational solution; order and efficiency, like that of the machine.

James Richards published extensively: a dozen books, and numerous articles on a great variety of architectural themes, but his primary role was that of Editor of the *Architectural Review*.[5]

Under the editorship of Richards, the journal had an enormous effect in formulating what modernism was taken to be and taken to mean in Britain. The longest-standing and most influential of its editors, Richards formulated its championing of modernism. In his advocacy, the rigorous exclusion of 'incorrect' architecture, and the careful way in which the 'correct' examples were interpreted, framed in relation to the necessary vision, was crucially also matched by a radical use of photography and layout. But an alternative bias mediated Richards' apparent dogma with particularly British concerns.

Certain other volumes published in Britain make a strong claim for influence and authority in their advocacy of modern architecture. Among them were those by the young English architect F.R.S. Yorke: *The Modern House*, first published in 1934 was followed three years later by *The Modern House in England* and *The Modern Flat*:[6] these emerged from Yorke's earlier writing in the pages of *Architectural Review*. Among those books published by accomplished modernist architects themselves, Gropius's book published in England as *The New Architecture and the Bauhaus* was seen by contemporaries as the most influential.[7] Of Le Corbusier's early defining publications from *L'Esprit Nouveau*, *Towards a New Architecture* was translated, possibly mistranslated, in 1927.[8]

Nikolaus Pevsner's first book, *Pioneers of the Modern Movement from William Morris to Walter Gropius* (1936) provided one of the first historical justifications for the adoption of this new form of architecture: a theme he would later extend as a contributor to the *Architectural Review*. Pevsner's book created an enduring but contentious link between the English Arts and Crafts tradition and the Modern Movement as defined for Pevsner in Gropius's early work. The making of the 'Modern Movement' thus ascribed to Pevsner has been, with justification, seen as the bringing together of widely divergent elements in a work of instrumentalist criticism. More recent appraisals of the historiography of modern architecture have emphasised both how such histories are constructed and how such interpretations subsequently become pervasive.[9] Tournikiotis's contrast of Pevsner's narrative with Emil Kaufman's history of modern architecture 'from Ledoux to Le Corbusier' (1933), provides only one alternative construct. In Tafuri and Dal Co's interpretation, Pevsner's book

> took on immense importance: it not only fixed an interpretation that exalted the role of a few prestigious leaders within a logical and progressive *movement*, but did so in a literary manner that inevitably ironed out the complexity of phenomena which, in reality, interacted both dialectically and contradictorily.[10]

Richards' own position took as read this interpretation, and developed its progressive programme more explicitly.

What also defined this modernist architectural culture is what it stood against: the wider sphere of British practice largely remained highly conservative. Richards, like others taking up the modernist position, saw the established figures of Reginald Blomfield, Vincent Harris or Herbert Baker as unwarrantedly smug.[11] And it is worth noting that only a tiny number of buildings built in Britain even in the later 1930s were in any sense modernist; public buildings, banks, houses were almost always built in a historicist language. While Richards and others wanted to ensure that this situation was transformed, they were doing so by means of effecting a shift in architectural discourse through their campaigns, publications and language.

As a campaigning body, the MARS group was founded in 1933 as the English counterpart of the modernist cause established by CIAM (Congrès Internationaux d'Architecture Moderne). The organisation's secretary, Siegfried Giedion, had influenced the formation of this group originated by Wells Coates and the writer Morton Shand,[12] replacing the more ambiguous earlier participation of Howard Robertson in CIAM. The group was deliberately exclusive, and according to Coates, 'certain people who are popularly and notoriously known as "modern" architects obviously do not qualify in our sense': they needed to talk the right language.[13] Its programme was not only of the dissemination of modernism as a practice, but the term 'research' signalled the intention to pursue both social research and research into materials; the group also participated in CIAM congresses from its inception. They attracted a young following such as the Architectural Association (AA) students, who forced a late revolution in their School's teaching and leadership in favour of modernism. With a much-discussed exhibition in 1938, the MARS group exerted an influence on British opinion which aligned with larger-scale concerns about social change in Britain. Like contemporaries in other fields, not least the political, the architects of MARS, including Richards, wanted to engage with the arguments for a wholesale reform of the physical conditions of human life.

The *Architectural Review*'s role

Within the architectural press, the *Architectural Review* (*AR*)[14] was already the voice of authority within British architecture; its earlier commitment was to the scrutiny of the British historical tradition and an almost complete opposition to the new. While it had, exceptionally, published Le Corbusier in 1927,[15] in 1929 Cecil Howitt's

Nottingham Council House had been its building of the year:[16] this version of 'new building' owed little to the twentieth century let alone to any of the versions of a modern tradition.

But it was with the editorship of James Richards in 1935 that the *Architectural Review* came to express and champion the modernist movement and became, more than MARS and more than any practice, the clearest manifestation of a new consciousness in Britain. Modernist buildings in Europe were lavishly documented, and built British work with the right aesthetic was championed. The work of Lubetkin, for example, frequently received much attention and extensive pictorial coverage. This policy, however, was not simply as dictated by CIAM doctrine and was open to kinds of work which, for Richards, saw architecture not as the expression of style, still less a matter of professional privilege, but instead inevitably related to society and its needs. However, this advocacy was highly exclusive, and the replacement of older traditions provided the underlying energy behind this new British practice. The look of the *Review* was perhaps equally important, and innovative layouts with a strong graphic quality and powerful full-page photographs embodied the chosen interpretation of this work.

This radical approach was juxtaposed with paradoxically opposed articles and the journal never became, as may have happened elsewhere, an exclusive expression of a single position. The MARS group may well have felt that the *AR*'s support was not quite as exclusive and wholehearted as they might have wished. Despite a reputation to the contrary, it never was a truly revolutionary instrument and continued, as it had before Richards' editorship, to explore and celebrate diverse positions within a reading of Englishness. Along with the role of Richards, there was the undoubted influence of H. de Cronin Hastings, who as long-term Editor and proprietor of the Architectural Press, exercised what Richards later called the 'remote control' of the journal and its editorial policy.

The role of the *AR* in changing architectural culture in Britain was one of the remarkable cases of change being fostered and expressed by a publication that captures the spirit of its particular age. Without it, modernism would no doubt have arrived in Britain. But the configuration that it took and the values it adopted were those that the *AR* developed: without that, a different form of modernism would have taken its place. An illuminating comparison may be made with the United States, similarly largely separated from the formation of what there came to be called 'The International Style'. The difference in the USA was that the growth of modernist work benefited from the arrival of a number of émigré designers, but was not as self-conscious or as coherent as a movement and, crucially, was devoid of the polemic of its British counterpart. Further, the very different political climate ensured that it had none of its social commitment, let alone its humanism, remaining as the term used in the USA suggests, primarily a *style*. Richards promoted an architecture that was the product of an enlightened social contract, that 'served' the people, with the result of giving a lower priority to the rigour of design. While such a comparison between differing situations can go only so far, it does illustrate that when modernism arrived, it did so transformed by the medium of its translation: the modern movement architecture of Germany, Holland and France influenced both Britain and the USA but its manifestation in those two countries was extremely different. The books and journals, processes of architectural education, and its adoption by institutions took different directions and formed two distinct cultures.

A later generation of architects grew up in Britain who accepted the existence of modernism as a given, and took it as the inevitable basis of their own practice: they were to be the generation involved in the large-scale building and re-building programmes after the Second World War. As Richards later wrote, 'today's architects take for granted freedoms and opportunities that would not be theirs if it had not been for the violent propagandists of the thirties.'[17] However, in this passage he was referring to Wells Coates, rather than himself and the other writers on the *Review*. Thus he modestly refused the role of revolutionary, even though the influence of his editorial position and his own publications was so widespread. It is highly significant that the properties of architecture he championed in the 1930s were those that later came into being in Britain; and through his continued role as *AR* Editor after 1946, he continued to effect architectural change, not least in his criticism of what had been achieved.

Richards described his architectural education which began in 1924 at the Architectural Association as characteristic of the prevailing tradition – his first design project being the typically *Beaux-Arts* theme of a hotel on a rocky promontory. He looked back at the period, however, as one when the students got more engaged with progressive notions than did the staff: Etchells' translation of Le Corbusier's *Vers une architecture* came out when Richards was in his third year, and following in the footsteps of Yerbury and Robertson, in vacations he and fellow students visited new buildings in Scandinavia and Germany.[18] After the AA, working in offices including that of Owen Williams, he soon came to a realisation: 'I would never make an architect. I was neither interested in, or competent at, the technical and business side and realised I had no talent for original design.'[19] In 1933 he was interviewed, one of seventy applicants, for a position as journalist on the Architectural Press, initially working on the *Architects' Journal*. Soon, however, Christian Barman as Editor of *Architectural Review* and later John Betjeman as Assistant Editor both resigned, with the result that Richards was appointed to the assistant position in 1935. 'Assistant', that is, to the largely absent Hubert de Cronin Hastings, *AR* Editor since 1927 and son of the then Architectural Press proprietor.

It is to a great extent through Hastings that the *Architectural Review* made and maintained its overall reputation: a series of campaigns continuing into the 1950s and 1960s were concerned with the visual quality (or lack of it) of British towns. While an enthusiast for modern architecture, Hastings was also responsible for its engagement with traditional values of craftsmanship and the picturesque, and a predominant interest in the strange and unfashionable, as if the visual vocabulary of the modern architect needed continual enlargement.[20] Against these prevailing preoccupations, what became Richards' campaign for the Modern Movement sometimes made for strange juxtapositions in the *AR*. Next to the dramatically illustrated coverage of a white-walled and sharp-edged representative of advanced and progressive ideas might be a feature on Dutch gables in East Anglia, or Baroque churches in Moravia.

There was nevertheless a perception that the *Architectural Review* under Richards' editorship was a very different and focused publication than it had been before: that Richards made the journal the focus of modernism in Britain.

As Hugh Casson, writer on the *AR*, later recalled:

> For nearly ten years the *Architectural Review* office under Richards was the centre point of the new movement in England ... [it] was at the height of its battle for modern architecture. Every issue carried its manifesto – a building by one of the pioneers, Max Fry, Tecton, Wells Coates or Connell Ward and Lucas – gorgeously illustrated by Dell and Wainwright and brilliantly analysed and described by J.M. Richards.[21]

Richards could and did express modernist fervour as an underpinning for the new thinking that the journal represented. Gropius was a particular hero, whose arrival in Britain in 1935 must have heralded great things, and Richards wrote on his contribution: 'For our own society (in this country and in others) to become intelligently ordered, the search for the standard must continue; so our mechanistic civilisation demands. The help and example of Professor Gropius will be invaluable.'[22]

Also early in his editorship, Richards wrote on the 'rational' in design which formed a manifesto underlying his later writing. 'Towards a Rational Aesthetic' argued that:

> To this new aesthetic the opportunities of rationalization that the machine brings, the progressive impersonalization of design, the new emphasis on the product rather than on the process of making it and the discovery of the abstract aesthetic virtues of machines themselves have all contributed. The difference is, in brief, that which lies between a humanistic aesthetic and an abstract one.[23]

There is also the central idea in Richards' position of the modern becoming the vernacular: rather than the creative individual architect, architecture must be a collective effort which does not depend on the aptitude and skills of the few. In *Circle*, in an article on 'The Condition of Architecture and the Principle of Anonymity', Richards wrote: 'Architecture cannot afford to be an affair of the individual. It is only when the individual innovation becomes assimilated into a regional tradition that it can be regarded as culturally valid.'[24] The historical model often referred to was an interpretation of the tradition, as in the Georgian house seen in eighteenth-century England, which was neutral, inexpressive and lent itself to repetition. Order, rationalisation, impersonalisation, abstraction, a new 'tradition': alongside the aim of moving towards a standard, a prototype of practice, these terms represented the core of Richards' belief and the origin of a new basis for architecture.

It is equally true that the forming of its position implied a distrust of the orthodoxies of Gropius, Le Corbusier and CIAM. A more commonly held sentiment in Britain was that of introducing a humanism which might be seen as lacking in those original sources of modernism: the doubts about this application of the Modern Movement in Britain expressed by Blomfield[25] were more widely pervasive. And, with a link to the enthusiasm of Yerbury, who initially opened the channels of communication with Scandinavia, a softer and less doctrinaire version of modernism became promoted, matching the intention of identifying a 'regional' tradition. As Richards wrote: 'Sweden, with her instinct for using materials well and her serious sense of social values, has set an example to all Europe of the way modern architecture can solve such problems as the housing of industrial workers.'[26] The *Review* in his period documented Scandinavian work, and also from time to time the bricky north European tradition which Yerbury had admired. Aalto was one of a number of architects to become alternative heroes,[27] with a pervasive influence in Britain.

THE MISSION OF MODERNISM

The aesthetic of modernism

The central irony to this discussion is that concerns about architecture as a social instrument, or as a reflection of industry, or as an expression of universal progress, surfaced only rarely in the pages of the *Architectural Review*. Far more frequent was a concern with how modern things *looked*. The *Review* of the 1930s worked very much as a visual document: the primacy of carefully taken and laid out photographs over the text; the large size of the page (28×35.5 cm) and the often very large photographs that bled off the page. Papers of particular texture and colour were used so that each month's issue appeared startlingly fresh: RIBA Librarian David Dean referred to it as an 'art object'.[28] This was true even early in the decade, with Hastings responsible for design: in August 1930, wood-inlay pictures by Carl Malmsten were tipped-in on blue cartridge, and even a piece of wallpaper bound in, to an issue on Sweden and its design: this as well as the use of full-page photographs and innovation in fonts and layout. This quality was enthusiastically extended by John Betjeman who was Assistant Editor from 1930, with his use of an eclectic mix of materials and papers, Victorian typefaces, extravagant colour and the best of printing.

2.3
Architectural Review, July 1936: layout by Laszlo Moholy-Nagy of an issue on the theme Seaside, pp. 14–15.

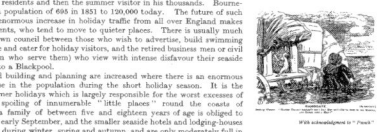

THE MISSION OF MODERNISM

2.4
***Architectural Review*, December 1936: modernist layout and photography, house at Iver by F.R.S. Yorke.**

Within a more modernist vocabulary of innovation, this expression of the visual in graphic ingenuity continued: the most extreme commissioned by Richards, the 'Leisure at the Seaside' article of July 1936, was designed by Laszlo Moholy-Nagy. He used strong blocks of colour in both abstract and representational contexts, cartridge paper perforated with circles, and an integration of text and graphics not seen before in Britain, as befitted the former designer of the Bauhaus publications. The article was also illustrated by his photographs, ironically contrasting in their expression of the 'new photography' with the text voicing a nostalgia for the English seaside's recent decline.[29] The visual quality, the image of the page, was constantly important in

43

the *Architectural Review*'s practice. While this certainly originated with Hastings as Editor, and was from time to time expressed particularly strongly by such a designer-contributor as Moholy-Nagy, it also became firmly associated with the modernist quality the journal gained, even before Richards' editorship. An examination of its coverage of certain key British modern buildings helps to illustrate this. The documentation in March 1933 of the early house by Amyas Connell at Grayswood in Surrey sets up the pattern: a full-page photograph, two smaller photographs, and a half-page site plan are supplemented by a short, and only descriptive, text. So half the allotted space is taken by a single graphically strong photograph, which thus becomes the predominant message of the building.[30]

2.5
Architectural Review, April 1938: modernist layout and photography, Electricity showrooms, Regent Street by Maxwell Fry.

THE MISSION OF MODERNISM

The design caution attributed to Hastings, 'details large, general views small'[31] can clearly be seen in the documentation in 1937 of another expression of British modernism, the house at Coombe in Surrey by Maxwell Fry.[32] The largest, a full-page image, shows the sun-room, modestly furnished but filled with sunlight and 'the large area of the window that can be thrown completely open'. Of the exterior photographs, the most prominent is of the paved roof terrace which faces south: other details show the sun-room from outside and living room with its long sliding windows. Again, the text does not attempt to do more than support and describe the images in terms of an understanding of what they intend to show: the house is seen in isolation (despite its suburban setting) and with minimal signs of inhabitation. The photographs, however, serve the house well in their depiction of a sunlit, calm and fulfilled world eloquently represented here.

Chermayeff's house at Bentley Wood in Sussex was given rather more lavish coverage in 1939. In most ways typical of the dominant use of photography in the time of Richards' editorship, the *AR*'s staff photographers, Dell and Wainwright, had been commissioned and produced numerous crisp, well-lit images of the exterior, the terrace, the living room, the dining room and such details as the terrace wall and sliding windows. They are images of an airy house, full of sun, placed in a clearing in a wooded landscape. The horizontal form of

2.6
Bentley Wood, Sussex by Chermayeff: photograph by Dell and Wainwright published in *Architectural Review*, February 1939.

most of the photographs emphasises the horizontality of the house and its long open terrace, and the Wealden landscape around. The sixteen pages allotted also include diagrams intended to explain the design of details, construction and services: these integrate photographs and expanded drawings with graphically spread text, a modest version of modernist typography. The narrative text in contrast takes up only a few pages, and serves to describe but not, at all, to analyse or critique.[33] The most memorable parts of the coverage are the lavish photographs and carefully arranged content, the visual relationship of the house, the placing of art works and the landscape: the most striking image shows the house in the distance placed in a panorama, trees spreading far beyond to the horizon, framed by the sails of the house's wind pump. What this documentation communicates is the achievement of the house as a consummate object, perfect in its isolation; it depicts a cultured and tranquil life, executed by an architect who had recourse to modern techniques and modernist language, and not at all to precedent. There is nothing absolute about this interpretation, or indeed about the choice to make it so prominent in the journal; but the language of this coverage is unmistakably that of an ideal which has been brought into being.

In interrogating the values of the *Architectural Review* in this period, the counterpart of its writing, also very important and not always taking a supportive role to the visual, did *itself* emphasise the visual qualities over detailed analysis of the programme and operation of a building. The early house in Bayswater by Denys Lasdun was also covered in 1939:[34] there is extensive discussion of it as a prototype of a town house, and illustrated discussion about how it might set up a typology to replace outdated Victorian villas. Numerous photographs, with the façade taken by John Havinden, and drawings and discussion of the furnishing of rooms and planning form the *AR*'s documentation. The pilotus central to the façade is described as 'not absolutely necessary' structurally; there is no grid of piloti, in contrast to the house's undoubted Corbusian model, the Villa Cook at Boulogne-sur-Seine. So it might be concluded that the *look* of the house, defined by its specific modernist pedigree, is seen as its main achievement. But, significantly, rather than embodying Le Corbusier's 'Five Points' of the new architecture, it is built of brick and has none of the spatial invention of the Corbusian original: however, since it looked modern it *was* modern, in the terms of the *AR*'s evaluation. It could be seen as itself a photograph of the Villa Cook: in his review of *The Modern House in England* published in 1938, Hugh Casson had written, 'a lot of these houses were images of houses'.[35] The documentation of a building which represented architecture as a series

2.7
Illustration from F.R.S. Yorke, *The Modern House*, Architectural Press, 1934, showing Le Corbusier's house at Boulogne-sur-Seine.

THE MISSION OF MODERNISM

2.8
House in Newton Road, Bayswater, by Denys Lasdun: photograph by John Havinden published in *Architectural Review*, March 1939; as Hugh Casson remarked, 'a lot of these houses are images of houses'.

of images, irrespective of its material qualities or use, or relation to modernist principle, became a common practice in the 1930s and is one of the further legacies of the period. The careful representation of the perfected visual qualities of the building came to be seen as the surmounting achievement of a work of modern architecture.

But in other cases, relatively rarely, the architectural intention lay elsewhere. 'Mass Produced Shelter' is the name of an article on Mount Royal Flats, Oxford Street published in January 1935.[36] Rather than an emphasis on the aesthetic of the building, modern in the sense of Erich

Mendelsohn rather than Gropius or Le Corbusier, the emphasis is on the research which, it is described, shaped the design process:

> Some two months of intensive study and experiment were put into this initial work, until the unit of the flats, 18 ft by 17 ft, was passed by all the parties concerned, architects, engineers, builders, building owners, as an efficient piece of machinery. The rest is mass production: the whole building is made up of this unit repeated 650 times and mounted upon a base of shops and services ... Each [tenant] has his 'cell', but he shares with his fellows a sort of communal life, the need for which is embodied in the public spaces on the first floor at Mount Royal (shops, café, post office) ... Mass produced equipment. The mass produced home. The mass produced town.

The connection here is with ideas, advanced by both Gropius and Le Corbusier, on mass production as one of the principal practices which a modern architect could adopt in order to relate architecture more closely to possible means of production, and also the idea of perfecting the type which then could be infinitely reproduced. It was, however, highly unusual for the *Review* to champion mass-production as an ideal; the idea of research thus outlined is nevertheless an occasion when it is relating with the concerns of the newly formed MARS group.

An early contribution to *AR* by Richards similarly took up design issues, and how they related to the social engagement of architecture rather than the more frequently expressed aesthetic concern. The Pioneer Health Centre in Peckham, designed by Owen Williams,[37] was a new type of building, provided as a mission for health in a deprived district. Photographs were taken by M. Dell and H.L. Wainwright, official photographers to the *AR* since 1930, but not always credited as such. Their work as seen here at Peckham is typically modernist in the emphasis on form and the assemblage of masses, of light and contrast, the rhythm of volumes, the exclusion of all but the most significant and edited signs of inhabitation. The telling detail became one of their most frequent strategies, and here the article is introduced by a photograph of sculpturally curved railings on the roof with the caption 'Fresh air and sunshine on the roof playground. The railings curve inwards so that it is almost impossible to climb up and fall over.' Very much indebted to the approach of German 'new photography' in parallel to the acknowledged Bauhaus influence on many of the architects whose work they photographed, Dell and Wainwright were not actually taught within that modernist tradition.[38]

The review article 'The Idea behind the Idea' by Richards has much on a philosophy of health as preventative practice, which links happily with his eagerness for the social improvement which architecture might bring about: Peckham might well have been a perfect building. He later moves on to architectural qualities: 'the detailed layout of each floor is a good example of the ultimate simplification of which really good planning consists'. However, he concludes with implicit criticism which cannot excuse poor detail design: 'this building is architecturally alive, and no crudity of execution can destroy that vitality – and more than elaborate consideration of detail can bring a dead building to life.'[39]

The most cursory look at the *Architectural Review* of the 1930s will disclose that over half of the pages of each issue do not carry editorial material; neither manifestos, commentaries, critiques, nor the coverage of new buildings. They do though, carry the advertisements by which manufacturers and the suppliers of services hoped to attract architects to specify or use their products. Many of these products were new: new materials and the means to adopt new techniques to effect the new architecture. Among a much greater number in one issue for March 1935 can be found: a proprietary flat roof system, the 'Paropa' roof; Henry Hope skylights (as used at Blackpool Pleasure Beach); Vernier cushion control lifts; British Aluminium grilles; Vitrolite coloured glass panels; 'Vita' glass that let in health-giving rays; 'invisible panel' warming; Williams' metal windows; 'Cullamix' cement and aggregate; and the necessary structural steel manufacturers. For a few of the advertisers, modern architecture was a mission that they were enthusiastic to support. Some advertisements adopted modernist graphics and layout: most, however, were content to follow where architects might steer them. It is interesting to note, however, that there was no particular urgency or drive on the part of industry for the necessity for new practices, which had been an argument adopted in architects' polemic.

The *Review* in the 1930s gave particular prominence to the work of Berthold Lubetkin and his practice, Tecton, despite the development of a modern 'vernacular' being Richards' primary aim: Lubetkin was anything but anonymous, although in his favour were his social commitment and purpose.[40] Soon after the completion of Tecton's first major building in Britain, Highpoint flats in Highgate, the *Review* covered it fully, with twenty photographs, one full page and one in colour, thirteen plans and diagrams, and an appreciation by Le Corbusier as well as one by Richards.[41] This marks, at a fairly early stage in his editorship, the opportunity to take account of a major achievement in British modernism: Highpoint became for some

2.9
Highpoint, Highgate: Berthold Lubetkin and Tecton, published in *Architectural Review*, January 1936.

years, in part due to the coverage in the *AR* the most renowned modern building in the country. It was clearly a coup to secure Le Corbusier as a critic. 'For a long time I have dreamt of executing dwellings in such conditions for humanity' he wrote, praising Tecton's use of a standard design: 'the result is an excellent quality in the smallest details; well studied, once and for all, they extend their benefits to the whole building.' He spoke also of the building as the 'seed of the vertical garden-city as opposed to the horizontal extension', as a response to the chaos and spread of London. For Le Corbusier, it appeared as a model for future development, a prototype which, it would also appear, he wished he had designed himself.

Richards takes a more critical view, starting his criticism with the observation that 'the time has come when we have the right to demand a high standard of finish and mechanical craftsmanship in modern buildings.' The revolution of the Modern Movement, he says with a degree of optimism, has arrived: so his attention is in pointing out the high standard of finish and detail as well as the thoughtfulness of the block's planning, against the poorer standard of earlier British modern work. The aesthetic, Richards says is one of 'restraint and simplicity' and the block is devoid of monumentality. He does make some negative criticisms: the badly designed name sign, a lack of individual privacy, low ceiling heights; but certainly praises the building as representing an ingenious solution to the development of a difficult site as well as providing a sense of communality in this block of private flats.

The photographs taken by Dell and Wainwright had sharp contrast and emphasised formal qualities, providing what came to be the standard views of the block. Atypically, though, there are three photographs of flats' living rooms, including Lubetkin's own, each showing the differing furnishing of identical space. With Highpoint, a major achievement which he is bound to praise, Richards' language is characterised by words such as 'standard'; 'plan' as in 'economically planned', 'detail and finish', and 'type'; while his adjectives include 'essential', 'pleasant', 'interesting' and most of all the reiteration of 'modern'. It is clear that these terms represent judicious appreciation, rational analysis and restraint. It would of course be possible for such a radically new building, the most fully achieved building of modernism in Britain at that time, to bring about genuine enthusiasm and passion; Richards' modest rhetoric remains understated. The language of his discussion and critique does not represent the uncompromising modernist rigour which other writers would have favoured.

Richards at the *Architectural Review* thus took a position paradoxically characterised both by polemic and caution: while convinced

2.10
Highpoint, Highgate; detail of entrance canopy: Berthold Lubetkin and Tecton, published in *Architectural Review*, January 1936.

of the rightness of a modernist strategy, he remained an architectural critic more concerned with the making of detail than with the writing of manifestos. The *AR* was, finally, powerful in reinforcing the visual interpretation of modern architecture in British architectural culture: feeling, in the sense of joy and fulfilment; thinking, in the sense of intellectual rigour, both remained unexpressed.

Richards' judgement

There is a counterpoint to the modernism for which the *Review* was renowned. All through the 1930s, many articles on the curious and unexplored buildings and artefacts of history had appeared. These were often the result of Hastings' interests but often too of Richards. The July 1937 issue of *Architectural Review* extensively covered Serge Chermayeff's reinforced concrete office building for Gilbey's, but also gave space to an account of the eighteenth-century Pantheon in Oxford Street as well as the minor nineteenth-century architect Alfred Darbyshire. In the January 1939 issue, Tecton's Finsbury Health Centre is given pride of place with eighteen pages of photographs, plans and description: alongside it is a survey of the visual quality of the buildings of the Isle of Man, and an account of a visit to the lost city of Angkor Wat.

For Richards, any and all of this could provide some kind of tangential education for the modern architect. Writing in the 1970s about this period, he pointed out: 'Discarding the historic styles as a source of forms and detail began a process of looking at them with very different eyes, of looking at the past in the same perspective as the present.'[42] The flattening out of history which he thus described had a long pedigree as a modernist practice, dating back at least to Picasso's appropriation of African religious objects. Such varied objects as Romanesque sculpture[43] or prehistoric earthworks were seen, quite irrespective of historical context, as phenomena capable of accommodating properties of modern art and abstraction. This ahistoricism and arbitrary selection made the whole of history a possible quarry.

Within this practice, there was a particular preoccupation with the English, and Richards began, together with John Piper, to document the anonymous buildings and objects of the urban and rural landscapes on a series of car journeys starting in 1938. Even before this, Piper's photographs and art work combined a romantic nostalgia for some lost and forgotten 'Englishness' with a quite modernist sensibility. In terms of architectural objects, the most significant of these early *AR* publications was Piper's 'The Nautical Style' of January 1938,[44] which focused on the lighthouse, jetty, buoy and seaside building. Piper saw these as having a strong functional element, nevertheless mediated by a consistent aesthetic. The article, illustrated with photographs by Piper, prefigured many of the interests of the post-war *AR*, which are pursued in Chapter 4 on 'The shift to the specific'.

At the beginning of 1940, Richards wrote the first of a long series of *Review* articles, 'Criticism', under the pseudonym of James MacQuedy: this alias perhaps enabled him to take a less avowedly partisan line than he had done in the Penguin *Introduction to Modern Architecture* published at the same time.[45]

> [N]ow we have reached a stage when we can take most of what modern architecture stands for granted. It should no longer be necessary to explain the functional basis on which the modern architect works; and as maturity develops, it becomes essential that we restore the practice of pictorial criticism. In doing so we are not retreating for the principles that gave modern architecture its validity ... But we are justified in judging buildings largely according to their appeal to the eye ... For modernity, like patriotism, is not enough.

2.11
The modern style: Housing, Kensal House Ladbroke Grove, London: designed by a committee led by Maxwell Fry, 1937.

THE MISSION OF MODERNISM

This is echoed by a retrospective comment he made in 1968:

> It might almost be said of architectural criticism in England in the 1930s that there was none – none, at least, in the sense of regular appraisals of new buildings as they were put up … [critics] were either for the modern movement or against it, and there was little incentive until the main battle had been won for those who were for it – the majority of the more objective writers about architecture – to discriminate between good and bad quality in modern buildings.[46]

Richards had at the time presented some criticisms of the most celebrated achievements of the modern movement, as in the case of Highpoint and the Peckham Health Centre, but clearly felt he had abnegated the role of critic and thus not been a genuine interpreter of the new architecture. In reading his work of the 1930s, one might

2.12
The modern style: Private houses, Frognal, Hampstead: Connell, Ward and Lucas, 1937.

feel he is being too critical of himself: but in 1968 he would have known how effective his championing of modern architecture had been, without the consequent transformation of the world he had wished for. His autobiography expresses his regret for what had been achieved, and his RIBA Annual Discourse of 1972 entitled 'The Hollow Victory' admits the dystopian rather than utopian consequences of his campaigning.[47]

In 1942 he found himself in the British Army and created a book which celebrated, at a distance (it was written on the North African coast), the peaceful joys of English suburbia. *Castles on the Ground*[48] is, as has been remarked, a surprising thing to have been written by the man largely responsible for introducing the forms and practices of modernism to Britain.[49] He talks of the joy and quiet of the suburban street, its secluded garden, its contained bourgeois respectability. And, in relation to the strictures of taste which he had so long been responsible for promoting:

> One moral of this book is that creative activity can only be encouraged among the mass of people by building on a foundation of their own existing modes of expression ... sophisticated standards of taste and criticism can conveniently be forgotten. The methods pursued under the guidance of such standards is to offer people 'good architecture' and hope they will come to like it by habit. New habits are all very well but they are not a product of feeling, and the art of architecture requires the support of intense feeling. People can only learn to feel intensely by starting with the things that already mean something to them emotionally, and while the values on which the critics insist on basing their idea of architectural right and wrong remain aloof ... they will have no feelings about architecture.[50]

Modernist architecture however correct, however appropriate it may have been, becomes an imposition, he suggests, if it is not related to people's own sympathies and passions. Only by making a relationship to existing systems of belief can it hope to become part of a legitimate tradition. The implicit notion of architecture as essentially an expression of a broader culture shapes much of Richards' writing and the *Architectural Review* had always been deliberately and specifically cultural in its approach. Writers (and readers) far beyond the limits of the architectural profession contributed to its breadth of subject matter throughout the 1930s and despite its references to the *Zeitgeist* and to 'progress', individual architects were always presented as 'artists'. Richards' characteristically English dislike of the rational as the basis for design comes through in *Castles in the Ground*; architecture is finally about feeling. It might also be added that to see architecture as a practice more rooted in culture, and the culture of a place, is to be in the right place to start.

The alternative personae of Richards as 'James MacQuedy' or the soldier in exile provide a re-examination of his own expressed position. Nevertheless, the shift of architectural practice into the post-war world represents a triumphant articulation of the values developed by Richards and the *Review* in the 1930s. As Lubetkin himself declared with respect to the modernist group of pre-war architects: 'the old reactionaries were out and the doors were open to us. We were established.'[51] The shift in British architectural culture from the conservative to the progressive had been accomplished: the forms of building, whether housing, commercial development, or public buildings, embodied the aesthetics, if not the radical programme, of modernism.

Notes

1. James Richards, *Introduction to Modern Architecture*, Harmondsworth: Penguin, 1940. Introduction, p. 9. The book was in print until the early 1970s with no major modification to its position.
2. Richards wrote an autobiography *Memoirs of an Unjust Fella*, London: Weidenfeld & Nicolson, 1980.
3. Colin Rowe, *The Architecture of Good Intentions*, London: Academy Editions, 1994, pp. 38–9.
4. A. Isozaki, Introduction in K. Karatani, *Architecture as Metaphor*, Cambridge, MA: MIT Press, 1995, p. xi.
5. Richards was Editor or Co-editor of *Architectural Review* from 1935 to 1971, apart from a wartime period. See J. Mordaunt Crook 'Sir James Richards (1907–92): a Bibliographical Tribute' in *Architectural History*, vol. 42, 1999, pp. 354–74 for a full bibliography.
6. F.R.S. Yorke, *The Modern House* (1934); *The Modern House in England* (1937); *The Modern Flat* (1937), London: Architectural Press.
7. James Richards' interview with the present author in December 1986: his review of the book appeared in *AR*, August 1935, p. 46. Gropius, *The New Architecture and the Bauhaus*. London: Faber & Faber, 1935.
8. Trans. Frederick Etchells, with the insertion of the word 'new' in the title and many textual changes. London: John Rodker, 1927.
9. Nikolaus Pevsner, *Pioneers of the Modern Movement from William Morris to Walter Gropius*, London: Faber & Faber, 1936. See P. Tournikiotis, *The Historiography of Modern Architecture*, Cambridge, MA: MIT Press, 1999.
10. M. Tafuri and F. Dal Co, *Modern Architecture*, London: Academy, 1980, p. 257.
11. See Richards, *Memoirs*, p. 87.
12. Shand's publication of articles in *Architectural Review* in July 1934 and later were among the first to attempt an interpretation of European modernist architecture.
13. See S. Cantacuzino, *Wells Coates*, London: Gordon Fraser, 1978, p. 47.
14. Founded in 1896 as the 'Architectural Review for the Artist and Craftsman'.

15 Howard Robertson on the La Roche house, Paris, in 'Some Recent French Developments in Domestic Architecture', *AR*, January 1927, pp. 2–7.
16 *AR* August 1929, pp. 76–8.
17 Quoted in Cantacuzino, op. cit., p. 49.
18 Interview with the present author, December 1986.
19 Richards, *Memoirs*, p. 87.
20 See Chapter 4 on 'The shift to the specific' for expression of one of the most important of these.
21 Hugh Casson, 'The Elusive H de C', *RIBA Journal*, February 1971, pp. 58–9.
22 Richards, 'Walter Gropius', *AR*, August 1935, p. 46.
23 Richards *AR*, December 1935, p. 211.
24 Richards in J.L. Martin, B. Nicholson and N. Gabo (eds) *Circle*, London: Faber & Faber, 1937, p. 184.
25 See Reginald Blomfield, *Modernismus*, Oxford: Macmillan, 1934.
26 Richards, *Introduction to Modern Architecture*, pp. 78–9.
27 Aalto's house at Munkkiniemi was published in *Architectural Review*, April 1938, pp. 175–8.
28 The *AR* is described as 'guide-book, totem, and art object': David Dean, *The Thirties: Recalling the English Architectural Scene*, London: Trefoil, 1983, p. 14.
29 *AR*, July 1936, pp. 7–28.
30 *AR*, March 1933, pp. 118–19.
31 Susan Lasdun, 'H. de C. reviewed', *AR*, September 1996, p. 69.
32 *AR*, November 1937, pp. 187–92.
33 *AR*, February 1939, pp. 63–78.
34 *AR*, March 1939, pp. 119–32.
35 *AR*, February 1938, p. 90.
36 *AR*, January 1935, pp. 11–19.
37 *AR*, May 1935, pp. 203–16.
38 On Dell and Wainwright see Robert Elwall, *Photography Takes Command: The Camera and British Architecture 1890–1939*, London: RIBA, 1994, pp. 66–78.
39 *AR*, May 1935, p. 20.
40 See John Allan's *Lubetkin: Architecture and the Tradition of Progress*, London: RIBA Publications, 1992.
41 *AR*, January 1936, pp. 5–18.
42 *AR*, November 1979, p. 302.
43 See John Piper, 'England's Early Sculptors', *AR*, October 1936, pp. 157–62.
44 *AR*, January 1938, pp. 1–14.
45 James MacQuedy, 'Criticism', *AR*, January 1940, p. 25.
46 J.M. Richards 'Architectural Criticism in the Nineteen-Thirties', in J. Summerson (ed.), *Concerning Architecture: Essays on Architectural Writers and Writing*, presented to Nikolaus Pevsner, London: Allen Lane, 1968, pp. 252–7.
47 *RIBA Journal*, May 1972, pp. 192–7.
48 J.M. Richards, *Castles on the Ground*, London: Architectural Press, 1946.
49 Based on his interest in the suburb, there is a Richards archive in the Museum of Domestic Design and Architecture at Middlesex University which incorporates his library.
50 Richards, *Castles on the Ground*, pp. 79–80.
51 Quoted in John R. Gold, *The Experience of Modernism*, London: Spon, 1997, p. 187.

CHAPTER 3

the forgetting of art

the Abercrombie Plan for post-war London

THE FORGETTING OF ART

> There is no doubt whatever that if the full resources of modern building science and the skill and imagination of modern architects are used in every house, whether a small two-storeyed house or a flat, [they] will be as good as the best that London has known in the past. A new London, clean, humane and beautiful will grow out of the County Plan.
>
> (*The County of London Plan Explained*, 1945)[1]

The County of London Plan of 1943, generally referred to as the Abercrombie Plan, provides an apposite focus for an enquiry into the project of rebuilding British cities after the Second World War, since it was the most completely articulated and well illustrated document among a considerable number of officially authorised plans for reconstructing British cities. It is the most significant of a very few publications which defined, and provided images of, the subsequent programme of urban rebuilding. Patrick Abercrombie was responsible for a considerable number of contemporary proposals,[2] and as such the Plan is very much the product of the matured British planning discourse of its time. It proposed an ambitious reordering of most of the city, with new roads, parks and reconstructed neighbourhoods, and brought with it the more abstract qualities of efficiency and order. It is also clearly the product of a commonly held set of beliefs – not necessarily the architectural programme of the developing modernist movement, but the project of modernisation which shaped other aspects of British life. It reflected the assumptions of the emerging welfare state, not least that of strong centralised government, and embodied assumptions of social control, seen largely uncritically in the years of wartime and immediately after.

The immediate context of the Plan was wartime. Britain's war had begun in 1939 and in the first two years London had suffered much from the Blitz which destroyed large parts of the capital. In the City alone, buildings covering 164 out of 460 acres were destroyed and the proportion in parts of the inner East End was considerably higher.[3] This destruction was accompanied by the contingent sufferings of wartime – danger, insecurity, shortages and loss – but also by an unprecedented level of state control. Empty houses could be taken over by the local authority; people with an empty room could be forced to take someone in; travel was restricted by the government, as of course was food. In almost every area of life it seemed that the state had assumed power. Myriad aspects of life were subject to control and direction, even when the reason for that control was not evident. But peace was also present in the imagination, and even when the war's outcome was seriously in doubt, the thought of a future redemptive peace, the post-war creation of a better world, could sustain and inspire. There was a momentous dialectic of peace and harmony after war and destruction. So during wartime there was a genuine wish for the creation of places where there was harmony, where conflict on a large or small scale could not develop. As Ralph Tubbs wrote in 1942:

> Today we are at war ... The war is no mere conflict between nations, it is part of a great battle for the establishment of a civilisation in which mankind may live in friendship, in conditions that make a full life possible. The preparation now to ensure that these conditions are realised is an essential part of our war effort.[4]

Such was the context of a widely ranging discourse of social progress in wartime Britain, notably including the 1942 Beveridge Report, which led to the foundation of the welfare state. An equally important counterpart of that was the idea of remaking cities – cities which had never been planned, which had been caught up in the nineteenth-century social explosion of the Industrial Revolution. Planners had positioned themselves to know what needed to be done: since early in the century, town planning had developed as a practice to be concerned with the inclusive planning of whole cities rather than the simpler *Beaux-Arts* intention of making the city beautiful. Trained as an architect, Abercrombie had become Professor of Planning at Liverpool in 1915 and later at University College London. From his prize-winning plan for Dublin of 1914 onwards, he proposed the wholesale reordering of cities and regions in a series of projects.[5] He described the planner's task as giving 'a guiding hand to the trend of natural evolution as a result of a careful study of the place itself.'[6] The outcome of the planners' work was to be a pleasant, organised and efficient city.

Town planning had the tools to approach the highly complex task of urban reconstruction. Among the books on planning published in wartime was Ralph Tubbs's 1942 Penguin Book *Living in Cities*: 134,000 copies were sold.[7] The cover of this popular book, which was also represented as travelling exhibition, is highly representative of the 1940s spirit of reconstruction. Four images show Salisbury and its Cathedral Close; a polluted industrial town of the Potteries; a street totally destroyed by bombing with the smoke still rising; and the hands of an architect at his drawing board, pencil in hand, with set square, parallel motion and compasses, drawing up plans for rebuilding the city.

THE FORGETTING OF ART

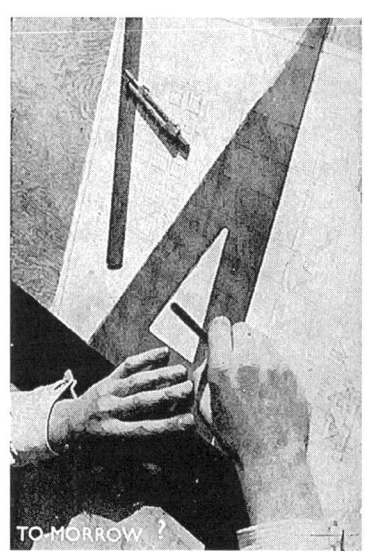

3.1
Yesterday-Today-Tomorrow?:
Illustrations from cover of Ralph Tubbs, *Living in Cities*, Penguin, 1942.

The message is that chaos will be replaced by geometry, disorder with order. The confusion and degradation represented by the industrial city is contrasted with the order and beauty of the medieval city. The architect (or planner) is represented as a healer, making by the lines on the paper a positive and redeemed future, one that will with patience replace the long-term degeneracy of the urban conditions created by industrialisation, and the immediate chaos in the city produced by bombing. The medieval city, it might be pointed out, was a highly structured and controlled society, ruled by the fear of God. It is significant that the only positive urban image is that of a highly ordered and controlled society. One could go further and assert that the planner and politician at this time, assuming power over the huge and complex process of bringing a city to order, were taking a god-like role, with, to a large extent, the assent of the people. Colin Rowe in *Collage City* is among those who have pointed out that the drive to build the modern city had a largely concealed utopian motive: the town planner and architect took on a messianic role. They brought, Rowe says, a 'message of good news.'[8]

Maureen Waller has described the popularity of the Abercrombie Plan's vision of London. There were 75,000 visitors to exhibitions of the Plan at County Hall and the Royal Academy: 'Like the Beveridge report which preceded it, Abercrombie's plan instilled hope for a better post-war world, a world in which poverty and squalor would be eradicated – a world worth fighting for.'[9] Nevertheless the Plan drawn up under the leadership of Patrick Abercrombie can be seen as embodying a set of values largely alien to the ordinary Londoner whose life it set out to improve. It can be seen as the product of a highly specific, narrow perspective, comprehensible both in its social context and in the context of the town planning traditions both of Britain and modern Europe, but highly reductive in the range of its concerns and priorities. There has been a long-standing British distrust of ideology, but its programme of rebuilding and reinvention represents a very strong ideology which accommodates no ambiguity, little self-doubt, and which makes clear the significance of the empirical, of what was seen as 'fact' in the developing processes of this enormous enterprise.

What makes this so very crucial from a historical point of view is how, to a very great extent, the programme which the Abercrombie Plan epitomises had a huge impact on actual British cities: cities were reconstructed on a scale quite without parallel in the thirty years after the Second World War. While urban plans were not carried out in any complete way, implicit intentions and assumptions led to what development there was, and make evident the background to the appearance of cities still seen today.

Abercrombie's context

One primary intention was erasure, and the reinvention of tracts of the city in terms of new principles which would create a new city with none of the bad qualities of the old – in other words, the construction of a utopia. The Abercrombie Plan, like other documents of the period, was illustrated with pictures of completely destroyed sections of cities, after intense Nazi bombing. The obvious distress at this is expressed: it is made clear nevertheless that it presented an 'opportunity', although of course cities could have been rebuilt on identical lines, as not only happened in European cities but even in parts of British ones. The joy which it gave those wanting to impose a new order was muted by the tragic circumstances: but, as has been remarked, far more of London and other cities were destroyed by post-war urban redevelopment than by the destruction of bombing itself, however extensive that may have been. Highly significant in any case is that the debate about urban reconstruction began before the start of war: The MARS group's town planning committee led by William Tatton Brown presented a proposal for reconstructing London to the CIAM Paris Congress in 1937:[10] a plan for the reconstruction of the centre of Coventry was exhibited some months before that city's destruction in the Blitz.[11]

The report of the Royal Commission on the location of the industrial population chaired by Sir Montague Barlow and published in January 1940 is also important as a background to the Abercrombie

Plan. It marked a complete transformation in the role of urban planning in Britain, changing the emphasis from regulating private enterprise to taking authoritative control. Connecting for the first time rural depopulation with metropolitan expansion, its brief was not only to report on the current situation and its disadvantages, but also to propose remedial measures. Its analysis concentrated on the overcrowding and continuous growth of London, and the bad location of existing industry. It proposed a central authority which would carry out the necessary measures, the decentralisation or dispersal of industry, and the redevelopment of central areas: industry could be refused permission to establish in the South East.

A *Dissentient Memorandum* by Patrick Abercrombie, who was a member of the committee, proposed considerably more powers for the suggested government body: 'Industrial control should be legislated on a national basis integrated with local and regional planning and a proper pattern or design must be given to the human environment, so that not only economic but social and artistic needs may be satisfied.'[12] He pointed out the major problem of the payment of compensation by local authorities for planning refusals, and the related problem of private profit on land which had been affected by public planning. This was in turn dealt with by the Uthwatt Report on compensation and betterment,[13] which saw the two as closely related: revenue from one was supposed to pay for the other. The specific proposals of the report were unworkable and changed when the principles came into legislation but the radical terms of reference of the report, that private ownership of urban land was to be put under severe restriction and government control, underlined the change in the climate of opinion in the previous decade.[14]

That the legislative framework emerged from the cultural context of the day is perhaps implicit: there had been a major change in both popular and professional opinion. Giles Scott, speaking as President of the RIBA in 1934, stressed the role of the architect

> as a planner ... with an invaluable contribution to make towards an improvement in the art of living ... 'Planning' is the key-word to a form of development peculiar to our own time. We cannot continue to tolerate the poverty, ill-health, waste and ugliness of disorder. The whole world is out of joint through lack of planning.[15]

Such a view of the possibilities of planning, that the efficient marshalling of existing resources could help to abolish poverty and urban ugliness, was commonplace in Britain in the 1930s. Few doubts were expressed, and ordinary people seemed to share the view that the role of planners and architects was the solution of the problems of city life through social engineering. Marjorie and C.H.V. Quennell, writing in the popular book *Good New Days* published in 1935[16] opposed the old world of congestion, squalor and rural despoilation with hints of an already existing new world, where communally based housing and facilities were to be situated pleasantly in parkland. Examples of flats by Gropius and Fry and Owen Williams' Peckham Health Centre, as well as flat-roofed concrete houses and sunny nursery schools, are seen as representative of the new order. Such attitudes, prevalent as they were in the 1930s and later, can be related to the tradition of Ruskin and Morris, and even Pugin's 'Contrasts' published in 1836, which countered an idealised medieval world to the industrial society then emerging. The idea of the busy, tightly packed metropolis characterised by major continental cities, had long been perceived with distaste by English observers who had seen the one-family house with a garden attached, perforce spreading over the countryside, as the proper way to live.[17] Alongside Barlow's arguments for decentralising the urban population were those from others who simply felt that over-population of the city should always be prevented. C.B. Purdom wrote in *How Should We Rebuild London?* on the city's need to reduce its population and lower its density: 'Here we are brought into contact with the mass of undifferentiated persons, persons who know neither us nor each other: out of these nameless and numberless the mob appears when dominated by a single emotion.'[18]

3.2
Expectation and *Fulfilment* by 'Batt': Illustrations from C.B. Purdom, *How Should We Rebuild London?* 1945, making clear the intention of urban erasure and replanning.

The threat of the working-class crowd was an important factor for Purdom and others from the 'Garden City' tradition. In his chapter on London pleasures, the illustration shows elegant couples in smart restaurants, the National Gallery, Shakespeare, the boat race, a game of cricket. The text comments on London's natural advantages such as the river, and spends much more time talking about playing fields than pubs. Deploring the large number of public houses, he comments:

> The number, size and amount of money taken in these places, especially in the old working class districts, is evidence of the place they fill in many hundreds of thousands of men's lives, and witnesses also to the discomfort and inadequacy of home life.[19]

Thus a puritan programme of moral improvement and disapproval of working-class activities is masked as a plan for urban progress.

But in addition to this English tradition, which is with justification described as anti-urban, a new and complementary influence, that of the avant-garde in modern architecture and urbanism, was in full flood by the late 1930s. Le Corbusier's influence on urban theory was paramount, and was the leading formative influence on the urbanism of CIAM; *La Ville radieuse* first published in English in 1933 is of particular relevance. Taking as its base line the disappearance of traditional city forms, it identifies the problems of the modern city: 'Modern society needs housing, parks and highways' and introduces the model of the radiant city with huge blocks set in parkland and wide highways carrying traffic unimpeded by crossings.[20] Places of work are strictly zoned: places of recreation amply provided. Abundant evidence of the model inhabitant is provided: his pleasures are those of physical culture and the joy of nature coupled with a spartan monasticism. Le Corbusier's extreme version of Ebenezer Howard's Garden City was a compelling image. Dedicated to 'Authority', the realisation of its precepts was dependent on the power to carry out the plan:

> I shall tell you who the despot is you are waiting for. The despot is the Plan. The correct, realistic, exact plan, the one that will provide your solution once the problem has been posited clearly, in its entirety, in its indispensable harmony ... And this plan is your despot: a tyrant, a tribune of the people. Without other help, it will plead its course, reply to objections, overcome the opposition of private interest, thrust aside outworn customs, rescind out-moded regulations, and create its own authority.[21]

The great appeal of such a utopian vision is that of a city without process or change, where everything in it is present in its inception, and which would determine definitively the life of the place. Its attraction seems to be its conceptual clarity, in other words its simplicity: by clearing a site and replacing its various buildings with a simple zoned and laid out city, there is the intellectual satisfaction of a problem solved.

Several precursors to Abercrombie made modernist proposals for re-planning London. The most significant debate took place in the MARS group town planning committee led by William Tatton Brown. A linear plan credited to Tatton Brown with neighbourhood planning and a series of green park wedges running through the city was produced in 1937. However, the committee members Arthur Korn and Felix Samuely formulated what came to be known as the MARS Plan for London, published in 1942. They wrote:

> The final aim of all town planning is to provide the maximum number of amenities for the population. They can be grouped under the following headings: Public Health, Culture and Leisure ... Provision of maximum benefits depends on three other items: Housing, Work and Transport.[22]

Its solution to these needed provisions is the gradual reconstruction of the entire city: improved efficiency is to pay the £1,200 million cost; districts of 600,000 people around a central transport artery are split into boroughs of 50,000 people.[23] While making a plan which begged a question – was it an exercise in modernist planning or a serious proposal to solve London's problems? – the Korn plan did advance a strategy seen later in a different form as basic to Abercrombie, that of forming small identified communities within the vastness of the city. The Plan argued:

> The vast crowds must be split into groups in which the individual does not feel so overwhelmed that he is forced to retire to his own home almost entirely for his social life. Only by forming clearly defined units, which in turn are part of larger units, can social life be organised.[24]

This principle of what came in Abercrombie to be called the 'neighbourhood unit' related to far earlier social theory: followers of Ferdinand Tönnies' book *Community and Civil Society*[25] had argued for a pre-urban model where, as in a small rural community, the abstracted relations of city life could be transformed into genuine

THE FORGETTING OF ART

human interaction. This could only be achieved if the city became a series of small communities, and this is what both the MARS Plan of 1942 and Abercrombie's Plan used as a basic strategy.

A 'modest proposal'

The County of London Plan, in valuing a pre-urban notion of community, can be seen as embodying values of both the English moral tradition of Morris and the 'Garden City' tradition of Unwin,[26] and rather less than Korn's plan, in compounding this with the modernist imperatives of Le Corbusier. Unlike earlier proposals, however, it had an official and highly serious basis: it was prepared in response to an official directive from the Ministry of Works: the Minister, Lord Reith, had requested the drawing up of 'a plan for the reconstruction of the county of London to assist the Ministry in considering the methods and machinery for the planning and carrying out of the reconstruction of Town and Country.'[27] Its brief requested

3.3
London, Social and Functional Analysis: from *County of London Plan*, Forshaw and Abercrombie, 1943; the basis of its planning was the division of the city into identified communities.

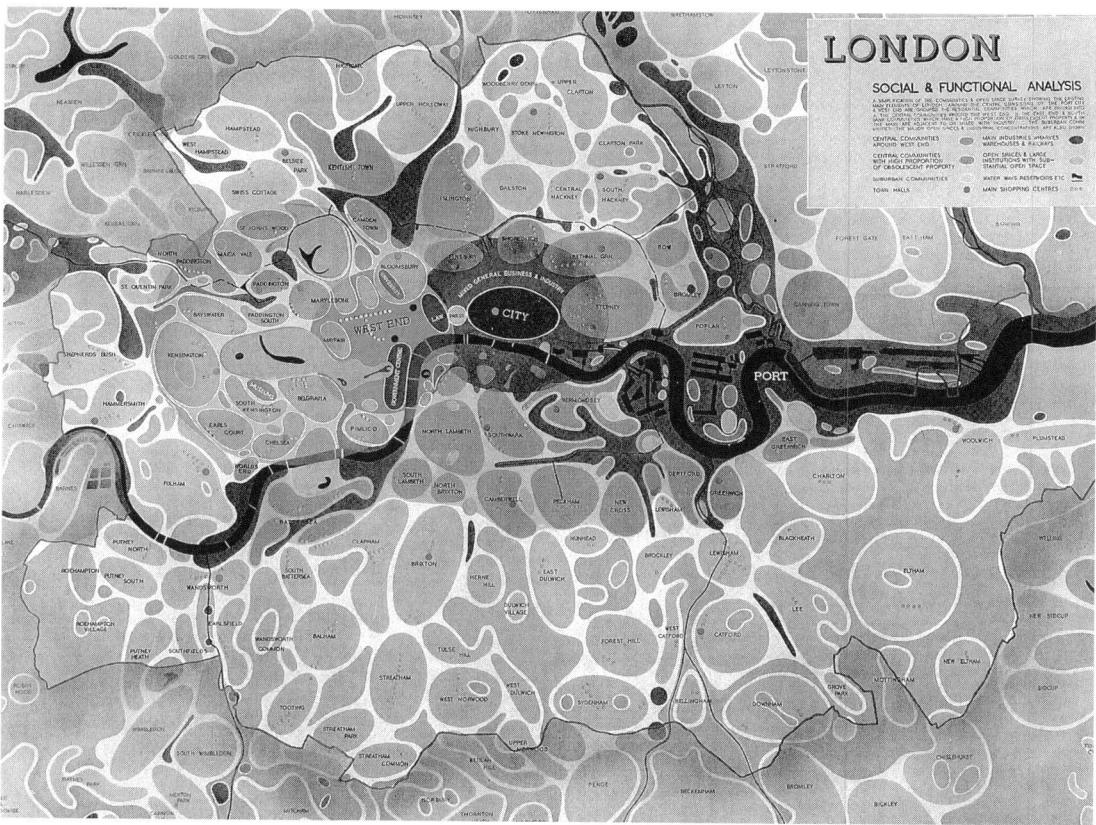

a realistic plan and one sufficiently flexible to provide a framework into which any post-war reconstruction and redevelopment could be incorporated. It also requested its authors to draw up their plan without regard to existing legislation or indeed existing local government organisation. The time had come, it seemed, for a strong and potentially radical plan to attempt a solution to what were perceived as the problems of London, and to act as an adjunct to the report of the Barlow Commission, of which Abercrombie had been a member. Its joint authors were the LCC architect J.H. Forshaw and Abercrombie. The small team of architects and planners was however responsible for much of the content, and here the leading figure was Wesley Dougill, after his death replaced by Arthur Ling, who was responsible for the planning of neighbourhood units.[28]

The official basis of the County of London Plan, requested at Cabinet level and created by the local authority, gave weight and moment to a document supposedly characterised by its attempt to incorporate the diversity of the desires and opinions of those involved in the life of London into a single perspective. Abercrombie was able to harness widespread contemporary dissatisfaction with the status quo in the same way that the Beveridge Report, for example, did. Couched in accessible terms, and with great care taken in its presentation with ample photographs and coloured plans, it was intended to be a popular document.

The presentation of the Plan is to lay out the basic problems as it perceives them in the preamble and first chapter, and the majority of its length is concerned with the reiteration of these problems, their articulation and the Plan's proposed solutions. The opportunity to re-plan London, the Plan says, is one presented both by widespread damage and the destruction of existing property and by the wartime pause in development. By establishing new principles by which to guide and control its further development, the Plan hopes to create a 'better-planned' London and one in which, it hopes, the city's problems will be solved. The problems dealt with and emphasised in the Plan are basically five: the congestion of traffic, causing waste of time and loss of life: the problem of 'depressed housing', the general drabness and dreariness of much of inner London; the inadequacy and imbalance in the supply of open spaces; the mixing of housing and industry causing environmental problems; and the continued sprawl of London to be ever-bigger with the consequent destruction of the surrounding countryside. The last of these problems is largely outside the boundary of the London County Council area and is consequently dealt with in the Greater London Plan produced by Abercrombie in 1944.[29] Further problems referred to in the preamble include the 'lack of coherent architectural development' (on the lines of, say, Regent Street), and the co-ordination of railway development.

Thus, the primacy of better road communication, meaning the construction of new roads, the zoning of areas as residential or industrial, meaning the renewal of one or the other, the large-scale provision of new parks, the reconstruction of inner-city areas on the grounds of their bad planning and general drabness, and the planning on more dignified lines of the central areas, are established early on as the problems the Plan is dealing with. These problems, having been rather briefly affirmed, are not questioned further: the process of dealing with them however is to be examined: '[A]re there to be flats or houses; high densities or low: open space of loose texture within or compactness and playing fields far off ... industry decentralised with population or one taken out and another left behind?'[30]

The Plan acknowledges contending interests, the different views of parts of the community and of 'different public authorities' in the formulation of specific proposals. Research involved finding the views of disparate groups, and an extensive 'civic survey' of the existing situation in London, to lead to the correct solutions. Nevertheless, the formulation of the Plan has little to do with consultation and discussion, as might have been evident thirty years later: it is the production of experts who believe they know best what should be done. In *The County of London Plan Explained*, the plan is described in these terms: 'The Plan was generated by the people of London and created by architects and planners aware of what the people want. Now it is before the people for them to turn into reality.'[31] Having adopted its five basic points, the Plan's authors proceed to relate all human activities to their framework. To them, seeing the city as a community 'where people live, work and play',[32] as a metropolis, the centre of government, culture and commerce, and as a machine in terms of its communication, cover its major aspects. The majority of the body of the Plan deals with such chapter headings as 'housing', 'reconstruction areas' and an 'industrial survey', discussing and establishing detailed points on these subject areas. The conceptual framework of the Plan, in its simplicity, has the advantage of being concrete in its clarity. By the concentration of the undeniable problems of London into five distinct areas, the consequent 'solutions' are equally clear: zoning, the removal of 'surplus' population, road construction, large-scale redevelopment of the inner suburbs, and rationalisation of the metropolitan centre.

The preamble of the Plan, referring to the current opportunity for 'better planning', refers to the new concepts of planning inherent

THE FORGETTING OF ART

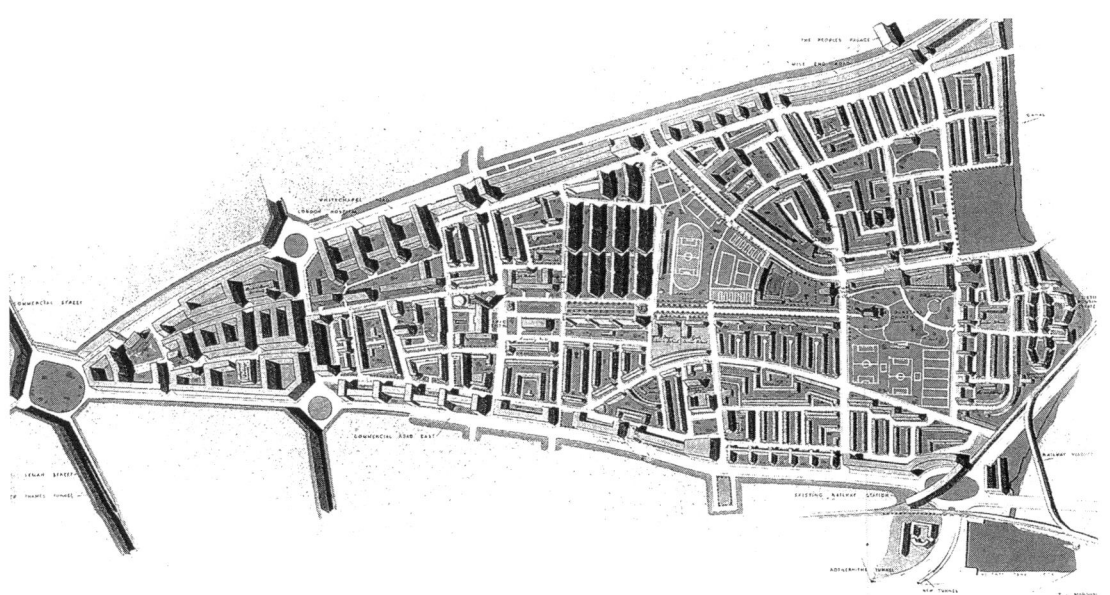

3.4
Axonometric of layout of Stepney as a 'reconstruction area', one of a number of areas of inner London to be totally replanned and rebuilt at a density of 136 people per acre: from the *County of London Plan,* **1943.**

in the Barlow, Uthwatt and Scott reports: it refers also to the possibility of extreme solutions, the razing of the existing city and its reconstruction according to a 'new theoretic conception' or its abandonment. A more modest possibility (and that embodied in the Plan) is 'to retain the old structure where discernible and make it workable under modern conditions.'[33] This avowedly modest proposal could be seen as having two separate parts: (i) tactical – new developments in housing and road construction, and (ii) strategic – to draw up clearly defined principles by which to channel development into appropriate directions. The working out of the Plan's specific proposals is based on the perception of the existence of small communities within the city, of a recognisable identity.

The basis of the plan is the 'neighbourhood unit', with a population of six to ten thousand the core of the Plan's reconstruction proposals, subtending down to the individual dwellings and upwards to the 'community' of the whole suburb. A Plan is drawn up dividing the whole of London into named 'communities' of varying size: while some of these communities clearly reflect existing social groupings, their rigid boundaries and relative homogeneity are debatable. Given the piecemeal and speculative developments which have characterised London's growth it might be seen as the forcing of an issue, again more concerned with conceptual and organisational clarity than empirical evidence: 'Community grouping helps in no small measure towards the inculcation of local pride; it facilitates control and organisation and is the means of resolving what would otherwise be interminable aggregations of housing.'[34] It could also be added that the point of a city could well lie in the advantage of living in a community of millions rather than a few thousand, and that only the very young and the very old need community in that sense. Nevertheless, E.J. Carter and Ernö Goldfinger in their explanation of the County of London Plan argue that it is the lack of planning that has caused urban dislocation:

> [The] idea of community life is the big human factor which the planners have detected and which underlies all their planning. They recognise, however, that in many parts all community feeling is dead – lost largely because lack of planning has had a disruptive, anti-social effect.[35]

Underlying this strategy is the substantial reduction of population in the city as a whole. The reduction of the total population of the London area by up to one million is proposed: in a somewhat different sense this is the forcing of an issue, relating to the Plan's calculations of optimum densities of population. Population density is in three tiers: for the central residential areas, 200 people per acre is allowable, while 136 is to be the norm for the inner city, including the specified reconstruction areas, and 100 for the outer areas. These figures are in turn based on another statistic relating to the need for open space, which is based on a standard of four acres per thousand people. The rigid 'flexibility' of density, irrespective of the employment of the resident population, or a myriad of local factors, is a clear example of the limits of the statistically based approach. One of the areas proposed for total reconstruction was Shoreditch. This borough was the most overcrowded in terms of the Plan's standards, and also the most recalcitrant in terms of zoning, with a small factory on almost every street, as well as a lack of parks. The proposal here was for the reduction of the population by more than half from 82,240 to 34,000.

Proposals on the location of housing, parks and open space, industry, the decanting of population and so on, take up a large part of the Plan, but equally significant are its proposals in terms of physical planning. These proposals include those on the Plan for a new system of road communications, the phased reconstruction of entire areas of the inner city, and new schemes for the central area, including the South Bank. The road schemes, originating from the basis of the economic cost of traffic congestion, include three concentric rings, vastly improved radial routes, several set in 'parkways', and three tunnels under the West End.[36]

THE FORGETTING OF ART

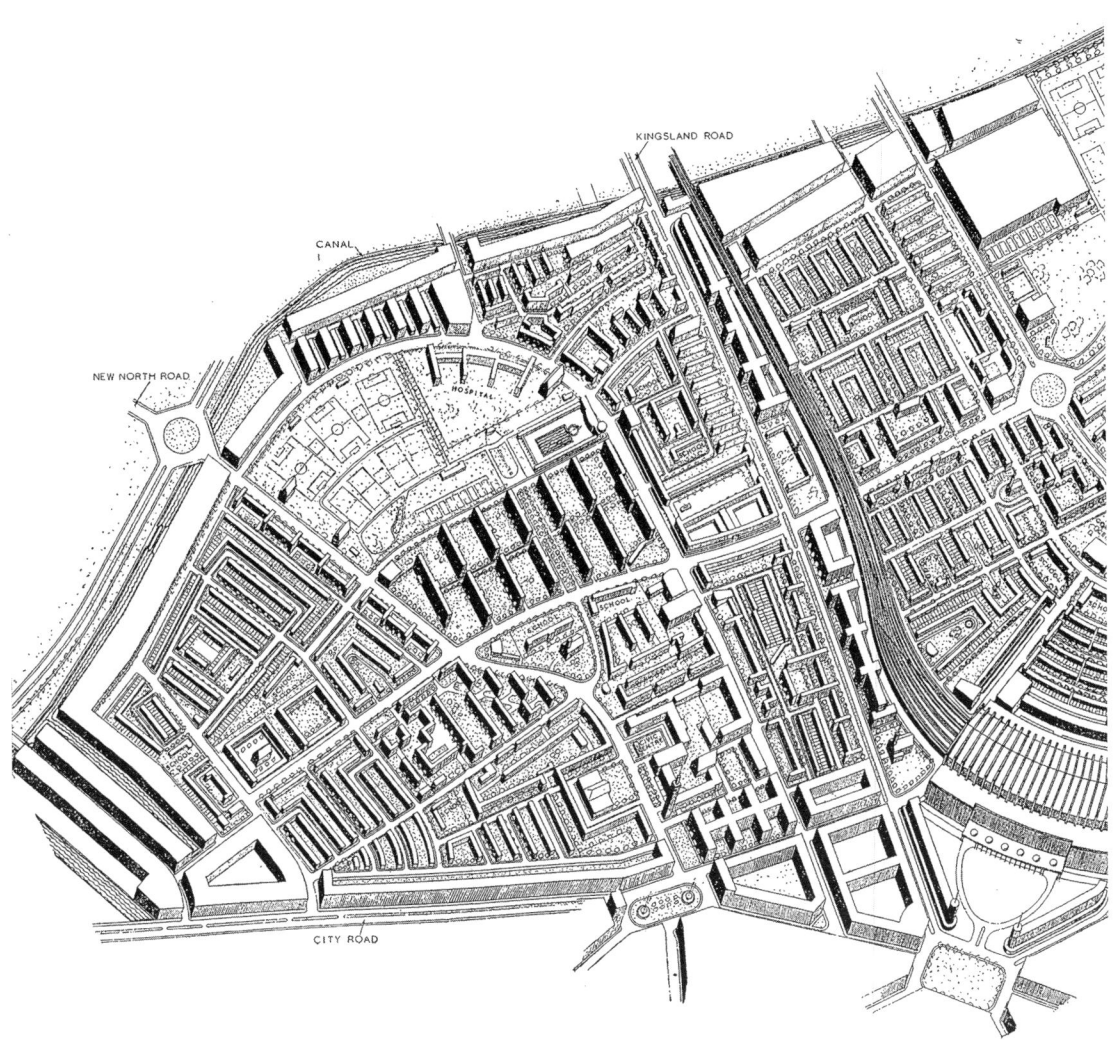

The 'reconstruction areas' as they are termed, are ten areas of the inner suburbs whose present condition is considered to be beyond redemption. The Plan proposes complete redevelopment of these areas, to eradicate substandard housing, remove industry to specific zones, introduce parks and abundant public facilities, and in general make the areas so attractive that the reduced population still living there includes young families. The statistical basis for its proposals is a survey of empirical 'information' on the location of industry, density of population, condition of property and so on. The concept of 'slums', i.e. property beyond economic modernisation, is a key one, 60 per cent being found in a studied area of East London. Old property in general is seen as 'obsolescent': in architectural terms much seems undesirable, Victorian schools for example being described as 'gaunt'.

3.5
Axonometric of the 'reconstruction area' of Shoreditch, proposed for total replanning and the removal of over half its population: extensive areas were later rebuilt with social housing, and a park created on part of the site shown: from the *County of London Plan*, 1943.

THE FORGETTING OF ART

These areas, which include Shoreditch and Hackney to the north east, and Bermondsey and Southwark to the south, are to be formed of several 'neighbourhood units', their size based on the catchment area for a primary school, estimated at 6,000 to 10,000. The layout of these units relates closely to this, with no main roads for children to cross on the way to these schools. The road system itself is reshaped using largely existing main roads, with the canting off of local traffic into service roads. Most of the existing back streets, described as redundant, are replaced with areas for housing in mixed developments of houses and flats, grouped in squares and tree-lined streets: 'Rehousing on large urban and central sites must be applied on a more scientific basis.'[37] In its perspectives, 'a relatively small number of ten storey flats are shown grouped together, usually near a park, and with the wide spaces between them laid out as gardens with tennis courts and playgrounds'.[38] As Lionel Esher has remarked, the design was 'trying uneasily ... to accommodate the two extremes – English Garden City sentimentality and German *Zeilenbau* geometry'.[39] Greatly increased open space is provided, smaller gardens subtending to open 'amenity spaces' with larger parks and school playing fields spaced through the districts. Shops are concentrated into compact areas, markets removed to planned squares. As far as public buildings are concerned, 'It seems likely that there will be a greatly increased demand for community buildings, for physical culture, dancing, dramatics, handicrafts, discussion groups, lectures, etc.';[40] this gives a clear indication of the kind of activities which, it was intended, members of these new communities would be offered.

The assumption of the rightness of the power to carry out these proposals in the common good, is never questioned. While the phased nature of reconstruction was to give the opportunity for future modification, the implications of the total design and control of vast areas of inner London were seen in only positive terms, the ability to eradicate social and environmental evils, as they were perceived. If the Plan is considered to be in a utopian tradition, then the significance of these reconstruction areas is clear: the availability of new territory, without history and tradition, is a necessity for the clear articulation of the utopian ideal.

The Plan also turned its attention to areas of central London where a single dominant function could be discerned. The government area around Whitehall, the University area in Bloomsbury, and the legal area of the Inns of Court were to become 'precincts'. As with the reconstruction areas, movement through the area is excluded, leaving it inward-looking and separate from the city outside. The

THE FORGETTING OF ART

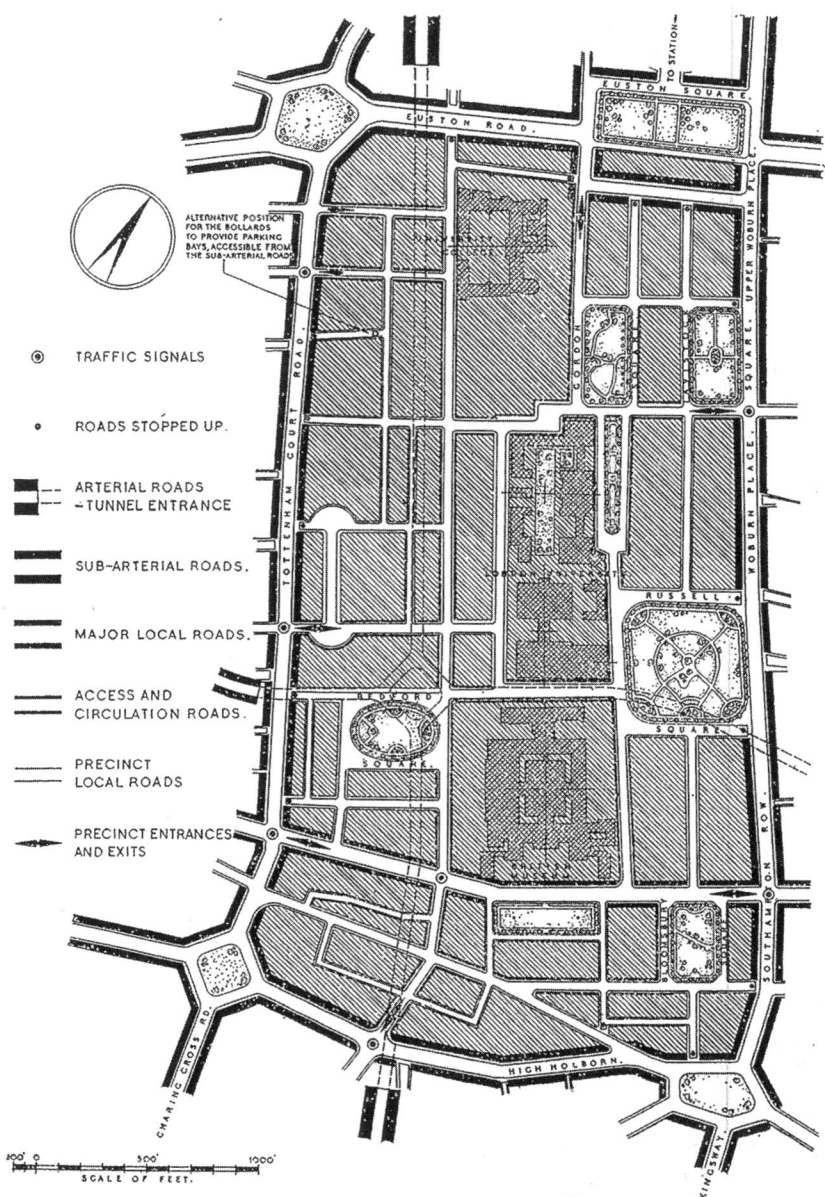

3.6
Bloomsbury 'university precinct', as proposed: roads on the periphery were to be widened and two underground road tunnels built: from the *County of London Plan* 1943.

originator of this idea, which came to be highly influential in postwar reconstruction, is H. Alker Tripp, Assistant Commissioner of Police at Scotland Yard. His book *Town Planning and Road Traffic*,[41] with a foreword by Abercrombie, argued for the necessity of planning and a clear hierarchy of road systems to reduce road casualties. Tripp's idea of the precinct, with all through-traffic excluded, was his basis of urban planning:

THE FORGETTING OF ART

> These pockets will be a leading feature of the whole town plan; from a traffic point of view they are merely pockets, but each will be a centre of life and activity and they will thus require a more ornamental name. Each pocket represents in its way a separate little community. The words 'precinct', 'close', 'purlieu', 'pale' 'circuit' are all possible.[42]

The term which became established also had particular relevance in London:

> An outstanding example of a real precinct, with all its abounding virtues, is already to be found in the Inns of Court in London ... Within quiet confines from which the general traffic has been totally excluded, lie those ordered precincts, adorned with buildings that are architecturally fitting, and relieved and softened by grass plots and growing trees. In preserves of that kind all men, and not only a favoured few, should be able to spend their working hours, and town dwellers their lives. While the lawyers' precincts will keep their own dignity and reserve, the shopping precincts will revel in colour and display, and in each business precinct the stockbrokers and merchants will be able to move freely without dodging between masses of buses and cars.[43]

One new precinct for central London was proposed, for the South Bank, with a series of office towers set in public gardens with a

3.7
Ten-storey flats proposed for the inner London reconstruction areas: from the *County of London Plan,* **1943.**

THE FORGETTING OF ART

3.8
Churchill Gardens, Pimlico designed by Powell and Moya 1946 and consistent with the Abercrombie Plan's reconstruction principles, showing blocks in the earliest section built 1950

cultural and recreational centre adjacent to Waterloo. A somewhat limited proposal for developing the river front on the south side, the only part of the metropolitan centre which the Plan dares to treat as a virgin site, it displays a particular paucity of imagination in its idea of the city.[44] Nevertheless, with or without Abercrombie, the proposed site became used initially for the Festival of Britain with several cultural institutions, and some offices, to follow.

Pieces of evidence

Although the County of London Plan was an officially originated and adopted document,[45] few of its proposals came to be realised. Its brief was to ignore the current legislative framework presumably as Lord Reith, its instigator, felt that stringent legislation should be forthcoming if opinion in favour of changes were sufficiently strong. Despite the current of opinion and the post-war Labour government committed to major social changes, the 1947 Town Planning Act when it came failed to solve the problem at the crux of any planned comprehensive redevelopment, that of the private ownership of urban land. Despite fierce powers of compulsory purchase embodied in the report, problems of compensation, insurmountable in any but a totalitarian state, made large-scale

THE FORGETTING OF ART

planning unworkable. The economic basis of the Plan, its enormous costs by any standards, are not really dealt with in the Plan except in terms of the self-justification that much of the work would be necessary in a piecemeal way, and that increased 'efficiency' would pay for itself.

There are numerous vestigial pieces of evidence of the Plan in infill housing on sites such as the Lansbury Estate, part of the Poplar reconstruction area, or the Tecton schemes on inner-city sites in Finsbury and Paddington. Traces of the Shoreditch plan can be seen in large tracts of redeveloped housing and an unloved park. Most of the road building proposals have not come to pass, despite enormous traffic increases since 1943, in the event coped with by sophisticated traffic management schemes: the proposed 'D' ring became the M25 several decades later and the Euston Road underpass and Shepherds Bush motorway spur are fragments of its grander schemes. The South Bank has been redeveloped in a somewhat different form, but nevertheless in its aspect as a 'culture precinct' must be ranked as one of the parts of the Abercrombie scheme to come to fruition. One can briefly note that Abercrombie's West Midland Plan, drawn up

3.9
Shoreditch reconstruction area: maisonettes built early 1960s.

in 1948, was to be somewhat more fulfilled in Birmingham: two concentric ring roads as well as arterial roads were built: whole areas of the inner city, on a smaller scale than London's, were reconstructed as six 'new towns': 'flatted factories' were constructed to house displaced small industry.[46] Even in an only partially fulfilled form, one can have some idea of the immense scale of such redevelopment; the new city which has emerged hardly seems something to envy on London's behalf.[47]

Abercrombie's other London plan, that for the Greater London area,[48] was also to be realised to a greater extent. Based on the assumptions of the County of London plan, and a way of managing the 'overspill' population intended to be decanted from inner London boroughs, it was also to propose, beyond the maintained greenbelt where development was severely restricted, a place where new industry could develop. The prevailing preoccupation with 'regional planning' begun by Patrick Geddes and the subject of earlier plans by Abercrombie,[49] was the basis, and it was, perhaps ironically, formulated after the plan for London itself. Its key proposals were for ten 'satellite' towns, each with a population of 60,000: these became built as the eight initial new towns from 1947. Among the ten sites chosen in the Abercrombie Plan, Harlow and Stevenage were later realised: they differed from others in being based on existing small towns rather than open sites which the majority were, proposed in a ring twenty miles or so around London. The Plan's developed proposals for Ongar, with its low densities and neighbourhood planning, foresaw the way the new towns around London came to be designed.

In this proposal for new towns, as in the various proposals of the County of London Plan, Abercrombie was developing earlier ideas. Just as the 'green belt' proposal of the Greater London Plan originated in 1910 with George Pepler,[50] so the plans for roads and parks can be traced to the publication of the London Society's papers in 1921; and the development of the South Bank is an idea which began its built realisation with the establishment of County Hall, started in 1911. Raymond Unwin in particular can be seen as the precursor of much of the body of the Greater London Plan;[51] it had become a commonplace that the growth of London must be halted and some of its population and industry encouraged or made to leave. No one could have defended the current (pre-war) state of London with its visual drabness, congestion and confusion. What was, however, a new element was that the form of the proposals of the Abercrombie and Forshaw plan was tinged with the flavour of modernism. To examine the plans or perspectives of the

THE FORGETTING OF ART

3.10
Harlow Town Centre, Frederick Gibberd 1958, planned as a precinct: Harlow was one of the first 'new towns' built around London after the Second World War, and proposed in Abercrombie's *Greater London Plan*, **1945.**

reconstruction areas, hardly Unwinian in their planning, or to consider the breadth of the conceptual sweep of its proposals, is to see a document imbued with the confidence of modernist polemic. 'Modern society needs housing, parks and highways'[52] wrote Le Corbusier in *La Ville radieuse*: not necessarily an original statement in 1933, and owing something to the English Garden City ideal, but one which Abercrombie's analysis starts from.

Evaluating Abercrombie

The Plan embodies a belief in planning as the instrument of change, change which is not only desirable but which is necessary and urgent, and which has a dialectical relationship to the possibilities of human fulfilment. It implicitly denies that wealth of human experience which cannot be incorporated into its measurement of problems and thus into its conclusions. Rebuilding a city is always highly complex and politically and emotionally charged. While the destruction of wartime and the bad living conditions of much of London meant some programme of rebuilding was necessary, outside the current discourse of planning, far less radical and inclusive proposals could have been made, as was the case with the reconstruction of most war-damaged European cities. Almost all were reconstructed with a far closer relation to existing patterns and practices.[53] Although Abercrombie and other contemporary authors of plans and proposals made assumptions which may be extensively criticised now, not least because of their ideas of the city, their work represents an exceptional case of the modernist discourse of planning in the sense of ordering and clarifying a city which in its terms represented disorder and even chaos. There are moments, exceptional rather than the rule, where the creation of a new pattern has worked. There was, however, no sense of the city dynamic in its living quality, with a fluid relationship of objects, people, life and events: a different relationship with the city that would be explored first in work of the 1970s and 1980s, which said that the city was both 'hard' and 'soft', built form and lived experience.[54]

Christopher Alexander has illuminated the processes of urban planning in 'A City Is Not a Tree'.[55] Activities and people are formed into conceptual hierarchies, and these hierarchies are represented quite literally in the forms and diagrams of the plan. Making a city involved the marshalling of its necessary elements in a rational, but, in the case of Abercrombie, a picturesque and visually pleasing order. The different activities of the city were rudimentarily summarised into four headings, which were then directly represented in the physical zoning of the rebuilt city. A need for better communications led to the design of new wide roads, a need for better houses involved blocks of newly designed modern housing, a need for separation of urban functions: housing, industry, commercial, public, led to the drawing of lines of zoning. All this in a direct and literal way. Other functions of the city in its diversity were acknowledged but they would, it was supposed, take care of themselves. There was also, as in modernist thinking developed prior to the war, the setting up of a *type* – the establishment of rules. The status of these, always arbitrary, is not acknowledged: neither is the consequent notion of standardisation – and it might be assumed that all the reconstructed inner-city areas would be largely identical. Thus the processes of the Plan were undertaken at a diagrammatic level with little account taken of site or programme, or the distinction between intention and construction.

THE FORGETTING OF ART

As in any document proposing action, the County of London Plan contains both a presentation of what is considered wrong with things as they are, and the presentation of proposals which aim to rectify these problems. There is not necessarily a dialectical relationship between what are perceived as 'wrong' and 'right' proposals; what there does seem to be, however, is the connection that the nature of the formulation of the questions asked determines the answers given. Further, it can be argued that the value judgements of the designer of such utopian schemes are embodied in the process of making decisions: while apparently collecting empirical data, the designer is building up to a solution presented as the only one possible, but actually inherent in the formulation of the questions posed.[56]

In the Abercrombie Plan and other contemporary documents, a further importance was the significance of *fact* as a basis for action. However the use of 'fact' was highly selective to the point of absurdity. As in Le Corbusier's *La Ville radieuse*, where the fact of *insolation* dictated the orientation of housing blocks over any other possible criterion,[57] so in the most arbitrary case, London's housing redevelopment areas would be developed around the size of a nursery school; itself surely not absolute, neither is the calculation of the likely number of nursery-age children in a given area. By working with statistics, and giving some great prominence in the processes of the Plan's development, the easy way was taken. Statistics about industry are considered as fact, but do not, for example, account for any possible decline in dock activity, which is seen as the continuing backbone of London's economic life. The tabulation of figures in relation to industry is based on the location and removal of factories in the various London boroughs, and the possibilities, borough by borough, of further movement. The economic basis of industrial location, the reason for it being there in the first place, is not considered as important and is presumably intended to take care of itself. More basically, the large and increasing numbers in non-industrial employment are not dealt with as a relevant issue. The idea of stopping any industrial development so it would move to the outer ring of new towns was little more than a hope, its many implications not fully considered. Urban equilibrium – which is the aspiration of the plan, against the dynamism of economic development – is one of its central contradictions. In general, the Abercrombie Plan was shaped by a static view of the region, supported by the marshalling of fact: change was not accommodated. The real determinants: economic processes, population movement, decline of urban industries and

the growth of others, let alone the global economy, left Abercrombie's proposals stranded.

For Manfredo Tafuri and Francesco Dal Co there was a great shift from the pre-war situation of avant-garde activity and the institutions of state: 'Architecture was left with no choice but to accept new parameters of confrontation, drastically curtailing the traditions of its rebellious years in a political activism of its profession.'[58] Ideologies became subservient to a political situation and had to appear responsible, and were no longer the province of the small radical group. Post-war urban developments in Britain were also remarkable in the context of the rest of Europe for Tafuri and Dal Co:

> They are perhaps the most advanced product that can be expected from the urbanistic ideas and means devised by one of the most original cultural traditions of our century. Yet, rather than a further development of that tradition, they represent, it would seem, its contradictory conclusion.[59]

3.11
Glasgow, flats built late 1960s: the city's reconstruction programme was responsible for the greatest number of multi-storey and system built blocks of flats in Britain.

81

THE FORGETTING OF ART

But the limits of the Plan's approach were evident. In the objective to bring the city to order, it corresponded with the most long-lasting of intentions, from Papal Rome to Haussmann's Paris. Yet as Adrian Forty has pointed out: 'The supposition that what looks ordered will be orderly, has, it must be said, been one of the great fallacies of the modern era.'[60] The argument against order in the city has been eloquently argued by Richard Sennett in his first book, *The Uses of Disorder*. Referring to modernist urban practice, he writes:

> [There is an] assumption that the planning of cities should be directed to bring order and clarity to the city as a whole. Instead of this idea, whose basis is found in mechanical ideas of production, the city must be conceived as a social order of parts without a coherent, controllable, whole form ... Encouraging unzoned public places ... would thus promote visual and functional disorder in the city. My belief is that this disorder is *better* than dead, predetermined planning, which restricts effective social exploration.[61]

Modern culture, it seems, needs a different kind of city, the rich, restless, chaotic modern metropolis recognised by Baudelaire or Walter Benjamin.

Such critiques are not only with the benefit of critical distance: as Ian Nairn wrote in 1959:

> [T]he city should be a place for everyone – tarts as well as good girls, spivs as well as model husbands and honest men. The city is a place of infinite choice, and what more important choice than that between good and evil or convention and freedom?[62]

For a later generation coming to maturity in the 1950s and 1960s, socially, politically and architecturally, the smug assurance and lack of dialogue of those responsible for urban reconstruction mirrored that of the conservative forces of the 1930s; against whom the generation involved in the rebuilding programme had fought so hard. The problems which the process of planning created, the too-large scale of its thinking, its rigid and highly limited approach, remained firmly within a scientific and mechanistic discourse. Science not art was the paradigm of the County of London Plan. In the plan, there was a disregard of the subjective and denial of the poetic of the city. In a different sense from the frequently cited unbuilt Wren plan for London, it represented a tremendous missed opportunity when there was a great popular agreement for change. The embedding of architectural practices into the social and political process led to the forgetting of art.

Notes

1. E.J. Carter and Ernö Goldfinger, *The County of London Plan Explained*, Harmondsworth: Penguin, 1945, p. 31.
2. Among them were plans for Plymouth (1943), Hull (1945) the Clyde Valley (1946) and the West Midlands (1947).
3. See W. Kent, *The Lost Treasures of London*, London: Phoenix House, 1947, p. 16.
4. R. Tubbs 'Tomorrow' in *Living in Cities*, Harmondsworth: Penguin, 1942, p. 27.
5. Patrick Abercrombie (1879–1957): on Abercrombie see Gerald Dix, 'Patrick Abercrombie', in Gordon E. Cherry (ed.), *Pioneers in British Planning*, London: Architectural Press, 1981, p. 103–30.
6. Dix, op. cit., p. 105.
7. Tubbs, op. cit.
8. Colin Rowe and Fred Koetter, *Collage City*, Cambridge, MA: MIT Press 1978, p. 11.
9. Maureen Waller, *London 1945*, London: John Murray, 2005, p. 445.
10. See p. 65 below.
11. See John R. Gold, *The Experience of Modernism*, London: Spon, 1997, pp. 145ff. and p. 171 for further discussion and examples of this.
12. Barlow Report, *A Dissentient Memorandum*, London: HMSO, 1940, p. 233.
13. Uthwatt Report, *Report of the Expert Committee on Compensation and Betterment*, London: HMSO, 1942.
14. In the Town and Country Planning Act, 1947.
15. Giles Scott, Foreword to the RIBA Centenary Exhibition Catalogue, 1934. Quoted by Gavin Stamp in 'Britain in the Thirties', *Architectural Design*, vol. 49, no. 10–11.
16. M. and C. Quennell, *Good New Days*, London: Batsford, 1935.
17. See S.E. Rasmussen, *London: the Unique City*, London: Penguin, 1960, pp. 215ff.
18. J.H. Purdom, *How Should We Rebuild London?*, London: J.M. Dent, 1945, p. 91.
19. Ibid., p. 93.
20. Le Corbusier, *Radiant City [La Ville radieuse]*, London: Architectural Press, 1967, p. 340.
21. Ibid., p.153.
22. 'A Master Plan for London', in *AR*, June 1942, p. 143.
23. See John R. Gold on the London MARS plan in Thomas Deckker (ed.), *The Modern City Revisited*, London: Spon, 2000. See also John R. Gold, *The Experience of Modernism*, London: Spon, 1997.
24. 'A Master Plan for London', op. cit., p. 145.
25. Tönnies's book *Gemeinschaft und Gesellschaft* was published in German in 1887 but only translated into English in 1940.
26. On Unwin, see Frank Jackson, *Raymond Unwin*, London: Zwemmer, 1985.
27. J.H. Forshaw and P. Abercrombie, *The County of London Plan*, London: Macmillan, 1943, Authors' note p. v.
28. See Gold, op. cit., p.180, for details and discussion of the Plan's context.
29. Abercrombie, *The Greater London Plan*, London: HMSO, 1944.
30. Forshaw and Abercrombie, op. cit., p. 6.
31. Carter and Goldfinger, op. cit., p. 5.
32. Forshaw and Abercrombie, op. cit., p. 7.
33. Ibid., p. 5.
34. Ibid., p. 28.
35. Carter and Goldfinger, op. cit., p. 19.
36. Based on the road plan by Lutyens and Bressey Highway Development Survey (Greater London), London: HMSO, 1937.
37. Forshaw and Abercrombie, op. cit., p. 77.
38. Ibid., p. 102.
39. Lionel Esher, *A Broken Wave*, London: Allen Lane, 1981, p. 61.
40. Forshaw and Abercrombie, op. cit., p. 103.

THE FORGETTING OF ART

41 H. Alker Tripp, *Town Planning and Road Traffic*, London: Edward Arnold, 1942.
42 Ibid., p. 75.
43 Ibid.
44 Forshaw and Abercrombie, op. cit., pp. 130ff.
45 It provided the basis for the County of London Development Plan of 1951.
46 Patrick Abercrombie and H. Jackson, *West Midlands Plan*, London: Ministry of Town Planning, 1948.
47 See Andrew Higgott, 'Birmingham: Building the Modern City', in Thomas Deckker (ed.), *The Modern City Revisited*, London: Spon, 2000.
48 Abercrombie, *The Greater London Plan*, London: HMSO, 1944.
49 Starting with Doncaster Regional Plan, 1922.
50 Paper at RIBA Town Planning Conference, 1910.
51 In particular in the paper 'Some Thoughts on the Development of London', in Aston Webb (ed.), *London of the Future*, London: Fisher Unwin, 1921.
52 Le Corbusier, *Radiant City*, op. cit., p. 340.
53 See Jeffry N. Diefendorf, *Rebuilding Europe's Bombed Cities*, London: Macmillan, 1990; the principal exception was Rotterdam.
54 Among key texts are Henri Lefebvre, *The Production of Space*, Oxford: Blackwell, 1991; Richard Sennett, *The Uses of Disorder*, London: Allen Lane, Penguin, 1971; Peter Ackroyd, *London the Biography*, London: Chatto & Windus, 2000 illustrates the point as far as London is concerned.
55 Christopher Alexander 'A City Is Not a Tree', *Design*, February 1966, pp. 46–55.
56 For this argument see M. Sjaasted, 'From Mind to Matter', *AA Files 1*, Winter 1981–2, vol. 1, no. 1, pp. 64–7.
57 Le Corbusier, *Radiant City*, op. cit., p. 159.
58 Manfredo Tafuri and Francesco dal Co, *Modern Architecture*, London: Academy Editions, 1980, p. 305.
59 Ibid., p. 316.
60 Adrian Forty, *Words and Buildings*, London: Thames & Hudson, 2000, p. 243.
61 Sennett, op. cit., p. 116.
62 *Encounter* 65, vol. 12, no. 2/59, p. 54; quoted in Brian Appleyard, *The Pleasures of Peace*, London: Faber & Faber, 1989, p. 124.

CHAPTER 4

the shift to the specific

the new interpretation of materiality in Brutalism and the Functional Tradition

THE SHIFT TO THE SPECIFIC

> We meant by 'as found' not only adjacent buildings but all those marks that constitute remembrancers in a place and that are to be read through finding out how the existing built fabric of the place had come to be as it was ... As soon as architecture begins to be thought about, its ideogram should be so touched by the 'as found' as to make it specific-to-place ... Thus the 'as found' was a new seeing of the ordinary, an openness as to how prosaic 'things' could re-energise our inventive activity ... We were concerned with the seeing of materials for what they were: the woodness of wood; the sandiness of sand.
> (Alison and Peter Smithson recalling the early 1950s in 'The "As Found" and the "Found"')[1]

Alison and Peter Smithson represent and embody a set of concerns which emerged in the first decade or so after the Second World War. Their mastery of polemic, however hermetic its concerns might have sometimes appeared, makes them an obvious focus of an enquiry into the ideas materialising in this period. However, such concerns were far wider-ranging and more deeply rooted than these two architects and their immediate circle: the emphasis on re-valuing what was there, the sense of the identity of place and identity of culture created a shift in architectural thought. For a new generation of architects, there no longer was the ideal of the universal, or, as expressed in J.M. Richards' position, the idea of a standardised, anonymous practice. The site of a work of architecture came to be seen as *specific* and to embody qualities, rather than neutral, abstract and general. Instead of the Purist pre-war Le Corbusier, who had designed ideally for a flat, physically undistinguished site, places were now seen to have their own narratives. At the same time, materials came to be seen as having innate and specific qualities rather than being subservient to abstract form-making. One key manifestation of a new understanding was developed in the *Architectural Review*, with its scrutiny of a wide variety of vernacular forms and materials, not to mention its consistent exploration of the sense of place. But the radical position taken up by such architects as the Smithsons, together with certain associated artists and writers, was to articulate a parallel re-examination of place and material in the architectural discourse of post-war Britain.

John Summerson wrote the introduction to the catalogue of the first exhibition of post-war British architecture: *45–55 Ten Years of British Architecture.*[2] In it he described the achievement of the pre-war ideals of modernism in public housing and the new towns, school building, public buildings such as the Royal Festival Hall, the

Festival of Britain itself, and an as yet smaller amount of private housing and commercial development. 'The buildings illustrated are, without exception, of a kind which before the war, would have been labelled as belonging to "the modern movement" . . . few would think that label worth applying now.'[3] There was no significant anti-modern position remaining, and modernism had arrived. In these post-war years, the architects forming the pre-war avant-garde transformed their roles, or in the case of Lubetkin, even gave up architecture. According to Anthony Jackson's later sardonic judgement, 'Fry, Yorke and Gibberd successfully evolved an indifferent modernism attuned to the democratic tastes of the community'[4]: while in 1959 Colin Rowe wrote that 'The long awaited recognition of modern architecture has turned out to be something of an anti-climax. The architect has, to an extent, superseded his own conception of himself.'[5] It became clear that simultaneous with the full realisation of modernism in Britain, a new ideology had to emerge.

The dialectic at the centre of this period was on one hand between those who believed that modernism needed to lose its uncompromising quality: as Herbert Read wrote in his revised *Art and Industry* in 1956, there was 'justifiable dissatisfaction with the bleakness of pioneering functionalism'.[6] The Festival of Britain typifies the approach of introducing both design individualism and specifically English qualities into the practice of a definitively modern architecture, also informed by international influences (perhaps most notably that of Russian Constructivism), but effectively overlaid with a presentation and detail characterised by whimsy. The exhibition site's layout was Picturesque rather than modernist, and it may be seen that the question of the Picturesque was one around which the crucial polarity of the period was developed. Banham later argued that Pevsner's role in articulating the term and developing a discussion on it, from 1942 onwards, was that of a 'betrayal'.[7] For Banham in contrast, the crucial strategy was not to 'lose nerve' and to maintain and develop the modern, for which he (particularly in the narrative of the 1960s) became the most significant figure as its erudite centre. Modern architecture for him was, crucially, to reflect the conditions of modern life and its technology while remaining undoubtedly a practice of art. Development of the modernist project was absolutely vital, but needed to be based on internationalism and a rejection of a historical basis for design. It is within this dialectic that the Smithsons' position may be located. The younger generation of architects, 'queuing to get into life' in Alison Smithson's phrase, rejected what they saw as a lack of rigour as well as compromise and missed opportunity in built modern work. 'Englishness' had for them made an unwelcome reappearance, especially in the Festival of Britain. The London South Bank site, established by Abercrombie as a cultural zone, effectively became an architectural exhibition for the summer of 1951.[8]

Alison and Peter Smithson saw themselves as 'setting ourselves the task of rethinking architecture in the early 1950s':[9] contemporaries observed the certainty with which they adopted this role in their generation of architects.

> In their own estimation, and that of a good many others, they were the leaders. Eduardo Paolozzi, their friend and collaborator, burst into a meeting with them one day, announcing 'Right! Make way for THE architects'.[10]

Other close contemporaries such as James Stirling could not accept their chosen role, largely based on one building and a great deal of self-assurance. The Smithsons had been students at Newcastle, at that time part of Durham University, in the years immediately after 1945, and subsequently worked in the London County Council's Schools division.[11] Their own school at Hunstanton, Norfolk, built as the result of a competition won in 1949 when Peter and Alison Smithson were 26 and 23 respectively, had gained much attention, particularly through publication after its completion in 1954.[12] The building of Hunstanton gave them an achievement which, although sometimes controversial, was extensively published and discussed; none of their contemporaries had any comparable success in building. Looking from a distance as if it had taken its formal clue from Mies van der Rohe in his buildings for the Illinois Institute of Technology campus, on closer view it demonstrated an approach which was already quite distinctive in this first building. Materials were used in a highly controlled way, structure was exposed, and along with the undoubted aesthetic of modernity, there was an attendant anti-aesthetic. They asserted that their use of materials intended to communicate 'the quality of real materials':[13] brick, steel and concrete were used in a direct and unaestheticised way.

The context of this work was, quite specifically, not only that of other architects of their generation but developed alongside that of artists, in particular Eduardo Paolozzi and Nigel Henderson. A relatively informal group, but consciously avant-garde, was formed in 1952 – the Independent Group, loosely attached to the London Institute of Contemporary Arts (ICA). Recent commentators have given this group greater significance than appeared to be the case at the time: the influence of artists and art theory on such architects as the

Smithsons is undeniable however, while artists including Paolozzi gained a role they would not otherwise have had.[14] In a way that has rarely happened in British architectural history, the thinking of architects was enriched and strengthened by art: lectures and meetings at the ICA were underpinned by more evidently social and conversational modes of exchange; frequent meetings at Reyner and Mary Banham's house, parties and Soho pubs.

The Smithsons' undoubted influence may well have been substantially expressed in the unrecorded modes of conversation and in the teaching of Peter Smithson at the AA School. But in terms of a larger arena of discourse, a debate was played out with a series of articles that punctuated the decade of the 1950s. The pages of *Architectural Design* (*AD*) and the *Architectural Review* (*AR*) were accessible to them, and it is in these articles and responses to them that their ideas were exposed and developed, and their reputation constructed. The appointment of Theo Crosby to the editorial staff of *AD* in 1953 helped: he had, with the Smithsons, been involved in the early meetings of the Independent Group, as had Reyner Banham, who had been appointed an Editor at the *AR* in the previous year. The articles include 'The Built World: Urban Re-identification', in 1955, which developed a critical position on the Garden City model; 'Cluster City: a New Shape for the Community', which proposed alternative urban form-making in 1957, a theme consistently followed, including in 'The Function of Architecture in Cultures-in-Change' in 1960. A critical examination of American culture was also pursued, for example in 'Mobility', published in 1958.[15]

According to Anthony Jackson, these writings by the Smithsons were characterised by assertion rather than reasoned argument, 'their terminology simple but obscure, their meanings seeming to

4.1
Alison and Peter Smithson: urban restructuring proposals for a multi-level cluster city 1952: from *Uppercase 3*, edited by Theo Crosby, 1960.

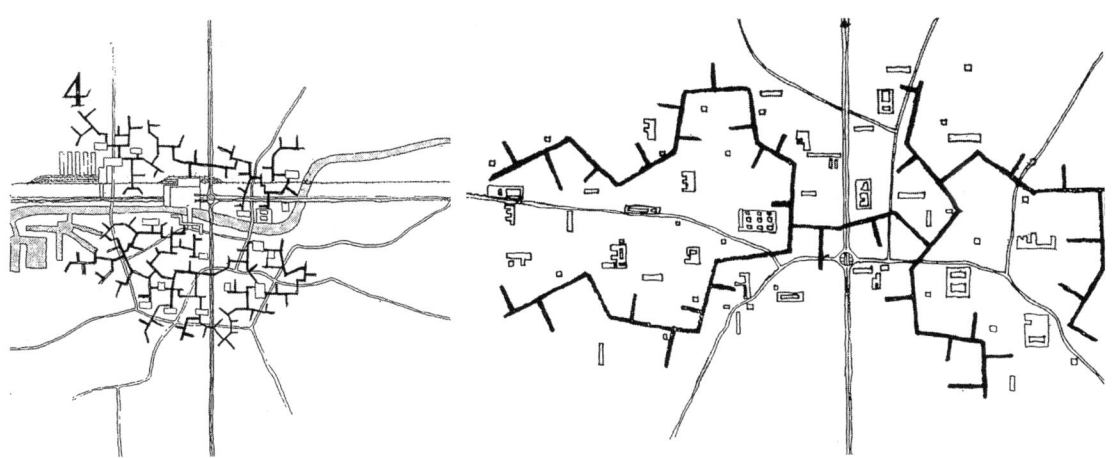

have been expounded elsewhere.'[16] A number were collected in somewhat altered form as a book *Ordinariness and Light*, but not published until 1970, and linked with their building of Robin Hood Gardens – which was somewhat ironic, when the dominant discourse of British architecture had moved on. In the development of their writing to articulate the values of their sometimes awkward buildings and projects, issues seemed at times hard to express. However, their starting point was clear:

> It is necessary to create an architecture of reality, an architecture which takes as its starting point the period 1910 – of de Stijl, Dada and Cubism ... An art concerned with the natural order, the poetic relationship between living things and environment. We wish to see towns and buildings which do not make us feel ashamed, ashamed that we cannot realise the potential of the twentieth century, ashamed that philosophers and physicists must think us fools, and painters think us irrelevant. We live in moron-like cities. Our generation must try and produce evidence that men are at work.[17]

The Smithsons' aspiration in this statement from 1955 reflects the ambition towards an architecture which was truly of its time, not compromised by tradition, not afraid to be uncompromising. Much of their writing deals with the question of the city, evidently a response to the contemporary European concern with construction and reconstruction: the starting point is their reaction to the extensive rebuilding of cities, as well as the construction of housing estates on the periphery of every British city and town, and the new town building programme emerging from Abercrombie. The reconstruction areas and low density, Garden City inspired estates seemed uninspired, lacking any urban quality, and most importantly did not work to create meaningful and rewarding places for those who lived there. The mediocrity of the results of the huge programme of building was clear and represented 'a true bankruptcy of sustaining notions'.[18]

Their alternative strategy, consistently expressed in a series of writings and projects, was focused on the making of new forms for the city, which would achieve far more in creating successful places in which to live and work, responsive to the conditions of modern life. Their use of language is key, and in the repeated use of particular terms, which almost become neologisms, the Smithsons expressed the possibilities of their new approach. Among these linguistic expressions are:

Association: 'a town is by definition a pattern of association' by which they meant different degrees of human relationship between the scale of the house, the street, the district and town as a whole;
Identity: that every place of dwelling should be specific and located, related to the human needs of its inhabitants;
Cluster: their proposed urban form: 'A close knit, complicated moving aggregation but an aggregation with a distinct structure'[19] which would create, in a random form and not focused on one specific centre, a new urban landscape;
Fix: urban identifying points against which other elements of the environment may change, which might be certain buildings either modern or historical, or the dominant form of an urban motorway.[20]

Embodied in this language was what for them was the key problem of urban re-identification, a process with an existential resonance, of creating new urban situations that would endow the modern city with meaning.

With the repetition of these concerns and expressions, engaged with the notion of urban relationship and identity, a real alternative was evolved to the dominant rationalist discourse of urbanism of CIAM on the one hand,[21] and on the other, the more immediate consequence of the poverty of British urban building. The Smithsons' global arena was their participation in CIAM and their critique of its precepts, leading to the evolution of Team X. The decisive moment for them was in 1953 when at the CIAM IX meeting at Aix-en-Provence they presented an alternative to CIAM's abstract categories of *Dwelling, Work, Recreation and Transport* with a new hierarchy of meaning: *House, Street, District and City*. More than earlier British architects, they made links with architects working in other European countries, and most importantly may be seen to have led them.[22] So for the first time, British architects made European discourse their own: an international dimension shaped British thought.

The discourse of Brutalism

Not only *identity* but also *material* became prime concerns of a new avant-garde. Material, rather than modernist concerns primarily interested in form, was seen as expressing the specific, resonating with life and memory and reifying the particular. It is this that lies at the heart of 'Brutalism', the term which not only articulates the

Smithsons' approach but that of a discourse developed in Britain in the 1950s. Traces of human activity, as seen in Nigel Henderson's powerful photographs of urban dereliction in bombed East London, or fossil-fragments in the roach-bed limestone of the Smithsons' Economist Building, or in the primal material form of the Cobb in Lyme Regis, described as a 'Parthenon' of this tradition by de Cronin Hastings. Material informing both surface and form: the Brutalist stance also drawing attention to the ordinary, the everyday, that which had hitherto been unvalued. Setting out as a consciously radical position – and an alternative to the humane (and in their eyes compromised) 'New Empiricism' earlier championed by *Architectural Review* (see p. 103) – Brutalism looked back to the origins of European modernism and took a firm line, emphasising 'raw' materials and the clarity of structural elements. As the Smithsons later put it: 'the woodness of wood, the sandiness of sand'.[23] The Smithsons' strictures on honesty of form and materials were very pervasive, seen in other Independent Group work and also mirrored in one of the consistent campaigns of the *AR*, that of championing the 'Functional Tradition'.

Reyner Banham's influential 1955 article *The New Brutalism* was a highly perceptive discussion which introduced his definition of Brutalism: 'Memorability as image, clear exhibition of structure, valuation of materials as found',[24] Banham argues that 'what moves the New Brutalist is the thing itself, in its totality, with all its overtones of human association'. Memory permeating material – which could be site-specific, or could be culturally specific, or could be formed as response to an aspect of the brief. Banham begins however by discussing the term itself, which is, exceptionally, both a campaigning banner and a historian's label: the use of 'new' opens up a historical perspective (as well as being a response to the 'New Empiricism'). The echoes of both *béton brut* and *art brut* are contained in 'Brutalism' which for him essentially is about *image*: the building as an 'immediately apprehensible visual identity . . . confirmed by experience of the building in use',[25] which is holistically the product of its functions and materials. Materiality becomes the primary concern about the architecture's communicability: as has been remarked, the visual in any traditional aesthetic sense is absent certainly from the truly Brutalist phase of the Smithsons' work. And, in an existential sense, the haptic rather than the visual is made the dominant sensation. In a 1959 interview, Alison Smithson argued that modern building before them was 'not built of real materials at all but some sort of processed material such as Kraft cheese: we turned back to wood and concrete, glass and steel, all the materials which you can really get hold of'.[26]

The Smithsons' Soho House project had been published in *AD* in

December 1953: referring to it as the first expression of 'the New Brutalism', Peter Smithson wrote: 'It was decided to have no finishes at all internally – the building to be a combination of shelter and environment. Bare concrete, brickwork and wood . . . our intention to have the structure exposed entirely'. This re-working of the London terraced house, however modest as a project, indeed manifested a new value to domestic space, primal rather than primitive. Its occupants (it was intended for themselves) would have lived in a series of rigorously formed spaces, simultaneously modern and archetypal. As Kenneth Scott's contemporary response to it said:

> Someone has said that the Smithsons build caves for men rather than houses. This idea comes from the feeling that one gets inside their buildings, of being in touch with the very nature of which the building is a part.[27]

The concern with authenticity of material and form could be embodied in a small and understated urban building.

Through the early 1950s the Smithsons' concern for authentic materials developed into a larger enquiry about the authentic, which owed much to the artists they knew, as well as a possibly second-hand appreciation of existentialist thought. Nigel Henderson's relationship to the Smithsons was formative, both in terms of their social understanding which they did acknowledge, and in their materiality which they didn't, although Peter Smithson wrote much later about the power of the *image* which Henderson created. Kenneth Frampton is one of the few people to have written of the decisive influence Henderson had on what he calls Brutalism's existential character.[28] Henderson was conscious of connections with Tapies and Dubuffet and the idea of *art brut*: his work was informed by Surrealism and he is far from the social documentarist which his Bethnal Green street photographs, used by the Smithsons in their CIAM grille of 1953 and again in the publication *Uppercase* 3 (1960), have suggested. In London, he became, through his friendship with Paolozzi, involved with such projects as the *Parallel of Life and Art* exhibition, and later, again with Paolozzi, he worked on the signs of inhabitation of the Smithsons' structure 'Patio and Pavilion' in the *This is Tomorrow* exhibition at the Whitechapel Art Gallery in 1956.

Henderson lived in Bethnal Green, East London from 1945 to 1954 in an urban landscape still socially cohesive but physically shattered by wartime bombing. His wife Judith Henderson was engaged in an anthropological project, studying the life of East London, of which his photographs were a counterpart. Although the life of the streets remained a subject, it was the material of the streets

THE SHIFT TO THE SPECIFIC

4.2
Nigel Henderson: photograph of urban dereliction, Bethnal Green London, c.1950.

themselves which was also a constant preoccupation: he took home mangled metal, wire and other urban detritus. He wrote of his fascination with the material quality of what he found: 'I feel happiest among discarded things, vituperative fragments, cast casually from life, with the fizz of vitality still about them.' The traces of time and human use transformed materiality:

> A new boot is a fine monument to man, an artefact. A worn out boot traces his images with a heroic pathos and takes its part as a universal image-maker ... Time works like an analytical chemist with its tinctures and titrations. It gives us intimations of the reality of things.[29]

The paradigmatic building of Brutalism is, perhaps, not the Hunstanton School or Soho House project, but the exhibition installation done for the *This is Tomorrow* exhibition at the London Whitechapel Art Gallery in 1956. Intended by its organiser Lawrence Alloway to represent a new synthesis of art practice and architectural practice, twelve groups of artists working with architects made installations. The Smithsons, collaborating with Nigel Henderson and Eduardo Paolozzi, evolved a project – 'Patio and Pavilion'. In a deceptively simple strategy, the architects designed the structure, the artists introduced marks of dwelling. The artfully primitive pavilion, made of salvaged wood with a corrugated plastic roof and a sand floor, was placed in a space clad with reflected aluminium sheets; thus the viewer is conscious of their place in the exhibition: both subject and object, viewer and viewed. This minimal shed perhaps did accommodate all fundamental human needs. The Smithsons wrote in the exhibition catalogue:

4.3a
'Patio and Pavilion' exhibition installation by Alison and Peter Smithson in collaboration with artists Eduardo Paolozzi and Nigel Henderson, *This is Tomorrow* Exhibition, Whitechapel Art Gallery 1956.

4.3b
'Patio and Pavilion' exhibit interior with portrait montage by Nigel Henderson and 'signs of inhabitation' by Eduardo Paolozzi and Henderson.

> Patio and Pavilion represents the fundamental necessities of the human habitat in a series of symbols/the first necessity is for a piece of the world/ the patio/the second necessity is for an enclosed space/the pavilion/these two spaces are furnished with symbols for all human needs.[30]

The idea of authenticity within this architectural discourse also extends to freedom of the individual inhabitant – not designing the whole environment but allowing the inhabitants and their life to take over. Life, in a way, knew best.[31] After some years of debate on the term they felt they had originated, the Smithsons wrote on the New Brutalism: 'Brutalism tries to face up to a mass-produced society, and drag a rough poetry out of the confused and powerful forces which are at work. [It] has been discussed stylistically, whereas its essence is ethical.'[32]

In terms of building form, their later expressed idea of 'conglomerate ordering' gave a retrospective value to such early projects as the Golden Lane and Sheffield University competition entries. Its qualities are not only anti-geometrical, but make an entirely new spatial model, based on elements distinct and whole in themselves, not reduced and 'designed' into combination. This quality, or a recognition of it, was already perceived by Banham in 1955. In the Smithsons' Sheffield University project, which for him exemplifies Brutalist form-making, 'no attempt is made to give a geometrical form to the total scheme; large blocks of topologically similar spaces stand about the site with the same graceless memorability as martello towers or pit-head gear.' Thus these projects represent an anti-formality, representing a shift from Hunstanton School and their Coventry Cathedral project and rejecting, according to Banham, 'beauty and geometry' in favour of 'more generalised concepts – image and topology'. By 'topology' he means a basic formal quality, 'Essentially primitive [but] reached only through immense sophistication.'[33]

Peter Smithson was teaching at the AA from 1955 to 1960. The architects' new strategy, against the prevailing idea (both traditional and modernist) of a building as a perfected object, was examined by him in his teaching. Further, in what should be interpreted as an anti-modernist stance, it examined site and context, inculcating a deeply rooted sensibility of place: 'It should therefore be with care, reflection and with love that we make changes.' He described his teaching of context as far from literal, measured or mechanistic:

> When I was teaching at the Architectural Association's School of Architecture in the mid-fifties the School's syllabus was reorganised in a very simple way to induce what I then called 'context

thinking' – that a new thing is to be thought through in the context of existing patterns. Thought through in the context of the patterns of human association, the patterns of use, the patterns of movement, the patterns of stillness, quiet, noise and so on, and the patterns of form, in so far as we can uncover them, and it was taught that a design for a building on building ground could not be evolved out of context. This sounded easy. But it cut against all inherited post-Renaissance tradition – of buildings as 'ideas', of buildings as 'obstructions', of buildings as simple mechanisms – and it cut against the simple force of fashion.[34]

The background to this position is also that of the model of an unelaborated architecture which is the product of an evident process, and is the manifestation of clarity. This would, in sharp contrast, be true of the prefabrication programme developed in the post-war years, for example in the much-praised Schools Building Programme of Hertfordshire County Council, with its integration of the skills of the manufacturer and the technologist, and a disregard for architectural convention.[35] There is also an undoubted connection to the Arts and Crafts movement which, despite the great changes over three decades, had never gone away; and the resonance of values of making, alongside a position characterised by modesty, supported the values of modernism as developed in Britain.

4.4
Interior of Sugden House, Watford 1956; Alison and Peter Smithson, with unplastered stock brick and untreated timber.

THE SHIFT TO THE SPECIFIC

4.5
Roach-bed Portland stone used as facing at the Economist Building, St James's, London, Alison and Peter Smithson, 1964; fossils in the stone indicating a narrative and manifesting texture.

For Adolf Loos, at an earlier stage of the development of a modern practice of architecture, it was learning (and convention) that obscured the possibility of a new architecture which was, primarily, building: an art, learned in its way, but rooted in the present. A sense of materials, their characteristics and appropriate use, lay at the heart of his strategy: a directness of form, economy of design, the discipline of material. It was also the expression of the strength of pre-modern traditions, and thus a counterpart to the vernacular without being identified with that as anachronistic. Loos's position, while indebted to the English Arts and Crafts tradition, did not adopt the anti-capitalism and opposition to industry of William Morris, neither was it expressive in a political sense of social morality. It was building of a comprehensive order: its absence of the utopianism which characterised later modern theories, its engagement with the humble role of building, links it with the newly emerging theories of the 1950s. The building strategy advocated by the Smithsons thus relates to the large, extended territory which, if the term were not so loaded, could be named vernacular: not historical quotation, but embodying the recognition of shared meanings. It is against the novelty of modernism, its heroism, the commitment to originality. It is what happens when modernism is a given, a strategy based on an analysis of contemporary culture.

This transformation of architectural practice was, undoubtedly, a synthesis evolved out of its own context, both intellectual and artistic. The members of the Independent Group had in common a wide and inclusive definition of culture. All activities and artefacts were the possible subjects of art and objects of attention: the 1953 exhibition *Parallel of Life and Art*, which for Banham was the first manifestation of the new sensibility, included all kinds of images, art and science, archaic and current, set in a non-hierarchical relationship. There was also a remarkable congruence of strategy with such artists as the American painter Barnett Newman, who wrote in 1948:

> We are creating images whose reality is self-evident and which are devoid of the props and crutches that evoke associations with outmoded images, both sublime and beautiful. We are freeing ourselves of the impediments of memory, association, nostalgia, legend, myth or what have you, that have been the devices of Western European painting. Instead of making 'cathedrals' out of Christ, man, or 'life', we are making it out of ourselves, out of our own feelings. The image we produce is the self-evident one of revelation, real and concrete, that can be understood by anyone.[36]

The renewal of the modernist impetus of renewal and reinvention can be seen in art and architecture alike, and allied with a new aim to transcend history and link with something more deeply rooted than that conditioned by culture.

Neither are there fixed values of beauty and ugliness. Symptomatic of this non-hieratic view is the movement, more truthfully a term, *art brut* founded by Jean Dubuffet and others in Paris to encompass certain work not only by artists but by the mad, the child, the 'primitive'; unformed by the cultural influences and institutions of art. It was not only anti-'modernist' but anti-ideal, against the Platonic idea of perfection of forms. Human expression, originating in the unconscious, was seen as authentic: but *art brut* also means *raw* art. Dubuffet, in his own work, creates a surface that is animated, constructed, and which incorporates tar, lead and cement; or, in a series of pastoral works, material of the landscape was formed into the image surface – humus, leaves, the layering deposit of the forest floor. *Let the Material Speak for Itself* was the catalogue of a 1955 ICA exhibition of Dubuffet's work written by Georges Limbour.[37] Limbour describes the process of Dubuffet's painting: 'For him, painting is *matter* rather than *form*'.[38] Each substance reacts differently to the hand – and the mind – which 'appeals to it and displays its own resistance or wilful intractability'.[39] The work of Jean Paul Sartre was much read, or at least much discussed, in Britain in the early 1950s. Sartre's existentialism implied not simply personal expression or 'freedom', but the profound and more authentic engagement with the world and its social structures.

The 'Functional Tradition'

The *Architectural Review* issue of January 1950, its issue for the mid-century, took as its theme what it termed 'The Functional Tradition', introducing it with a criticism of modernism as it had developed until then. Its judgement is based on the scale of the object of the architect's attention: that of the town plan or larger, rather than the actual processes of building at a human scale:

> Far too often in recent years the progressive architect's attention has been directed to the big idea, the town plan, the national plan, the cosmic pattern, to the exclusion of more local and particular interests. The result has been that he has begun to lose his ability to see other than with his mind's eye.[40]

The second problem for the *AR* is the prevailing emphasis on the processes of technology and on knowledge, rather than aesthetics or the exercise of the skills of design:

> One might say that the more sensitive architect today staggers under the weight of his realisation of the facts of life. The burden of technical awareness hangs heavily on the student and practising architect alike and the sense of social responsibility often assumes the proportions and character of an incubus as well as a stimulant. A wholly satisfying virile architecture cannot flourish unless in its practice social justification is lavishly compounded with personal pleasure – a wholesome delight in the creative process itself as well as an appreciation of the end in view ... Let the modern architect then drop his mental gaze from the great distances, sufficient to notice the qualities of the ordinary things around him ... Let him study the surface of a rock, for instance, and experience afresh the sudden realisation of how the values inherent in its textural qualities have re-occurred in walls, buildings, roads, giving them a complexity and vitality which are completely passed by in the present-day townscape.[41]

Thus working with the immediate visceral sense of material, and not least working with what is there, appreciating the qualities of architecture created outside modernist discourse. While this argument is presented as newly relevant, it relates to a parallel and sometimes hidden narrative in the *AR* of the 1930s (see p. 51). This issue on 'The Functional Tradition' can be seen as a coming together of interests on the part of editors H. de Cronin Hastings and J.M. Richards: the latter had begun, with John Piper, to document the anonymous buildings and objects of the urban and rural landscapes, including mills, railway buildings and seaside architecture, on a series of car journeys starting in 1938.[42] Even before this, Piper's photographs and art work combined a romantic nostalgia for some lost and forgotten 'Englishness' with a quite modernist sensibility. Such varied objects as Romanesque sculpture[43] or prehistoric earthworks were seen, quite irrespective of historical context, as phenomena capable of accommodating properties of modern art and abstraction. In its ahistoricism and arbitrary selection of an element of a work, this approach was in the modernist tradition of appropriating an artefact for qualities quite different from those of its original context. In terms of architectural objects, the most significant of these early *AR* publications was Piper's 'The Nautical Style' of January

1938, which focused on the lighthouse, jetty, buoy and seaside building. Piper saw these as having a strong functional element, nevertheless mediated by a consistent aesthetic: 'even lighthouse builders have never banished taste altogether from their buildings'.[44] The article, illustrated with photographs by Piper, prefigured many of the interests of the post-war *AR*.

This became one of the *Architectural Review*'s most consistent campaigns, gaining a new relevance at this point in the post-war years: the exploration of the vernacular, of the anonymous architecture which forms a constant but unnoticed part of the urban and rural landscape. Such work, writers in the *AR* felt, had a strength and integrity lacking in more specifically architectural design. Eric de Maré made these observations in an *AR* issue on canals in 1949:[45]

> Throughout the history of English – or for that matter of any other – architecture, there is a continuous thread running parallel with the historical styles but owing little or nothing to them. It might be called a timeless tradition of functionalism if the term had not become confused by being used to define a far more sophisticated phase of contemporary architecture. For its constituent elements are geometry unadorned, and it owes its effects to the forthright, spare and logical use of materials. To this extent it has affinities with the architectural effects sought by the modern architects of today, which no doubt explains why, looking back over the centuries, our own eyes are especially apt at picking out structures that owe their charm and quality to this tradition of functionalism.[46]

The argument that the modern architect could use the powerful forms and spare detail of the 'Functional Tradition' was a new one, and the publication of the issue on canals, entirely written and photographed by de Maré, marked the beginning of the influence of this form of building. De Maré outlined the history of canals and documented canal life as well as such architectural concerns as bridges and locks. The quality of these structures was communicated by the strength of his photographs, even more so than by his text. A section entitled 'Sculpture by Accident' took this aesthetic interest further, with pictures of lock valves, balance beams, and bollards of iron and timber. De Maré saw an unconscious artistry in these objects – in machinery worn, angled, made picturesque: perhaps the bollard, with its simple form and function, could be seen as the quintessential symbol of this newly discovered beauty.[47]

THE SHIFT TO THE SPECIFIC

4.6
The Cobb sea wall at Lyme Regis, Dorset, published in *Architectural Review* January 1950, described as 'the Parthenon of the Functional Movement.'

The key example in the *AR* on the Functional Tradition was the Cobb, the sea wall at Lyme Regis in Dorset, which has much of the qualities De Maré had expounded in his article of the previous year:

> In plan it has what appears to be a free form, full of interesting sweeps and curves, which at closer inspection are seen to be dictated by the position of the reef on which it is built, and the need for a seaward face that will carry the force of the sea away from its entrance. Seen in section, this curve is repeated in the manner of a glacis to seaward, and cut off abruptly within the arc, so that an oblique view provides a most interesting exercise in masses. On still closer inspection, what in cold fact is literally no more than a half-mile of stone sea wall, reveals such a wealth of detail and such a variety of surface and pattern that almost every yard of it becomes an object lesson in surface treatment, from the natural indentations of the rock itself to the haphazard continuity of paving and the restrained application of the whitewash that edges stone steps and the tops of parapets ... it is a unique example, on a magnificent scale, of form conditioned by the strict discipline of function, yet so remarkably virile and expressive as to deserve the title of the Parthenon of the functional movement of the twentieth century.[48]

The journal also illustrated and described the

> products of what might be called the functional as opposed to the folk tradition – jetties, marine objects, traffic signs, lettering, street furniture, railway and river equipment: and some, perhaps least recognized of all, are to be found in the nature of the materials themselves, the textures of surfaces, the character of matter which, whether combined with stylistic trimmings or not, are in fact the very stuff of the functional idea.[49]

The purely visual qualities of buildings were thus emphasised, and nowhere was this more pertinent than in the town: the quality of a 'Townscape' was seen as dependent on the quality of its detail:

> Before townscape can be treated as a serious issue, the anonymous, the unacknowledged, the visually unidentified elements and objects of the urban scene must be collected, analysed, brought into consciousness, so to speak – accepted or discarded according to whether they fulfil the requirements of the contemporary idiom.[50]

THE SHIFT TO THE SPECIFIC

4.7
The Cobb, Lyme Regis: a *glacis* of figured Portland stone, partly rebuilt in the early nineteenth century.

The article picked up de Maré's emphasis on the contemporary relevance of these found objects, but had a much more hard-nosed sense of utility when it came to deciding whether they were germane to the current practice of design.

Eric de Maré had become a student at the Architectural Association in 1928. He worked in Sweden, and later joined the Architectural Press, employed by de Cronin Hastings as acting Editor of the *Architects' Journal* from 1943 onwards.[51] It was a fruitful partnership: early evidence of this was the *AR*'s championing of a new tendency in Swedish architecture, the 'New Empiricism'. This term, evolved by Hastings, effectively redefined functionalism to encompass that which had seemingly been excluded – the 'psychology' of the users of the new architecture:

> The new objectivity was not always so objective, the houses did not function as well as had been expected . . . The new human beings were not so different from the older ones. Man and his habits, recreations and needs are the focus of interest as never before.[52]

103

THE SHIFT TO THE SPECIFIC

However the *Review's* writers were collectively at pains to point out that modern architecture had not 'abdicated' in favour of a vernacular revival: instead, their position was in favour of a plurality in modern architectural design rather than a narrowly functionalist focus. The consistent tone of the journal does also imply a dilution of modernist rigour, and a softening both in terms of humanism and the use of such forms as the brick load-bearing wall and pitched roof. Its influence was widespread, but seen as hopelessly weak by the more progressive. It may well be this which led such architects as the Smithsons and their associates in the Independent Group to see the *Review* as the 'enemy'.

In the *AR*'s developing discourse, Eric de Maré's photographs formed an important element. More than any polemic or lengthy rationale, they helped to create a new language which expanded the possibilities of architectural design in post-war Britain. In 1956, following the success of his work on canal structures, he was commissioned by Richards to travel throughout England on the trail of early industrial buildings. He expanded the pre-war researches of Piper and Richards himself, gathering other suggestions for subject-matter and finding many undocumented examples of buildings. This was pioneering work: de Maré photographed textile mills,

4.8
Eric de Maré: photograph of Stanley textile mill 1813, Stroud Valley, Gloucestershire used in *The Functional Tradition in Early Industrial Buildings*, 1958.

THE SHIFT TO THE SPECIFIC

4.9
Eric de Maré: photograph of Albert Dock, Liverpool described in *The Functional Tradition* as 'a study in materials, functionally used: granite setts, iron bollards, stone steps and steel covering plates. Each creates its characteristic texture, which is intensified by the effects of wear'.

docks, warehouses, breweries – the whole range of surviving industrial architecture from the eighteenth and early nineteenth centuries. The end result was a powerful body of work, which was published as a special issue of the *Architectural Review* in July 1957.[53] The buildings illustrated had a consistency, vigour and energy rarely evident in architectural production. Some, such as the naval and civil dock buildings, had a raw scale and power uncompromised by aesthetic considerations. Others, such as the textile mills, showed a robust simplicity of detail. Materials were used with an honesty and fitness for purpose which seemed invigorating: several buildings successfully combined iron with masonry construction. Beyond this, the buildings' simplicity embodied a purity of form and clarity of function. Staircases were often separate elements; constituent parts of a building forming their own strong and uncompromised volumes. As a whole, this collection of architectural forms was unselfconscious and powerful – and far more convincing than work then being built in Britain and elsewhere.

In the history of twentieth-century architecture, this new recognition had a real pedigree. Gropius had promulgated the architectonic power of the grain elevators of Buffalo and Montreal in the

THE SHIFT TO THE SPECIFIC

Deutsche Werkbund Yearbook of 1913. Le Corbusier's dictum, 'eyes that do not see', encompassed a range of industrial productions whose functionality was a clear lesson for architects entrenched in anachronistic issues of style.[54] Richards' intention in assembling the material for this issue was similarly to reconstruct a history:

> [bringing] into focus another episode in our architectural history when the functional values that we look up to now were dominant ... may serve to put our own age in its proper perspective (and thus to allay the feeling that there is anything alarming or subversive in our preoccupation with functionalism) and at the same time, perhaps, furnish some useful lessons about the range and subtlety of the aesthetic effects of which an architecture dominated by functionalism is capable.[55]

His aim was thus also to provide a useful work, a source of reference – the journal was re-issued in an expanded book form the following year.[56] This new edition contained 265 photographs: 202 were de Maré's, some of the rest were by Richards and Piper. As Richards generously observed in his Foreword: 'This is primarily a picture book, and is, therefore, more Eric de Maré's creation than mine. Its main interest and purpose lie in his splendid series of photographs.'

The *AR* issue and subsequent book were received with surprise, as early industrial architecture had not been a general area of interest at that time.[57] Soon, however, the book became celebrated, catching the imagination of those involved in the search for form. One such architect was James Stirling, who wrote in *Perspecta* acknowledging the influence of this article on the 'Functional Tradition' and placing it in the broader context of Le Corbusier's use of vernacular elements in both Ronchamp and the Maisons Jaoul.[58] Stirling and Gowan were themselves influenced by Liverpool warehouses, with their articulation of brick and stone, in their design for the Ham Common flats of 1955. Stirling gave a further reason for the relevance of this type of building: 'Their merit ... as seen by an architect today is that they are usually composed of direct and undecorated volumes evolved from building usage and particularly from the functions of their major elements.'[59] This observation reveals a link with the work and theory of Louis Kahn, who was then becoming better known in Britain. Kahn believed that a building had to be composed of powerful volumes and honest materials: elements such as staircases and service ducts were given separate forms – the 'servant' and 'served' spaces evident in both the Yale Art Gallery and Philadelphia Laboratory projects. In the same way that Kahn saw the form of the castle keep as a paradigm, Kahn's followers adopted the powerful masonry forms of those early industrial buildings as a reference.⁶⁰

AR campaigns

The *Architectural Review*'s progression from a historical valuing of the Picturesque tradition, melded with a deeply rooted appreciation of the historical fabric of British towns, led to several preoccupations developed in the late 1940s and early 1950s. These became a series of campaigns about the visual quality or lack of quality in British towns and cities, generated by de Cronin Hastings, and which figured in the pages of the *Review* in the 1950s and beyond: the most significant were *Outrage, Subtopia* and later *Manplan*.

The idea of 'Outrage' reacted to what was often termed the 'visual clutter' of street furniture and signs; 'Subtopia' attacked the lack of urbanity of the suburb; and the hypothesis of Townscape. It contested the acceptance of the existing visual urban landscape as a given: architecturally impure, and certainly never 'planned'. The qualities of a town or city were appreciated as something experienced by moving through it, bringing changing experiences of space and the objects perceived. This polemic expressed a reaction to the axial planning and uniform street line, both of the *Beaux-Arts* tradition and of modernist urbanism. Variety, elements of surprise, the conjunction of disparate built objects were valued; rather than looking at the massing of these buildings as abstract form, appreciating their detail and their material texture. Towns were also seen as specific, as if there was a quality in each place, the *genius loci*, which could be teased out and enhanced. That this was a critique of current planning operations goes without saying: and the *Review* proposed a number of models for the modification of streets and towns starting with Lyme Regis in the January 1950 issue which set out many of its concerns.

Gordon Cullen, initially the Assistant Art Editor from 1946, is remembered particularly for his Townscape drawings, both of existing urban sequences and of possible improvements to scenes of civic disaster, which are perhaps the most lasting evidence of the campaign to revalue the juxtaposition of buildings and the space between them. Ian Nairn's vehement 'Outrage' campaign expressed passion for the quality of urban design – and fury at those who fell short of that standard. In Cullen's later published book on *Townscape*, the text introduces the principle:

THE SHIFT TO THE SPECIFIC

4.10
Gordon Cullen: *Townscape* **drawing envisaging a typically picturesque redesign of the Square, Lyme Regis, from** *Architectural Review,* **1950.**

> If I was asked to define townscape I would say that one building is architecture but two buildings are townscape. For as soon as two buildings are juxtaposed the art of townscape is released. Such problems as the relationship between the buildings and the space between the buildings immediately assume importance. Multiply this to the size of the town and you have the art of environment; the possibilities of relationship increase, manoeuvres and ploys proliferate. Even a small congregation of buildings can produce drama and spatial stimulation.[61]

Cullen's pervasive imagery was a significant part of the new British modernism. Streets were pictured as full of leisured, comfortably off people: there was bunting, the planting of trees, café tables. While such a scene may have been glimpsed in the microcosm of the Festival of Britain site on the London South Bank, Cullen's depiction of life in British towns of the 1950s was very wide of the mark. A more extensive judgement of the Townscape ideal might point out that it made many more conscious of the qualities of their existing environment, and certainly was a powerful influence in the later development of a conservation lobby. It foreshadowed an almost universally agreed strategy of buildings designed to infill into existing contexts, the consensus for which developed in the 1980s. 'Townscape' reached its own apotheosis in the project for 'Civilia, the end of suburban man'.[62] The project, generated by Hastings and illustrated with collages by Kenneth Browne, verged on the Surreal with a series of montages of all manner of existing buildings with no believable site or programme. As Peter Davey has remarked: '[A]s usual with Hasting's prescriptions for the betterment of his country, his last had little or no foundation in social, economic or political reality; image was all.'[63] Hastings retired in 1973; the old AR, of Townscape and visual idiosyncrasy retired with him, its circulation down, with financial losses – and on a larger scale, with the profession, and the country, in crisis.

The longevity of the Townscape idea nevertheless indicates that it did seem a valuable strategy for many. What is already there, it said, was a given: its qualities should be valued and it should provide a basis for future development rather than be swept away. That there would be a contrary reaction to this was inevitable: Reyner Banham argued that the position seemed to 'justify, even sanctify, a willingness to compromise every "real" architectural value, to surrender to all that was most provincial and second rate in British social and intellectual life.'[64] A further critique by Joseph Rykwert was published of the planning strategy advocated by the AR, in other words Townscape:

> the weakness at the foundations of the Review is a concern for surface and a neglect for structure. This is true at every level: in the matter of town planning, to take the salient instance, the Review is concerned with traffic signs, the pattern of advertising, street furniture ... street surfacing, all the paraphernalia of 'townscape' occupy infinitely more space than the ... speculative or even strictly technical aspects of the subject.[65]

Putting both the credit and blame for this in the hands of the 'visualisations' by Gordon Cullen, Rykwert says that these vociferous campaigns actually had little effect on the contemporary development of British towns and cities, their 'failure to register an influence on the bulk of current architecture'.

The particular and identified

'That a building's first duty is to the fabric of which it forms part is, we believe, that understanding which separated the third – Team X's – generation of the Modern Movement from the one which preceded it' wrote the Smithsons in *Italian Thoughts*.[66] In a larger context, their projects exemplified the key shift of post-war architectural thought to inhabited space rather than space of the abstraction of function. This is what Peter Smithson has called the *shift to the specific*[67] that is to say, not universal, not a strategy applied at a large scale, but individual. Not the product of a mechanistic process, like *La Ville radieuse* and the architecture of high modernism; instead, particular and identified, responding to context as specific, and responsive to human use. It was seen, equally, in the *Architectural Review*'s aesthetic concern with urban context – Townscape – and the buildings of what it called the 'Functional Tradition'.

Banham wrote critically in 1964 about the apparent 'Picturesque' aesthetic in Smithson projects:

> It is difficult to see how the Smithsons' insistence on 'accepting the realities of the situation' as put into effect in their Berlin project ... really differed from the Picturesque injunction to 'consult the genius of the place in all.' Again, the line pursued by the *Architectural Review*, for instance, in insisting that when new buildings were to be inserted into existing environments, then they should be 'sympathetic, but still avowedly true to their own time', differs from the Smithsons' problem of three new houses in an existing street chiefly in the tone of voice and choice of words employed in arriving at the same conclusion.[68]

The Smithsons had indeed appropriated Cullen, the visualiser of Townscape, for drawings of their Economist project, perhaps proving Banham's point.

However, the contrast of the Smithsons' position is that prevailing ideas of British town planning, particularly the development of the Townscape idea, were based on a concept of the pictorial. And in response to ideas that their own work was about an aesthetic, they had written that 'its essence is ethical ... [and is] an attempt to be objective' [with] the forces which are at work'.[69] There is a far more rigorous concern with form, rather than appearance – with a poetic of human existence, rather than the creation of urban scenography.

In his scepticism about the Smithsons' work on a far smaller scale, 'Patio and Pavilion', Banham expressed suspicion of any engagement on their part with, as he saw it, 'tradition and the past'.[70] By their implicit reference to some fundamental, ur-model of the house and its territory, they appeared to be making a break with the primary need for an engagement with modernity. For him, developments in the next decade were to be more suited to his beliefs on this, although those later clearly related to the re-engagement with history. Banham and his contemporaries would have argued that the urgent need to respond to the modern world – huge social changes, developments in technology, the real values of modern architecture, made the *Review*'s approach in particular hopelessly trivial. It could also be the case that there was, typical of Britain, an element of class here. The 'Establishment', in the shape of the *AR* editors and its preferred architects, were comfortably middle class, with a liberal public school education. But the generation coming to maturity in the 1950s, whatever their background, rejected its values and searched for the new, equally in what was socially more egalitarian.

Some engagement with historical forms was found quite generally in the 1950s. Alvar Aalto, Louis Kahn, Ernesto Rogers and even the dominant figure of Le Corbusier, among others, worked with forms embedded with cultural memory, without of course, rejecting modernity and the radical discontinuity with the past that it represented. For each of them, however diverse their positions might appear, the Modern Movement was the central referent: their aim was to renew and reposition modernism. A version of Primitivism is one such manifestation: echoes of archaic forms in Le Corbusier's Ronchamp Chapel, later in Van Eyck's interest in non-European cultures and later culminating in Bernard Rudofsky's 1964 exhibition *Architecture without Architects*. Underpinning this and encompassing a wider position is the search for the authentic: a concept at the centre of Existentialism. Sartre had written that life should be lived in a state of heightened consciousness, which challenged the apathy created by social structures. He wrote of Giacometti: 'He has chosen to sculpt the situated appearance, and has shown that in this way the absolute may be attained. He shows men and women already seen. But not seen by him alone.'[71] The counterpart in architecture may well have been the authentic version of the absolute attempted by the Smithsons with 'Patio and Pavilion', or Le Corbusier at Ronchamp.

The move in this 'shift to the specific' from the ideal to the grounded was expressed by James Stirling in his comparison between the Jaoul houses and Villa at Garches. Of Jaoul he said that: 'they are built by and intended for the status quo … whereas Garches anticipates and participates in the progress of twentieth century emancipation … a way of life which has not generally arrived'.[72] Earlier, an article by Colin Rowe published in the *Review* in May 1950 examines the basis of modernism in systems of Classical order. Referring to *Towards a New Architecture*,

THE SHIFT TO THE SPECIFIC

a fundamental dilemma becomes evident as an incapacity to define an attitude to sensation. An absolute value is consistently imputed to mathematics, which are 'sure and certain' and order is established as an intellectual concept affirmative of universal and comforting truths.[73]

Rowe's emphasis was on the necessity of a deliberate and more complex form-making on the part of modern architects.

The influence of these new bodies of work on architectural culture was considerable. Foster recently wrote that de Maré's photographs and research influenced him while a student in Manchester.[74] At around the same time, Stirling was exploring his formal language in the series of buildings exemplified by the Leicester Engineering School, which he referred to as rooted in a reading of the functional tradition.[75] The *AR*'s larger contribution as the valuer of context and the visual quality of the environment was evident in the development of the conservation movement, the foundation of local Civic Societies, and perhaps a growing tradition of infill buildings.

Any re-evaluation of the discourse of Brutalism has to acknowledge two distinct reactions. One is that, like other authoritative discourses, it was immediately influential on many: the combination of *béton brut*, shuttered and unadorned concrete, and asymmetrical, apparently random planning, shaped a new convention, not least with the contemporary generation at the AA. One such project is Pimlico School, designed by John Bancroft of the Greater London Council in 1967. The other is that Brutalism, rather than communicating its values and quality with an existential immediacy has, highly ironically, been seen as alienating by most. The new urban morphology which the Smithsons projected has, largely, been unpopular. Golden Lane led to Park Hill in Sheffield, designed by Lynn and Smith: the powerful image of the building dominating the east of the centre of the city is far more ambitious than other housing, but has been far from successful. Such buildings as the South Bank Cultural Centre in London, taking their formal *parti* from the Smithsons, its deck from Haupstadt, and the distinctive materiality of shuttered concrete, also have been seen negatively almost since their completion. Since the 1990s, however, a reappraisal has evolved and a new generation, not only of British architects, has engaged again with the issues raised by Brutalism. *As Found* is the title of a 2001 book by Claude Lichtenstein and Thomas Schregenburger,[76] which describes the anti-utopian artistic culture of Britain in the 1950s. Practitioners such as Caruso St John, Peter Salter and von Balmoos Krucker have acknowledged their indebtedness to the Smithsons.[77]

4.11
Pimlico School, London: John Bancroft of the GLC Schools Division, 1967–70; raw ribbed concrete and industrial patent glazing contribute to one of the most Brutalist of contemporary buildings.

THE SHIFT TO THE SPECIFIC

4.12
Park Hill housing estate, Sheffield, by Jack Lynn and Ivor Smith of the city architect's department, 1957–60. Expressing at the large scale of almost 1,000 flats the possibilities of a new urban form, this celebrated scheme's dominance of the city skyline is matched by a continued parallel existence in the architectural media.

Thus, the shift to the specific occurred in several parallel strands in British architectural life, in the linguistic formulation of the Smithsons, and the essentially visual arguments of the *Architectural Review*. Against purity, against utopia, but for inclusion, for individuality – this shift, though, took place very much against the background that the revolution of modernism had irrevocably occurred. But more than that, the idea of progress, of the possible achievement of an ideal, had gone. The idea of the image was paramount, as in Henderson's photographs which showed a material world which embodied life, which had a history however mundane, and which exemplified grain and texture. Materials that existed in time and had been shaped by the lives of people. Materials – and places – have their narratives, and the radical position developed in the 1950s was to introduce this into architectural discourse.

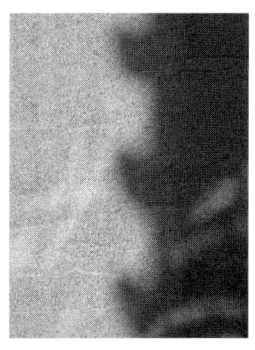

4.13
Barbican estate, London, Chamberlin, Powell and Bon, 1958–75: massive wall of pick-hammered concrete with granite aggregate, typical of the scheme's exterior surfaces.

Notes

1. Quoted in D. Robbins (ed.), *The Independent Group: Postwar Britain and the Aesthetics of Plenty*, Cambridge, MA: MIT Press, 1990, p. 201.
2. John Summerson, *45–55 Ten Years of British Architecture*, London: Arts Council, 1956. This included work by the younger generation of Leslie Martin, Powell and Moya and the Smithsons along with that of Lubetkin, Yorke and Gibberd.

113

THE SHIFT TO THE SPECIFIC

3 Summerson, op. cit., p. 6.
4 Anthony Jackson, *The Politics of Architecture*, London: Architectural Press, 1970, p. 179.
5 Colin Rowe, 'Review of Student Work', *AA Journal*, Sept./Oct. 1959, pp. 60–3.
6 Herbert Read, *Art and Industry*, London: Faber & Faber, 1956, p. 7.
7 R. Banham 'Revenge of the Picturesque: English Architectural Polemics 1945–65', in John Summerson (ed.), *Concerning Architecture*, London: Allen Lane, The Penguin Press, 1968, p. 265.
8 A full documentation and later reflection on the Festival of Britain in M. Banham and B. Hillier (eds), *A Tonic to the Nation*, London: Thames & Hudson, 1976: see also E. Harwood and A. Powers (eds), *Festival of Britain*, London: Twentieth Century Society, 2001.
9 Quoted in Robbins, op. cit., p. 201.
10 Quoted in M. Girouard, *Big Jim: the Life and Work of James Stirling*, London: Chatto & Windus, 1998, p. 54.
11 A full biography is yet to be written, but their own writings include much of a personal narrative.
12 *AR*, September 1954, pp. 152–4.
13 *Architectural Design* (hereafter *AD*), September 1953, pp. 238–48.
14 See extensive coverage and discussion in D. Robbins, op. cit.; the Smithsons' own account here underplays the specific role of the Independent Group.
15 'The Built World: Urban Re-identification', *AD*, June 1955, pp. 185–8; 'Cluster City: a New Shape for the Community', *AR*, November 1957, pp. 333–6; 'Mobility', *AD*, October 1958, pp. 385–8; 'The Function of Architecture in Cultures-in-Change', *AD*, April 1960, pp. 175–205. See also Alison and Peter Smithson, *Ordinariness and Light*, London: Faber & Faber, 1970, and the Bibliography in Helena Webster (ed.), *Modernism without Rhetoric*, London: Academy, 1997, pp. 214–19.
16 Jackson, op. cit., p. 184.
17 Smithsons' statement of 1955, reprinted in A. Smithson, *Without Rhetoric*, London: Latimer New Dimensions, 1973, p. 2.
18 A. and P. Smithson, op. cit., p. 9. They were not alone in immediately seeing the poverty of results of new town building: see in particular J.M. Richards, 'Failure of the New Towns', *AR*, July 1953, pp. 29–32.
19 See *AR*, November 1957.
20 See *AR*, January 1960.
21 The Congrès Internationaux d'Architecture Moderne founded in 1928: its ideas of urbanism expressed quintessentially in the Athens Charter emerging from CIAM IV. See U. Conrads, *Programmes and Manifestos on Twentieth Century Architecture*, London: Lund Humphries, 1970; K. Frampton, *Modern Architecture: A Critical History*, London: Thames & Hudson, 1992, pp. 269ff.
22 The Smithsons' CIAM grille presented at Aix-en-Provence is discussed by them in *Uppercase* 3, ed. Theo Crosby, London, 1960: it led also to the 1954 Doorn Manifesto with the collaboration of Aldo van Eyck, Jacob Bakema, John Voelcker and others.
23 Quoted in Robbins, op. cit., p. 201.
24 Reyner Banham, 'The New Brutalism', *AR*, December 1955, pp. 355–61.
25 Ibid., p. 358.
26 *Zodiac* 4, 1959, p. 69.
27 K. Scott, cited in *AR*, April 1954, p. 274.
28 Frampton, op. cit., p. 263. On Henderson see Victoria Walsh, *Nigel Henderson: Parallel of Life and Art*, London: Thames & Hudson, 2001.
29 N. Henderson in *Uppercase* 3, 1960, unpaginated.
30 *This is Tomorrow*, London, Whitechapel Art Gallery, Catalogue, 1955, p. 6.
31 See S.W. Goldhagen 'Freedom's Domiciles: Three projects by Alison and Peter Smithson', in S.W. Goldhagen and R. Legault (eds), *Anxious Modernisms*, Cambridge, MA: MIT Press, 2000, p. 84. She develops a reading of the Pavilion informed by Existen-

tialism, which also incorporates a rethinking of the contemporary Smithson projects, The House of the Future and Sugden house.
32 *AD*, April 1957, p. 113.
33 R. Banham, 'The New Brutalism', *AR*, December 1955, p. 361.
34 Peter Smithson, 'The Slow Growth of Another Sensibility: Architecture as Townbuilding', in J. Gowan (ed.), *A Continuing Experiment: Learning and Teaching at the Architectural Association*, London: Architectural Press, 1975, p. 58.
35 See Andrew Saint, *Towards A Social Architecture*, New Haven: Yale University Press, 1987.
36 Quoted in C. Harrison and P. Wood, *Art in Theory 1900–2000*, Oxford: Blackwell, 2002, p. 580.
37 G. Limbour, 'Let the Material Speak for Itself', in *Jean Dubuffet: Exhibition of Painting, Drawing, Sculpture*, trans. P. Watson, London: Institute of Contemporary Art, 1955.
38 Ibid., p. 7.
39 Ibid., p. 2.
40 *AR*, January 1950, pp. 2–66.
41 *AR*, January 1950, p. 45.
42 *AR*, January 1938, pp. 1–14.
43 See Piper's 'England's Early Sculptors', *AR*, October 1936, pp. 157–62.
44 Ibid.
45 *AR*, July 1949, pp. 1–64.
46 Ibid. The issue was published as a book: Eric de Maré, *The Canals of England*, London: Architectural Press, 1950.
47 See *Eric de Maré Photographer: builder with light*, London: Architectural Association, 1990.
48 *AR*, January 1950, pp. 9, 11.
49 Ibid.
50 Ibid.
51 Relevant here is de Maré's editing of *New Ways of Building*, London: Architectural Press, 1948.
52 *AR*, June 1947, pp. 199–204 (Sven Backström, quoted).
53 J.M. Richards (ed.), 'The Functional Tradition as Shown in Early Industrial Buildings', photographed by Eric de Maré, *AR*, July 1957, pp. 3–73.
54 Le Corbusier, *Vers une architecture*, 1923.
55 Richards, op. cit.
56 J.M. Richards (ed.), *The Functional Tradition in Early Industrial Buildings*, photographs by Eric de Maré, London: Architectural Press, 1958.
57 Birkin Haward in conversation with the present author, July 1990.
58 James Stirling, *The 'Functional Tradition' and Expression*, Perspecta 6, 1960, pp. 88–97.
59 Ibid.
60 For a more extensive account of de Maré, see A. Higgott, 'Eric de Maré and the Functional Tradition', in *Eric de Maré*, London: Architectural Association, 1990.
61 Gordon Cullen, *Townscape*, London: Architectural Press, 1961, p. 133. See also Introduction, p. 9ff. On Cullen, see David Gosling, *Gordon Cullen: Visions of Urban Design*, London: Academy Editions, 1996.
62 *Civilia* was published as a book under the pseudonym Ivor de Wolfe, London: Architectural Press, 1971.
63 Peter Davey in 'AR on AR', *AR*, May 1996, p. 71.
64 R. Banham, *The New Brutalism: Ethic or Aesthetic?*, London: Architectural Press, 1966, p. 13.
65 J. Rykwert in 'Review of a Review', *Zodiac* 4, 1959, p. 13.
66 A. and P. Smithson, *Italian Thoughts*, London, 1993, p. 66.
67 Afterword in Walsh, op. cit., p. 150.
68 R. Banham, *The New Brutalism*, p. 74.

THE SHIFT TO THE SPECIFIC

69 *AD*, April 1957, p. 113.
70 Banham, *The New Brutalism*, p. 64.
71 Pierre Matisse Gallery, NY, 1948. Cited in Harrison and Wood, op. cit., p. 612.
72 J. Stirling, 'Garches to Jaoul', *AR*, September 1955, p. 145.
73 Colin Rowe, 'Mannerism and Modern Architecture' *AR*, May 1950, p. 295.
74 David Jenkins (ed.), *Norman Foster Works*, vol. 1, London: Prestel, 2002, p. 12.
75 Stirling, 'The Functional Tradition'.
76 C. Lichtenstien and T. Schregenburger, *As Found: the Discovery of the Ordinary*, Baden: Lars Müller, 2001.
77 See, for example, *Architecture Is Not Made with the Brain: the Labour of Alison and Peter Smithson*, London: Architectural Association, 2005.

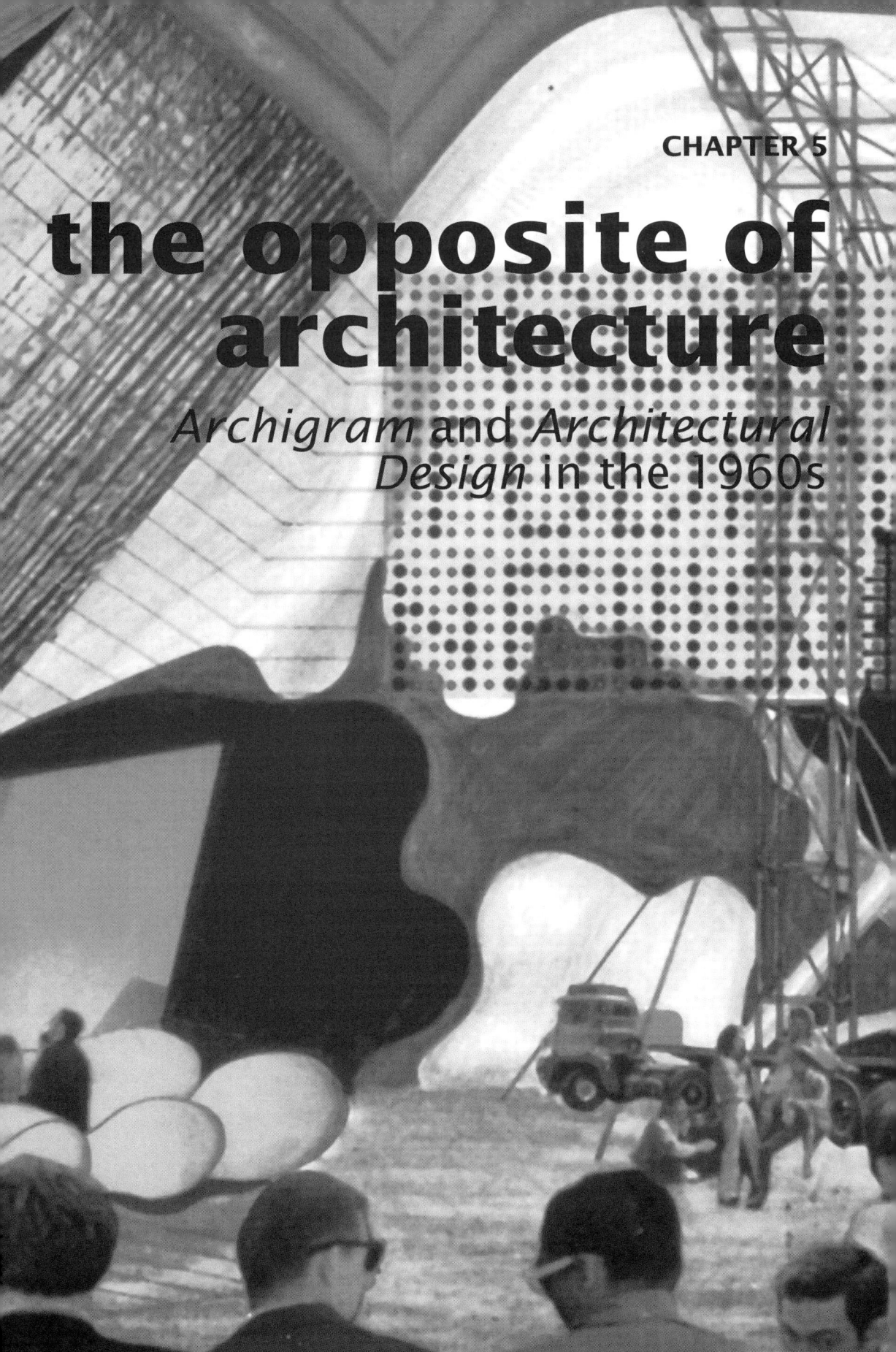

CHAPTER 5

the opposite of architecture

Archigram and Architectural Design in the 1960s

THE OPPOSITE OF ARCHITECTURE

> Architecture, as a service to human societies, can only be defined as the provision of fit environments for human activities. The word 'fit' may be defined in the most generous terms imaginable, but it still does not necessarily imply the erection of buildings. Environments may be made fit for human beings by any number of means ... Architecture, indeed, began with the first furs worn by our earliest ancestors, or with the discovery of fire – it shows a narrowly professional frame of mind to refer its beginnings solely to the cave or primitive hut.
>
> (Reyner Banham, 'Stocktaking: Tradition and Technology', 1960)[1]

The article, written by Reyner Banham in the *Architectural Review* at the beginning of the 1960s, expressed the real possibility of starting afresh with the eternal problems of building houses and creating cities. For him and for many of his contemporaries, this exciting potential was the result of transformations in technology, enabling the making of structures in ways inconceivable even in the recent past. The article, remarkably written as two parallel texts – 'Tradition' and 'Technology' – presents on the one hand the way that the tradition of architecture has recently developed, with such tendencies as the revivals of classical geometries, neo-expressionism, and even neo-modernism. On the other hand, as a parallel text he puts forward the radical material and structural advances of the time. Concrete shells, fibreglass units and lightweight space frames have as yet, he admits, hardly effected any change in the practice of architecture. For Banham the provocation of technology demands a response from architecture: he warns that existing architectural ways of working cannot accommodate the changes in environmental servicing and building construction. Architecture was on the threshold of something entirely new, not at all dependent on tradition: an architecture based on serving the needs of human activities, in fact the opposite of architecture as it had been practised. He admonishes architects in a manner reminiscent of Le Corbusier's polemic in *L'Esprit nouveau* forty years earlier, for their over-indulgent concerns with style and their blindness to the technological transformations around them.

In the same year Banham published his first book, *Theory and Design in the First Machine Age*,[2] a history of modern architecture which was an implicit revision and repudiation of the kind of instrumentalist history earlier written by Nikolaus Pevsner. Based on his PhD thesis – his was the first British PhD on modern architecture – its rewriting of history was radical, giving prominence to the work of the

THE OPPOSITE OF ARCHITECTURE

Futurists and rejecting the reading of the English Arts and Crafts as the key pioneers of modernism in the book by Pevsner (paradoxically his PhD supervisor), which was still in print.[3] Banham introduced other themes which in his hands became a complex story, notably the classical formal elements in much modernist form-making, not least that of Le Corbusier. But apart from this historical revision, he reversed the customary terms of its discussion: talking not of buildings but ideas, not of objects but of theories. There was a section of photographs of buildings as a counterpart to the narrative of presentation and analysis of theoretical positions, but they were there as representative images to remind rather than inform about the physical existence of buildings or drawings. His emphasis, instead, was on architectural programmes and manifestos from Choisy, through Loos, Sant'Elia, De Stijl and Le Corbusier to Fuller. As Colin St John Wilson has remarked, 'It was Banham who started it all'[4]; 'it' being in this case the discussion of architectural ideas as privileged over the discussion of buildings, the overweening attention no longer being paid to the architectural object. The book thus introduced a new kind of history which began the long-sustained emphasis on theory, and which developed an account of architectural culture. Buildings were not fundamentally interesting in their own right *as* buildings, but as the product of ideas and intentions. As he introduces the section on the Futurists, what was important was their programme: 'The qualities which made Futurism a turning point in the development of modern theories of design were primarily ideological and concerned with attitudes of mind, rather than formal or technical methods.'[5]

The last chapter of the book was an addition to Banham's thesis and made clear that he too, like Pevsner and Richards, was an instrumentalist historian, keen to champion particular views and influence architectural practice. Buckminster Fuller, a self-styled 'inventor' of new forms, far outside the orbit of Pevsner's historical account, is introduced in the final pages and may be a contradiction to the preceding narrative of the book. For Banham acclaims him in highly positive terms, referring to his 1927 Dymaxion House project:

> [H]ad it been built, [it] would have rendered [the Villa Savoye] technically obsolete before construction had even begun. The Dymaxion house was entirely radical, a hexagonal ring of dwelling space, walled in double skins of plastic . . . and hung by wires from the apex of a central duralumin mast which also housed all the mechanical services.[6]

Thus the rich historical story carefully drawn up by Banham seems negated by Fuller's technological form-making, and in his last page he writes:

> It may well be that what we have hitherto understood as architecture, and what we are beginning to understand of technology are incompatible disciplines. The architect who proposes to run with technology knows now that he will be in fast company, and that, in order to keep up he may have to emulate the Futurists and discard his whole cultural load, including the professional garments by which he is recognised as an architect.[7]

Responses to *Theory and Design* were positive and remained so, establishing Banham's authority as a historian and critic. Nikolaus Pevsner was no doubt quietly shocked at how much his student had diverted from the orthodoxy he had done so much to establish.[8] Others, such as Sibyl Moholy-Nagy, felt he had over-emphasised the role of books over buildings. His contemporary Alan Colquhoun reviewed the book, expressing doubt as to Banham's conscientiousness as a historian, particularly where Fuller was concerned. In his enthusiasm for Fuller, Banham had seen his work as 'pure' technology in a way it scarcely was; and certainly not as any sort of absolute contrast to the realisations of Le Corbusier or Mies van der Rohe.[9] For the young generation, particularly the architecture students of the early 1960s, Banham's historical revision was fresh and even electrifying: the Futurists were a revelation, the emphasis on modernist polemic right for a time ready for fresh thinking. His stress on the importance of a new technological form-making was a complement to the advanced technology daily manifested in the world: the machines beginning to appear in every Western home, and the race to conquer outer space.

Banham was to leave the staff of the *AR* two years later[10] and became a full-time academic, initially at the invitation of its students, at University College London. As the decade progressed, it became clear that the *Review* was losing its long-time position as the pre-eminent British journal: Banham's natural home was in any case increasingly to become a wider field, writing numerous academic articles, a regular column for *New Society*, and, eventually, some eleven books.[11] A more sympathetic environment for the development of the kind of technocratic attitudes he promoted was later provided by *Architectural Design*: but a more immediate relationship can be drawn to the projects and publication of the loosely formed group of young architects, Archigram.

Within a new spirit of architecture this engagement with technology was to become pre-eminent, but there were several other directions. The linear development of modernist building programmes continued, influenced to a greater or lesser extent by the ideas or at least the aesthetics of Brutalism. There was a huge housing programme, by this stage entirely modernist, throughout the decade; the 1960s saw the building of tower blocks of social housing by the hundred.[12] In parallel, a vast commercial building programme evolved, with office towers, shopping 'precincts' and other town centre development. Such new technology as was used, was mostly evident in prefabrication, particularly the development of 'systems' later in the decade, although with some resistance from architects. Large-scale projects became the paradigm: the example of Cumbernauld Town Centre, completed in 1966, was much discussed as an example of what came to be called megastructures.[13] Behind this extensive building programme was an underlying optimism: the political and economic situation was stable, and it seemed that anything was possible. The 1960s effectively saw the slow and much-delayed realisation of a post-war world where the building of a new environment was finally attainable. There was also a consensus politically: relatively right-wing Labour governments and socially liberal Conservative ones competed in terms of numbers of council houses built. The loosening of social structures and liberalisation in many fields led to the most astonishing creative period in British culture, in the broadest and most inclusive sense. And just as British music, fashion and film became globally successful, so did the renown of certain of its architects.

Making *Archigram*

> A new generation of architecture must arise – with forms and spaces which seem to reject the precepts of 'Modern'
> REJECT – curtains – design – history – graphpaper
> DIG ACCEPT ENDORSE – homogeneity – travelators – Monk – expendability . . .
> WE HAVE CHOSEN TO BYPASS THE DECAYING BAUHAUS IMAGE WHICH IS AN INSULT TO FUNCTIONALISM.
> you can roll out steel – any length
> you can blow up a balloon – any size
> you can mould plastic – any shape[14]

This extract was written by Peter Cook and David Greene for the first edition of *Archigram*, published in May 1961. Edited by AA student David Usbourne and the product of work by Cook, Greene and Mike

THE OPPOSITE OF ARCHITECTURE

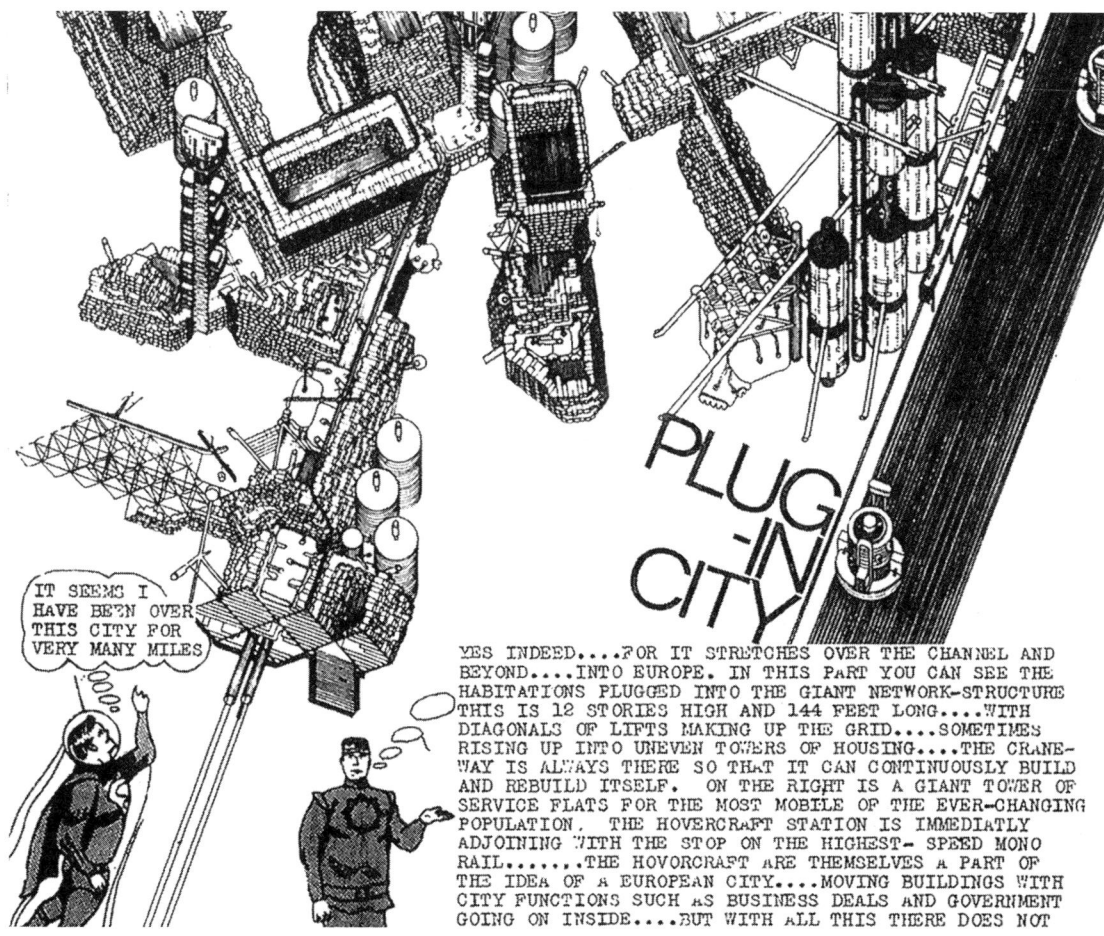

5.1
Peter Cook: Plug-in City from *Archigram 4*, 1964: the project – in its graphic form – becomes integrated with the journal's layout which is 'in orbit with the space comic/science fiction bit'.

Webb, it consisted of two pages, sold 300 copies, and included a montage of images of a variety of student projects, both from the AA and what was then Regent Street Polytechnic. *Archigram 1*, perhaps unsurprisingly, did not look like Archigram in the sense of its retrospective image and seemed to emerge from Brutalist discourse, with an assortment of expressive but unaesthetic shapes. Cook had recently graduated from the AA, Greene and Webb from Regent Street; what they had in common was a rejection of the way that the energy and iconoclasm of modernism had been turned into a formula. They also expressed boredom with (perhaps rather than anger about) current British practice, and felt that what was being produced by their own generation was genuinely innovative – but had no outlet for its publication.

It was in the second issue a year later that a more developed position was expressed. Projects by Ron Herron, Warren Chalk and

Dennis Crompton were included (each of them then working at the London County Council Architects' department on the South Bank project), as was work by Cedric Price.[15] Projects included some from the Brutalist tendency: others more obviously innovative, such as Mike Webb's Entertainment Centre for Leicester Square, a dynamic structure of spiral ramps with platforms making spaces for dancing, bowling and restaurants (as well as an office block 'to make it pay') covered by a lightweight curved roof. Adrian Sansom's East End housing project was a prefabricated expendable building with moveable internal partitions and a thirty-year building life: David Greene's project for a sprayed plastic house introduced organic form-making. Herron, Chalk and Crompton joined Cook, Webb and Greene to form what came to be called the Archigram group. But the group was not a group in the sense of a shared practice; each did projects singularly or in collaboration, with joint exhibition installations and, later, competition entries. The six members of the group were invited to work on the Euston Station project at Taylor Woodrow, with Theo Crosby, formerly Technical Editor at *Architectural Design*.[16]

Archigram – the word – started with the publication not the group of architects. 'Architecture – telegram': an instant communication through technology; thus their activity was intrinsically about publishing work and ideas, rather than designing or building them. For these architects, as important as having ideas and drawing them was to propagate them to a wider audience or, as Warren Chalk put it, to 'put noise into the system'. The third issue, published in August 1963 and titled *Expendability: Towards a Throwaway Architecture*, was technologically inflected in the way the work of Archigram came to be recognised. Cook wrote an editorial:

> Almost without realising it, we have absorbed into our lives the first generation of expendables ... food bags, paper tissues, polythene wrappers, ballpens, EPs ... so many things about which we don't have to think. We throw them away almost as soon as we acquire them ... Our collective mental blockage occurs between the land of the small-scale consumer products and the objects which make up our environment ... it will not be until such things as housing, amenity place and work place become recognised as consumer products that can be bought 'off the peg' ... that we can begin to make an environment that is really part of a developing human culture.[17]

Or, as he succinctly put it later: 'For us, the prepackaged frozen lunch is more important than Palladio.'[18]

THE OPPOSITE OF ARCHITECTURE

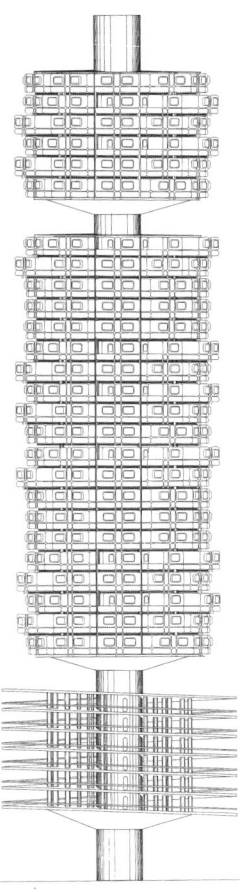

5.2
Warren Chalk: Capsule Tower from *Archigram* 6, 1965: a set of prefabricated and mobile dwelling modules plugged into a service tower.

The projects published in *Archigram 3* illustrate the idea that housing, streets and infrastructures can be rapidly made and equally readily discarded: Warren Chalk's capsule project was a service tower into which highly serviced plastic capsules were plugged. Chalk also proposed, with Herron, a City Interchange: a complex of communication systems which would service a sequence of office and communication towers. The graphic quality of the magazine and the drawings themselves were equally important: a propensity for organic forms – certainly no graph paper – and graphics that owed something to comics and something to pop art. Pages were a montage of words, flows and textures, communicating through their graphic as well as images and words themselves. Each of the Archigram architects, in their distinctive ways, could certainly draw, but *Archigram 3* in particular can be seen as the first full realisation that architectural ideas could be presented in this original and tremendously immediate way. Drawings, captions and montaged photographs formed a vivid and at the time shocking contrast to the way that architectural projects were supposed to be presented.

A subverted space fiction cartoon formed the first pages of *Archigram 4* – the ZOOM issue, with a pop art cover designed by Chalk, appearing in May 1964. Comic book heroes and heroines are given speech bubbles to articulate architectural thought:

> These space comic cities reflect without conscious intention certain overtones of meaning – illuminate an area of opinion that seeks the breakdown of conventional attitudes, the disruption of the 'straight-up-and-down formal vacuum . . . necessary to create a more dynamic environment.[19]

Within it, one version of Cook's most celebrated project – 'Plug-in City': the axonometric drawing published in *Archigram 4* – became one of the group's most reproduced images and variations of the project also formed part of later issues. It presented the jagged and irregular Futuristic form of buildings piled up on top of each other, with an emphasis on movement and connection. But unlike Sant'Elia's *Citta Nuova*, it genuinely was Futuristic as it embodied the principle of dynamic change, with each of its parts slotted into a highly extended serviced structure, subject both to removal and replacement.

> Yes indeed . . . for it stretches over the channel and beyond into Europe. In this part you can see the habitations plugged into the giant network structure. This is 12 stories high and 144 feet long . . . sometimes rising up into uneven towers of housing . . .

THE OPPOSITE OF ARCHITECTURE

the craneway is always there so it can continuously build and rebuild itself ... the hovercraft station is adjoining with a stop on the high speed monorail.[20]

Cook thus described 'Plug-in City', the expression of *Archigram*'s concerns with expendability, the appropriation of new technologies, and the matching of new and more dynamic lifestyles with a new way of envisaging architecture. Rather than a project to be analysed to the most extreme level, however, it should be seen as part of the group's programme of communication and publication: the image, in this and its later forms, was the message.

The fifth *Archigram*, following swiftly in November 1964, dealt with the theme of *Metropolis* and apart from later-celebrated projects by its own members – 'Walking City' by Ron Herron and Dennis Crompton's 'Computer City' – there was a wide sweep of city form projects, tending to what were described as 'high molehills'. Historically, Henri Sauvage from the 1920s and Ronald Jones' 1950 AA project appeared, as did contemporary work by Yona Friedman,

5.3
Archigram 6 **cover designed by Geoff Reeve in red and green, 1965.**

by Hans Hollein from Vienna and the Situationist New Babylon by Constant.

Archigram 6 followed in autumn 1965 with a dazzling red and green cover designed by Geoff Reeve. The tradition of student projects was continued, now with some of Cook's students including the AA thesis project by Nick Grimshaw 'University Network', which was, he said, a new kind of environment

> which throws a heavy responsibility on the user ... it is my firm belief that the individual will begin to realise his own potential and develop it. Once this is achieved society will be making far, far greater demands on its sensory and psychological environment – demands which are not even acknowledged by the majority of designers.[21]

The theme of new and responsive environments was seen in other projects, even though some seemed far more megastructural than flexible: but there was also a 'historical' section looking at the 1940s. It consisted of a montage of 35 mm film strips of images including blimps, war production, frogmen, steel structures, power stations: by comparison, the mid-1960s had only a 'few objects worth talking about'. The real contribution of the 1940s, it said, was the 'creative breakthrough' of the industrialised system of building.

Each issue of *Archigram* re-thought not only the content of the magazine but also how its ideas and work would be presented. Of the nine issues, there is no standard format, in terms of layout, page size or even 'look'. *Archigram* 7, appearing in December 1966, was not the most spectacular but consisted of 14 loose leaves in a folder of montaged images printed in red – 'free time mode' by Ron Herron and Barry Snowden. It included two pages of cut-outs: pieces of design such as a Tony Dugdale ramp, Price shed or Fuller icosahedron could be reassembled:

> Your two sheets of cut out can be played with just like a cut out of Noah's ark or St Paul's cathedral, after all the paraphernalia of current architecture is quite as pretty as anything ... But take a closer look at the bits ... there is no pattern set out for you.

Just as the loose-leaf form meant there was no predetermined order in reading the journal, so architecture might be a randomly assembled kit of parts. The most significant projects published were David Greene's 'Living Pod' and Mike Webb's 'Cushicle'. Both provided, in Greene's words, a house that 'is an appliance for carrying with you',[22]

THE OPPOSITE OF ARCHITECTURE

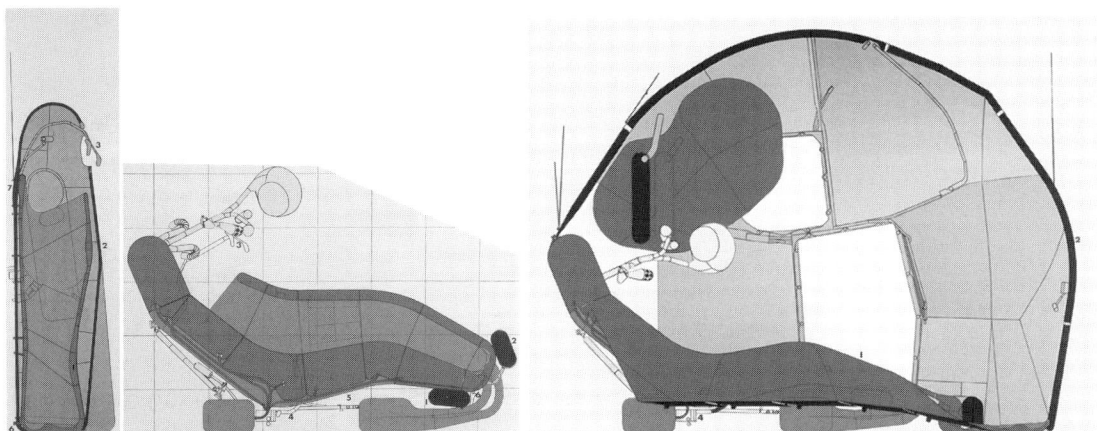

a small-scale, highly serviced enclosure for a modern nomad. The 'Cushicle' could be carried as a suit, opened out when needed into a inflated pod complete with water supply, projection television and reclining bed.

Archigram 8, published in 1968, was also, according to the editorial, 'entirely concerned with the problem of direct personal provision of comfort, facility, satisfaction, enquiry and above all the effect of all kinds of phenomena upon each other.'[23] The explicit programme of the issue was to develop architectural issues through non-architectural means, the provision of human needs through strategies that were not determined through the making of permanent buildings. As Peter Cook asserted: 'We have no buildings here, the boundaries are down'. The most significant projects published were the Ideas Circus and similarly conceived Instant City, worked on by Cook and Herron. Urban communities could be 'tuned up' through the arrival of a travelling urban circus which would erect screens, suspend inflatables, set up electronic communication systems and so on. Cities did not thus have to be reconstructed bur rather reconnected with new cultural forms, all by means temporary, low-cost and lightweight. The writing and projects in *Archigram 8* were flagged with a series of key words: *Metamorphosis, Nomad, Indeterminacy, Comfort, Hard-Soft, Emancipation, Change* and *Response*. So a series of distinctions was set up which made the transformation of life the focus, rather than the making of a serious piece of solid building.

The final issue of the journal, *Archigram 9*, appeared two years later in 1970. With the time lag comes a loss of energy and also of content; and it appears softer, less urgent and more established. It even provides a format which could have become standard: eleven

5.4
Mike Webb: Cushicle from *Archigram 7*, 1966: 'an invention that enables a man to carry a complete environment on his back. It inflates out when needed. It is a complete nomadic unit – and it is fully serviced'.

THE OPPOSITE OF ARCHITECTURE

5.5
Peter Cook: Instant City montage from *Archigram 8*, 1968: later Archigram projects by Cook and Herron moved towards the expression of urban tuning-up rather than purely technological realisations.

double-width pages printed on both sides with, evident on the cover, higher standards of production. (Although it does have a packet of seeds included, embellishing Greene's project 'Experimental Bottery'.) The editorial refers to politics: the group had been bruised in an ill-received presentation at the Paris *Beaux-Arts* in the wake of the 1968 near-revolution. 'Since we are English, we are most attracted to the characteristically Anglo-Saxon tactic of infiltration as contrasted with the characteristically Latin emotion which demands confrontation'.[24] What it says is necessary is the concerted effort of continual invention, which now possesses an international scale through the action of *Archizones* – Archigram's international exchange for like-minded people. The issue contains an announcement about the International Institute of Design session to be held in the summer in London. Led by Alvin Boyarsky, this very event, an archizone itself, was the seed of the AA as it developed in the following two decades, in which most of the Archigram architects were to play a full part.

Placing the subject

The talk of Archigram was consistently about the dissolving of the city into a dynamic field of forces, dazzled by movement and enriched by the creation of atmospheres. The city was, rather than a vast hybrid structure, a collection of events. This seems in ironical

128

contrast to much of the content of the issues of *Archigram* which presents, however radically and powerfully, a collection of *things*. While these objects were themselves flexible and mutable, and one may question in what sense they were finally resolved propositions, there remains a paradox at the core of their enterprise. David Greene has recently recalled:

> What Archigram consistently did was to draw and make models of the city. The city and architecture were still seen very much as objects, aesthetic objects that architects can design – and if Archigram designs them everything will be OK – rather than actually concentrating on the events.[25]

Greene has also referred to the artist Joseph Kosuth, whose influential article 'Art after Philosophy' was published in London in 1969.[26] Kosuth's work, widely seen as one of the foundations of conceptual art, radicalised art practice by removing the prime activity of the artist from the making of the work of art. The creation of an 'object' was not privileged; any art object has, for him, only historical relevance. Thus in his argument can be seen the transfer of the notion of the artist's production from visible aspects of the work to the intellectual processes that ultimately formed it: art is not aesthetics. The implications of this position have been comprehensively manifested in architectural discourse, but largely by the generation that was to come after Archigram.

Outside the production of the journal through the decade of the 1960s, Archigram realised a number of group projects, including the exhibitions *Living 1990* in 1967 and *Milanogram* at the Milan Triennale in 1968. The first to be realised was the *Living City* exhibition, opened at the Institute of Contemporary Arts in June 1963. Initiated by Theo Crosby, it provided an opportunity for a more public arena for their work: it burst them into prominence in the London art scene. As an installation, this was the first project to be set not in the pages of a magazine but in real space. The introduction by Peter Cook eloquently presented the key issue:

> *Living City* has come about as the reply to the situation as it appears to us, who are involved in the creation and evaluation of the environment. We are in a long-established European city, of long established precedents and no clear way for us to build upon them. The re-creation of environment is too often a jaded process, having to do only with densities, allocations of space, fulfilment of regulations: the spirit of cities is lost in the process.[27]

THE OPPOSITE OF ARCHITECTURE

5.6
Archigram group: 'Living City' exhibition installation, Institute of Contemporary Arts, London, 1963: the first project outside the pages of a magazine.

The intention of the exhibition was, rather, to present the total environment of the city: the city as a complete and inclusive condition in which all activities have validity. A new approach to the city would re-include the fleeting moment with the fundamental structure, and the subjective with the rational.

> In a living city all are important: the triviality of lighting a cigarette, or the hard fact of moving two million commuters a day. In fact they are equal – as facets of the shared experience of the city. So far, no other form of environment has been devised that produces the same quality of experience shared by so many minds and interests. When it is raining in Oxford Street the architecture is no more important than the rain; in fact the weather has more to do with the pulsation of the living city at that given moment. Similarly all moments of time are equally valid in the shared experience. The city lives equally in its past and its future, and in the present where we are.[28]

Described as a 'total environment', the exhibition produced a series of spaces ('gloops') with distinct atmospheres created both by spatial differentiation and the montage of images, lettering and colour. The themes were *Survival*, *Crowd*, *Man*, *Communications*, *Situation*. Cutting the spectator off from existing relationships and assumptions, the exhibition aimed to give new and unprecedented experiences to the viewer, empowering them to feel as well as to think. The 'living' city was one experienced rather than built, and the structure that enclosed the exhibition clearly less important than the perceptions created. Architecture, it might have been said, was less important than people, especially architects, assumed. Instead, the focus was on *situation*:

> Situation – the happenings within spaces in a city, the transient throwaway objects, the passing presence of cars and people – is as important, possibly more important, than the built demarcation of space ... As the spectator changes, the moving eye sees. Situation is related to individual perception, and the place of the individual in the environment.[29]

Thus the *Living City* exhibition installation was consistent with the intention which underlay Archigram's polemic to make new possibilities available and new sensations experienced. The city was seen as a potential field for the expansion of human experience and potential, transcending their evident love for the dynamic and electric *stuff* of the architecture they created.

Looking at the slim pile of published *Archigram* magazines,[30] one gets a quite different impression than from looking at the 1972 Studio Vista *Archigram* book, assumed to be a collection of the journal's content.[31] The book seems homogenised, and while it certainly has better production values, is more slick and evidently about image; there is a loss of rawness and of the wild extensive field of ideas. *Archigram* was like no other architectural journal – it was improvised, sharp, immediate, inventive, wilful, colourful. It was also transient, the reader intended to relate to it with visual immediacy – or not. Beyond that, it had a bold programme of reinterpreting what architecture was about: an ambition that radical change was urgent, and possible. Architecture, it said, is appalling, irrelevant, 'grey', and must be confronted.

Even though its major contributors were long-time ex-students, there is a sense, articulated particularly in the first and last issues, that 'students' are what the undertaking is about, with the possibility of their carrying forward a new agenda. The journal also makes clear that its contributors were a much looser group – not just the six 'Archigrammers'[32] but a far wider cluster. Cedric Price was represented in every issue except the first, and many foreign figures were included, from Europe in particular but also from the USA.[33]

Each issue was an experiment with format: strong colours, different size paper, radical graphics. With certain issues you could put it in your own order, with none more important than another: each issue had more inventiveness than a year of an established journal. The drive behind *Archigram* was not that the six members of the group would have an outlet for their work, but the spirit of invention and energy for change. Image – the creation of the memorable image – seemed the prime business of the journal. Along with this highly effective communication, there was the sense that these images were not serious projects, in the sense that they were necessarily what would be built but, rather, injections into the discourse of architecture. Even Le Corbusier's planning schemes, however immense, were created as if they were serious and realisable. Thus *Archigram* represents a new relationship to discourse and thus to the media: in the sense of the enquiry of this book, its projects exist *as* media.

The positive reception of *Archigram* was unparalleled, and its intended audience of the younger generation immediately took it up with great enthusiasm. Peter Murray, then a student at Bristol, has recalled that it appeared to his cohort of students as 'everything we had been searching for'. But longer lasting while less immediate was its influence on architectural *education*, particularly in Britain, which it was to transform. Banham wrote in 1965 that Archigram 'make no bones about being in the image business – like the rest of us they need to know what the city of the future is going to *look* like.'[34] In a contribution to the Archigram book, he described their work as 'designing for pleasure, doing your own thing with the conviction that comes from the uninhibited exercise of creative talent braced by ruthless self-criticism.'[35] For Colin Rowe, Archigram was making 'picturesque images of the future' with 'all the famous ingredients of Englishness now given a space-age gloss'. He concluded, oblivious to its many other tendencies, that their work was 'townscape in a space-suit'.[36]

A reaction to its instant popularity and to its obvious provocation was more widespread: even the AA's journal had a highly critical review, primarily targeted at *Archigram 8*. Objects from pop culture were, it said, presented 'without rhyme or reason' in a disjointed collage technique which 'achieves what seems largely to be a graphic effect'. Its approach was 'over-simplified' and its authors, rather bizarrely, include a long list of suggested texts for Archigram to read: transportation studies, scientific reports and urban modelling.[37] The idea of a scientific basis for design, based on rational processes of research and analysis, was indeed the antithesis of Archigram, and a parallel development of the decade. Richard Llewelyn Davies, head of University College London's school from 1960, was its leading proponent, seeing architecture primarily as an environmental practice. Ironically, Peter Cook was to take up his old position in 1990, demonstrating that the 'unserious' was, for many surprisingly, actually of more long-lasting relevance.

Architectural Design's agenda

At the end of the 1960s and for a few years beyond, *Architectural Design* (*AD*) took up the mantle of *Archigram* and became the immediate and urgent communicator of ideas, in continuation of the work of its more improvised predecessor. *AD* had also, during the decade, supplanted *Architectural Review* (*AR*) as the journal which best represented new thinking and practice in British architectural culture. Peter Murray, who worked on *AD* from 1969 to 1973, has described the readers of the *AR* as dressed in 'sports jackets and flannels' rather than any fashionable contemporary gear.[38]

Whatever the accuracy of that, the *AR* was never to catch up with the mood of the age as British culture transformed. That role was adopted by *Architectural Design*, under its long-term editor Monica Pidgeon, and a talented succession of Technical Editors, effectively deputies, from the 1950s to the 1970s. Pidgeon, a Chilean-born Bartlett graduate, became Editor in 1946, a role she continued to develop until leaving to edit the *RIBA Journal* late in 1975. Theo Crosby, as Technical Editor from 1953, introduced the Smithsons who published a series of influential articles (see p. 89) and, along with them, an engagement with contemporary issues. Crosby was succeeded by Kenneth Frampton from 1962 to 1965.[39] Frampton's tenure saw increasingly accomplished writing on the buildings of the day and in this period the news section was extended which was, along with more conventional coverage of buildings, news of innovation in the architectural world at large.

Turning from the *Architectural Review* to *Architectural Design* of the early 1960s one notices the lack of magisterial quality, the authority of voice that so characterised the *AR*: the distinctive editorial voice of Hubert de Cronin Hastings and indeed of Richards is substituted by a more neutral tone. If there was a 'special issue' in *AR* it would be introduced with much consequence – 'This is an important subject which you should listen to' – while *AD* would announce on the cover 'Italy' and that would be that. It becomes apparent that the *AR* was very much a campaigning journal, despite its apparent conservatism in this period. In the early 1960s *AD* by comparison simply presented work with apparently less editorialising. There was also a quieter and more modern layout in the latter and (in this similar to *AR*) very well-designed covers, conceived by its Technical Editors, notably Crosby.

The financial survival of *AD* was always perilous, and it was produced highly economically from a single room in Bloomsbury Way in London. The content was mainly the 'professional' coverage of new buildings in a standard format with photographs and descriptive text and, increasingly, critical commentary. The November 1963 *AD* provides a good example of the way its scope was becoming broader and perhaps more relevant for the generation of *Archigram*: what was considered appropriate to architectural discourse became wider than the coverage of significant buildings by significant architects. Pages of 'world news' are followed by a half page on the Fulham study, which saw the Archigram group's ideas applied in a project led by Theo Crosby. But innovative work in this issue is of a far broader origin, with a project by Yona Friedman 'Towards a Mobile Architecture', Frei Otto's lightweight fabric structure for Hanover, as well as Mike Webb's entertainment centre for Leicester Square. There are also features with coverage of technical innovation, on multi-storey suspension structures and the work of Jean Prouvé.

June 1964 saw the start of an annual *AD* 'Grand Project Award' series, aiming to present architectural developments in Britain and 'give public recognition to the work of relatively unknown architects'. The unbuilt (but commissioned) projects given awards included the winner, Peter Womersley's surgery unit at Edinburgh Western Hospital, others were the new architecture school for Marylebone Road by the LCC, the shopping development in Portsmouth (later named the Tricorn) by Owen Luder, and housing by Peter Phippen for Hatfield new town. With the exception of the latter, these and other prizewinning schemes were universally large and aggressive form-making of in situ concrete which had become, in the wake of an interpretation of Brutalism, the accepted approach for public commissions.

Dramatically different in its utopian ambition and scale, the same June 1964 issue of *AD* also had the first extended British publication of Constant's project 'New Babylon'.[40] No doubt parallel to, and an influence on, the indeterminate architecture of Cedric Price and Archigram, it had earlier been exhibited at the Institute of

Contemporary Arts in London. Constant proposed a future environment for *homo ludens*, leisured man in a technologically advanced society, where flexibility transcends functionalism:

> Every element would be undetermined, mobile and flexible. For the people circulating in this enormous social space are expected to give this space its ever-changing shape; to divide it, to vary it, to create its different atmospheres. The sector ... is a spatial system of levels ... the sector floors are primarily empty. They represent a sort of extension of the earth's surface, a new skin that covers the earth and multiplies its living space.[41]

This megastructure, potentially on a world scale, was (perhaps paradoxically) to enable the spatial liberation of a future politically liberated society: it emerged from the Paris-based Situationist International,[42] whose political concern with the form of the city as a means of control underpinned much of their strategy. On the more modest scale of a building, it could be seen as a revelation, as a new form of building which would enable rather than control.

It was with the appointment of Robin Middleton as Technical Editor in 1965, later succeeded by Peter Murray, that *AD* really came into its own as an inspiration to at least one generation of British architects. Its role, which did not transform overnight, was to become an essential and defining journal for architecture in a period of crisis and transition. That was to come later, however, and preceding the sense of the fracture of British architectural culture which it came to represent was an important period of optimism. Here, it seemed, architecture could step out of conventions which said that architecture was a highly serious and responsible activity which demanded overweening respect for existing traditions. The hierarchy of the profession was challenged, and existing architectural conventions mistrusted: the limits of British architecture were cast aside in favour of a new internationalism.

In November 1965 there was a given theme – Housing – with an op-art inspired cover: the news pages, now expanded to 'Cosmorama', included built projects from Japan, Venezuela and Austria, as well as prototypes for mobile and plastic-formed housing. More conventional coverage included two new Cambridge houses by Colin St John Wilson, and public housing at Greenwich by Chamberlin, Powell and Bon. The final editorial pages are given over to the first extensive survey of Archigram work, with a vast number of illustrations of their projects, and discussion and illustration of the magazine. 'Housing' as a discussion could thus include Plug-in City as well as an LCC scheme, a mobile home as well as St John Wilson's thoughtfully proportioned concrete-block houses. What it did not include, except vestigially, was a deeper questioning of the building of housing, either public or private, on a small or large scale. The kind of political, social and economic discussion which would have later been central was subordinated to an investigation of architectural form.

The October 1966 issue of *Architectural Design* had fourteen pages devoted to Cedric Price's 'Potteries Thinkbelt' project, together with an article by Price, 'Life Conditioning'.[43] A Price drawing was also on the cover, although this was balanced by twenty pages on the educational built work of Lyons Israel and Ellis, whose expressive

5.7
Architectural Design, October 1966: cover with Cedric Price drawing of the view from a railbus, 'Potteries Thinkbelt' project.

concrete forms provided a contrasting extension of the spirit of modernism. Cedric Price's project provided the absolute antithesis of that established kind of school and university building that gives massive and monumental expression to isolated buildings that dominate their site. Price's project received fullest coverage in the pages of *AD*, with numerous drawings on large and small scale and an extensive explanation of his strategy. Most radically, 'Potteries Thinkbelt' proposed a university without a building. It clearly forms a critique of the contemporary new university building programme, with ultimately 20,000 science and technology students dispersed over a series of sites spaced over north Staffordshire (the centre of the declining pottery industry) and connected by existing railways. Faculty areas were to be temporary in nature and located in mobile units on the tracks themselves, while housing integrated accommodation for students, university workers and local residents.

Along with the implicit agenda for a truly 'open' university, Price's strategy is for an immediately responsive and indeterminate architecture, utilising architectural means but with a highly original approach: the design and evolution of forms does not predominate. The emphasis on *thinking* rather than doing as the core of the architect's work is also new, and relates to the imperative of technology, in the spirit of Banham's warning in *Theory and Design*, to develop new ways of working. In this as in other projects, Price made clear his commitment to technologically relevant solutions but there is little of the delight in technology to be seen in most of *Archigram*. Perhaps most radically of all, Price professed not to be concerned about the aesthetics of the buildings he projected.

For his other early project 'Fun Palace', we have to look elsewhere as it was not published in *AD* but in the *Architectural Review*.[44] This was a project for a building to house cultural activities in the broadest sense, and Price's design is revolutionary in that, rather than each activity (dance, film teaching, jazz sessions, science playgrounds) being given a particular space, the building could be constantly changed: in fact, no configuration was likely to be used twice. Users controlled what was effectively a kit of parts: flooring panels, projection screens, lighting baffles, nylon tensioned canopies, cubes with panel infill, all disposed within the frame, serviced by a gantry crane. In his description:

> the whole complex, in both the activity it enables and the resultant structure it provides, is in effect a short-term toy to enable people, for once, to use a building with the same degree of meaningful personal immediacy that they are forced normally to reserve for a limited range of traditional pleasures.[45]

5.8
Cedric Price: 'Fun Palace' project begun in 1961, aerial night-time perspective from helicopter.

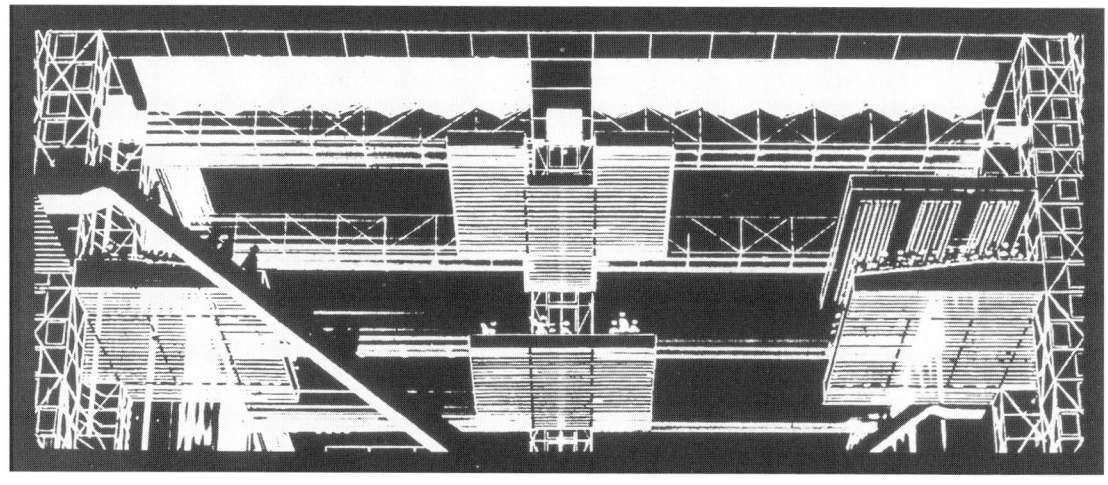

5.9
Cedric Price: 'Fun Palace' project begun 1961: perspective within frame, titled 'assembly'.

It thus linked architectural intervention inextricably to the activities it contained, and attempted to make architecture, for once, like life. While in some ways related to Archigram projects, Price's work is simultaneously more engaged with the solution of immediate problems and less committed to them taking architectural shape.

Architectural Design's special issue for February 1967 had a man in a space-suit on the cover and was entitled *2000+*. Dealing with 'the future', according to Robin Middleton it 'began with the suggestion that more attempts might be made to communicate the idea of technical innovation to an architecture still largely hidebound by a vision of the fine arts'. But Middleton talked also of the importance of the visual image as the counterpart of scientific understanding to inflect architectural practice: 'it may be suggested, however, that the imagery of technology may be as powerful an agency of change as the rational understanding of its scientific and technical basis.'[46] John McHale, a former artist and member of the Independent Group who was an enthusiastic interpreter of Buckminster Fuller, had assembled the material and wrote 'The Future of the Future'. Fuller wrote in an article at the beginning of the issue:

> Much of the most exciting and important point about tomorrow is not the technology or the automation at all, but that man is going to come into entirely new relationships with his fellow men. He will retain much more in his everyday relations of what we term the naiveté and idealism of the child.[47]

That social intention was not necessarily carried through in most of its contents, which largely consisted of a detailed examination and illustration of machinery and hardware. The sections on 'Outer Space', 'Inner Space' and 'Man+' dealt respectively with space capsules, space stations and moon landing craft, submarines and undersea laboratories; equipment for the body – the artificial hand and other medical devices, a 'computer and graphic console with a light pen'; and robot prototypes. While *AD* had included such devices in the past and would continue to do so, this issue in particular extended its involvement with advanced technologies both as a warning to architects that technology was advancing, and expressing for many in the 1960s a real excitement at its possibilities. *AD*'s conclusion warns of too great a fascination and says that any design should be limited to 'the degree to which any design assists or constrains human activity.'[48]

AD July 1967 covered the Montreal international exhibition, *Expo 67*. It neatly brought together the two prevailing themes of the journal: the coverage of completed new buildings and the importance of innovation. The two major buildings given most prominence were Buckminster Fuller's USA Pavilion, by far his most prominent achieved building, and the West German Pavilion by Frei Otto. Both effectively demonstrated that lightweight (and temporary) enclosures could be made with unprecedented techniques, in Fuller's case the Geodesic dome and in Otto's a plastic skin tent. It was a cause for optimism on the part of the younger generation that governments should commission revolutionary new building, and it seemed that such new technologies were set to replace the old.

Public housing was, however, in practice the daily concern in the 1960s of a very large proportion of architects, and it was returned to with a new *Housing Primer* in September 1967. The issue examined, both in theory and extensively in practice, the forms of low-rise and high-density development, realised largely in Greater London and the new towns. Alternatives to the high-rise or mixed development had been completed in increasing numbers and others were going on site: Michael Neylan's Bishopsfield in Harlow and Rosemary Stjernstedt's Central Hill for the borough of Lambeth were among those given coverage.

November 1967 returned to the theme of structural innovation with the School Construction Systems Development (SCSD) for the system-based construction of High Schools in California. Like some of the buildings completed at Montreal, SCSD seemed to be the shape of the future, a lower-cost system which would allow for the mass production of buildings of high quality. The pages of 'Cosmorama' in this issue are a record of other concerns of the period: projected vast new developments of towers in Paris; the demolition of St Pancras Station and its surroundings; Drop City, a squatter settlement of domes in Colorado; a projected Russian new town of prefabricated aluminium components; and an artificial island proposed for Monaco. Ambition was high, technology seemed to enable all the above and far more to happen, and the scale of many projects was enormous. Even, as the same issue points out, the Greater London Council's architect would build £75 million worth of work in 1967.

The following year saw a return to *AD* of both Cedric Price and Buckminster Fuller, the latter as he was awarded the RIBA's highest award, the Gold Medal for Architecture for 1968. Price guest-edited an issue *What About Learning?* in May 1968. For him, 'Education today is little more than a method of distorting the individual's mental and behavioural life to enable him to benefit from existing social and economic patterning'.[49] Theories of learning and technologies for learning were examined: a proposition for an electronic World University explained; and two schemes by Price illustrated. His *ATOM* project for the provision of learning facilities in a non-urban setting was to allow 'free-range self-pace learning', while on a smaller scale was the enabling of a London building as a 'public skill and information hive'. Both continued the theme of the Potteries Thinkbelt's open and inclusive learning structures, through strategies which involve far more (or perhaps far less) than the design of buildings.

Also in 1968 was an issue edited by AA students *Pneu World*.[50] While the subject of inflatable structures had been dealt with by *AD* before, the enthusiasm of the editors provided a rich field of student projects as well as military and other uses, and speculative projects such as Mike Webb's 'Cushicle' and several by the French *Utopie* group. In October, the issue was on James Stirling's recent buildings: undoubtedly one of the most highly regarded practising architects of the time, the work was introduced by Alvin Boyarsky.

But two issues later in 1968 stand out as moving very far away from that kind of model of an architectural journal, providing critical coverage of the production of a well known practitioner. August saw *Architecture of Democracy*, with writing by John Turner and others. Turner's provocative title: 'The Squatter Settlement: an Architecture that Works' was a political broadside on the complacency of all those architects concerned with housing, and an argument in favour of empowering individuals to make their own choices in the making and siting of their dwellings, however impoverished. For Turner, this was a complete overturning of the assumptions which led housing programmes and their concomitant social control.[51] Squatter settlements both in the Third World and in American cities were analysed, as was a project of MIT staff and students working with deprived communities in Roxbury. The 'inhuman monotony' of architect and planner-led housing construction was seen as a totalitarian drive which had to be unmasked by political will.

The December 1968 issue was guest-edited by Jonathan Miller, the satirical actor turned cultural commentator. *In Search of the City* was a collection of essays related to the idea of the city by writers from many fields of intellectual activity, but not by architects. The city, it argued, was a cultural palimpsest, rich, complex and impossible to know fully. As Miller pointedly wrote, 'architects and planners only know half of it.'[52] Astutely, the issue indirectly provided a penetrating criticism of the undertaking by architects and planners to remake cities: they were far too important for that. Writers and themes included were to gain much prominence later with the development of an appreciation of the culture of the city, and the issue seems particularly in advance of its date. D.P. Walker wrote on 'Poneropolis' (the city of the wicked), Francis Haskell on 'Doré's London', Frances Yates on 'Architecture and the Art of Memory' and Philip Hobsbawm on 'Cities and Insurrection'. But, however differently presented, it does match concerns aired elsewhere in the decade: *Archigram*'s observation about the rain being more important than the building at a moment in the city is also a criticism of architectural hubris.

Architectural Design in March 1969 asked 'What did they do for their theses? What are they doing now?' of a large number of recently graduated students from three London Schools – the AA, the Bartlett, University College and the Polytechnic (formerly Regent Street, later Westminster). Unusual as it was to devote an issue of a professional journal to student work, it matched the democratic mood of the time, and more importantly, like *Archigram* before it, presented student projects as of intrinsic interest. It was assumed they would express originality and be worthwhile in themselves at a time when architecture needed fresh input, not simply exercises in a school context. It also underlined that architectural education itself was the subject of much new thinking.

Also inclusive of the contribution of a large number of individuals, many of them non-architects, was *Despite Popular Demand*, the issue edited by Royston Landau in September 1969. Landau saw architecture primarily as 'problem solving' and the main thrust of its enquiry was to face what seemed to be a crisis in architecture with attempts to develop new ways of thinking which would enable its practice to be renewed and strengthened. Among many contributions are Cedric Price's 'Expediency', which considers architecture in relation to housing provision, and Gordon Pask on the architectural relevance of cybernetics. But closest to Landau are the philosophical enquiries of Karl Popper and Imre Lakatos who, ultimately, question the scientific model of deduction and, by extension, simplistic architectural thinking. Thus these special issues comprehensively questioned the fundamental practice of contemporary architecture on political grounds, on cultural grounds, as well as on the basis of its thinking – and had also considered that students might know better. While it might be premature to say that architecture was in crisis, these four AD issues over thirteen months in 1968 and 1969 asked the questions that came to be asked more urgently in the following decade.

A very odd issue of *AD* was that for June 1969, which nevertheless in some ways sums up the entire journal at this point at the end of the 1960s. Called *Treasure Island*, 150 people, from John Lennon to William Burroughs, from David Hockney to Ossie Clark, from Nikolaus Pevsner to Norman Foster, were asked to name a special, extraordinary place in Britain. Some were buildings but very few were

THE OPPOSITE OF ARCHITECTURE

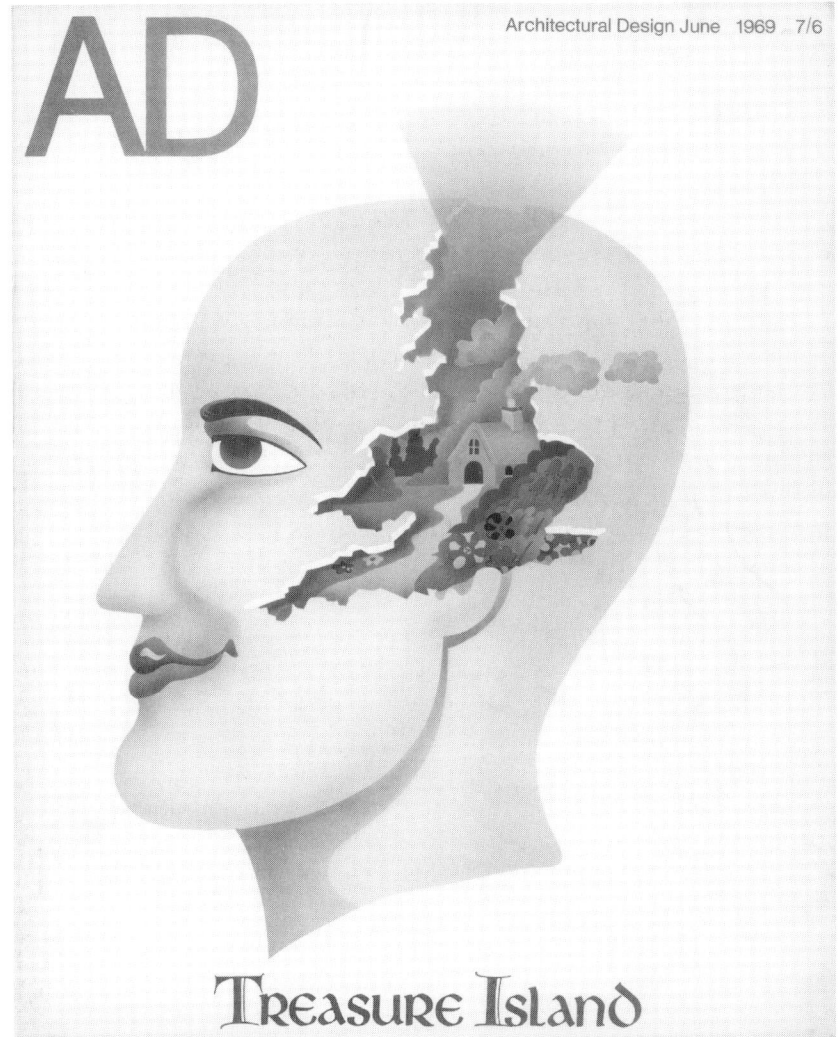

5.10
Architectural Design, June 1969, cover by Alan Aldridge: 'Treasure Island' issue in which 150 people including John Lennon, Nikolaus Pevsner and William Burroughs were asked to describe a special place in Britain.

'high' architecture: Stourhead landscape garden featured several times, as did iron age hill forts; there were allotments in Lewes, London's Westbourne Grove, the riverside walk east of Greenwich, Jodrell Bank Radio telescope and a fairy glen in north Wales. It is anecdotal, even 'celebrity'-led long before the term had entered the vernacular. But it was important to say that places, all kinds of places, meant something to people: and that this emotional connection was nothing to do with architecture as such, but was the subjective relation to space through memory, association and the imagination. In its simplicity, it cut through all the arguments about future directions in architecture, and the detailed criticism of what recent practice had produced. Instead, it provided a rich reminder of the limits, but also the possibilities of architecture as it was and might be. Some time later, an editorial by Robin Middleton explicitly touched on similar issues:

> We have been trying to figure out why architects today rarely succeed in creating environments that work out at a human scale – comfortable places, buildings that look as though people actually use them ... The most successful *places* are those where time and organisation have overlaid the environment with a complex assortment of patterns, styles, mistakes, feelings – the environment moulded by usage to the style of its inhabitants.[53]

Architectural Design in the 1970s

In January 1970 the balance of *Architectural Design* changed: the 'Cosmorama' section of news and short pieces at the beginning was extended and also now printed in colour. In October it changed again, and the entire magazine was printed on sugar paper with offset printing: the loss of shiny photographic paper meant that the old-style coverage of completed buildings was effectively stopped, as if 'Cosmorama' had taken over. But this did not affect the circulation, which was far higher than a decade earlier, as the sense of a more informal, collaged, and speculative magazine was what its readers wanted. 'Architecture' in the sense of completed buildings was still looked at, although often critically. Most of the completed buildings were, anachronistically, large and concrete, given the time-lag then of sometimes a decade between design and completion. But included also was a new kind of architecture, represented by Foster Associates, whose recent work was published in May 1970.[54] This included the since-demolished Fred Olsen Millwall Dock terminal and an inflatable office building in Hemel Hempstead. Certainly not yet a dominant tendency, its lightweight and sleek structures were responsive to the technological imperative of the time. Renzo Piano's work was also published, in March 1970, including a glass reinforced plastic sulphur plant near Rome,[55] as was Richard Rogers' 'zip-up enclosures' prototype.[56]

There continued to be an emphasis on 'systems' and on technological means: 'Frei Otto at work' in March 1971 and plastics, including recent projects by Chrysalis in March 1972. Low-cost enclosure systems, whether prototype shelters or tents for pop festival sites, made a frequent appearance, as did 'throwaway' housing, or thrown

THE OPPOSITE OF ARCHITECTURE

5.11
Architectural Design,
March 1971: Page from
'Cosmorama' section
showing a
polyurethane house
designed by Rudolph
Doernach and a glass
reinforced plastic
prototype shelter.

away in the case of Martin Pawley's 'Garbage Housing',[57] which was ironically placed in the February 1971 *AD* opposite the Smithsons' precast concrete St Hilda's Garden Building in Oxford. Housing continued as perhaps the most urgent issue – for the poor especially in the developing world (see 'Barrios are Not Romantic' in *AD* October 1971), but also for Camden housing, with *AD* March 1972 showing completed schemes of this London Borough's architects' department with a political and social analysis of the acute problems it faced.[58]

Highly contrasting new conceptual work and projects began to appear, such as those by the Italian avant-garde groups Archizoom and Superstudio:[59] and new historical discoveries were analysed,

145

such as Wittgenstein's house in Vienna.[60] But despite the overall emphasis on new and experimental forms of building, seen on a monthly basis in 'Cosmorama', any discussion of *AD* would be incomplete without reference to the myriad of other subjects discussed: Nick Roeg's film *Performance* was enthusiastically reviewed, Richard Sennett's first book dismissed, and accounts of the work of such contemporary artists Gilbert and George and Donald Judd regularly appeared. Writing for the magazine at that time was a new generation such as Bernard Tschumi[61] and Robin Evans[62] as well as frequent contributions by Cedric Price ('CP Supplements' edited by Peter Murray appeared from 1970 to 1972)[63], Martin Pawley, Peter Cook and Alvin Boyarsky.

It is perhaps fitting to give the last word to Boyarsky, whose photograph was on the cover of *AD* in April 1972, the sun shining out of his jacket pocket. Recently appointed as chairman of the Architectural Association School, he was to take up the agenda developed by *AD* as the programme for the School. Its concerns were mirrored in the structure of its teaching and many of its regular contributors joined the AA staff. 'Come and join us and help develop the idea through participation'[64] he wrote, referring to IIAD (International Institute of Design) Summer Session, but perhaps equally to the AA, which he was to reshape over the next two decades.

To sum up the larger significance of *Architectural Design* in the later 1960s and early 1970s, perhaps more than any other architectural magazine at any other time its ear was firmly on the ground to pick up whatever was going on, in an inclusive and undoctrinaire way. Even history (in fact Robin Middleton's abiding interest) in terms of new evaluations and discoveries was included, although certainly not as a basis for design. Architecture was, rather, something to be made new: the aim to revive and to re-orientate the programme of modernism in light of a more inclusive understanding of architecture's role, and a repudiation of the authoritarian hierarchy in which architecture had become implicated. Architecture was, instead, to serve 'the people'. Its emphasis was consistently on the new, on innovation in thinking and in practice, and in technologies – especially the latter.

Architectural Design created a new architectural culture through reiteration. Just as in the 1930s James Richards' *Architectural Review* continued to advance the cause of the acceptance of modernism through the frequent repetition of themes and language, so *AD* with its reiteration of the themes of flexibility, lightweight structure, mobility, communication, new technology, the user and so on effectively made them architecture's agenda. Each issue had inflatable structures, domes, moveable dwelling units, capsules, pieces of hardware. Confirmed by *AD*, they became the preoccupation of many architects in Britain: they seemed to represent the future of practice. But there is also evidence of a deeper crisis in practice: *AD*'s other, perhaps more subliminal, message is that however well-wrought a future architecture of capsules and lightweight enclosures might be, it would not be enough to respond to the political and cultural crisis into which architecture was heading, and this would seem to be Robin Middleton's own position as the generator of much of *AD*'s material over eight years.[65]

Breaking with practice

The larger picture of the 1960s in Britain would be one of optimism as yet untinged by doubt. A diffused sense of personal liberation as progress, rather than a deeper political reordering; architecture had been left behind, looking back rather than forward, and the architect should make use of technology that was available, to enable the human subject to experience the world with visceral immediacy through the means of architecture. The form-making of 'Walking City' and 'Plug-in City', megastructures with the properties of flexibility and change, does not necessarily seem to effect that. But projects by Mike Webb and David Greene of Archigram in particular and, especially, Cedric Price, create architecture to enable its users' life to be enhanced.

Thus the shift to the specific developed during the 1950s was totally reversed by this new tendency: existing traditions were to be disregarded and the modern world required something completely, radically, new. The role of such work as that of Archigram represents that the discourse of architecture moved back to the universal; it was also thus international. British work was at the head of international discourse, and became the generator of innovation in modernism rather than the maker of images of it. There was also a shift *away* from the specific within individual buildings: whether the Fun Palace's open and specifically unspecific framework, or Piano and Rogers' Pompidou project, which has little regard for the permanent art collection which it includes.

The Pompidou Centre in Paris, the subject of a competition won by Renzo Piano and Richard Rogers in 1972, is the most paradigmatic of the built work emerging from the British architectural discourse of the 1960s. Their building covered only half of the available site: each of the floors was an uninterrupted span but provided with

THE OPPOSITE OF ARCHITECTURE

5.12
Pompidou Centre, Paris: Piano and Rogers; competition 1972, completed 1977. Echoing the concerns of Archigram and Price, Rogers wrote 'We want our building to be adapted and changed by the people who use it': it is however doubtful if a new experience of architecture was created in this first full realisation of such ideas.

demountable fixtures such as wall hanging panels and enclosures. Most extraordinary however was the exterior: not only were the structure, lifts and escalator placed on the outside but so too were all the services – plumbing, air conditioning and so on were made into brightly coloured features of the building's appearance. Projection screens, electric newspapers and other gadgets were to make the main façade a constantly changing and lively surface. Rogers wrote in *AD* July 1972:

> We want our building to be adapted and changed by the people who use it ... We want to stop the architecture being a straitjacket inhibiting ideas ... Things change all the time ... maybe one day our museum might become a supermarket.⁶⁶

In the event, the building which opened in 1977 had changed from this initial vision, with the façades capable of little modification and the other half of the site – left for spontaneously generated activities – largely unoccupied. The flexible plan and plugged-in services remained: and the externalising of so much which would normally be in the core of the building gave an apparent complexity which was entirely caused by the intention to make the building's interior

148

THE OPPOSITE OF ARCHITECTURE

simple. However, the building in use has shown that the indeterminacy of the plan – the library, for example, being identical to a gallery capable of showing large works – has been less than ideal. Contrarily it could be argued that the building is not flexible enough: unlike the Fun Palace project, the floors are not moveable: not allowing then the free, open space for possibilities.

The 1970s saw the development of a plurality of discourses. One was that the material and urban thinking of the 1950s continued, its most successful realisations being the London Barbican Estate and National Theatre, which were only completed in the mid-1970s, and because of that delay were not fully appreciated until much later. The development of the practices of Rogers and Foster on the other hand emerged from the discourse of the enabling role of technology of the 1960s. Of one of the main generators of that discourse, Peter Cook, it can be said without irony that he invented a new way of being an architect; teaching, publishing, lecturing, acting as a critic, taking up the Headship of University College Bartlett School, and finally building. Each of the surviving members of Archigram, for their part, were awarded the RIBA's Royal Gold Medal in 2002.

As Royston Landau has written, Empiricism – the British tradition of Locke, Berkeley and Hume – has a great and long-standing role:

> [It] encourages a love of facts, evidence, and being practical, which is combined with an open-minded pleasure to be sought from innovation, experimentation, and novelty ... all very different from that other equally powerful cultural prerogative, the Rationalist European tradition, which places the priority on thinking it through before acting, and demands theoretical prescription first, and action second.[67]

The prevailing inductivist logic allowed British architecture in the 1960s to revert to what it was most comfortable with, the making of an object, even if an object unrecognisable as architecture: architecture which responded primarily, even exclusively, to programme and had nothing to say about site.

The central change of the 1960s was very significant since it meant the shift of the central concern of architecture from object to subject. In other words, it was possible to shift from the making of architecture in a physical sense to defining the role of architecture as fulfilling a purpose in relation to the human being inhabiting it. So (rather than the phenomenological reading of the experiencing

5.13
Helicon office development, Moorgate, London: Sheppard Robson, 1996. The ideologies of the 1960s later became the origin of a style, called High-Tech, bearing only traces of the radicalism of its source.

149

subject) architecture became the enabler of certain activities; and in the context of that happening immediately rather than eternally. So architecture could be flexible on a daily or hourly basis – the building was a kind of prosthetic device, like a false limb, to extend what the human being could do. Thus in a sense it became architecture without all the concerns of the tradition of architecture such as aesthetics, space and material: something that was the *opposite* of architecture, something *without* architecture, architecture with a disappearing object. The thinking of Price and his Fun Palace project, and Archigram's Living City in particular embody this position. But, while traces of it remain, the opposite of architecture simply became a *different* kind of architecture in the new formulation of modernism which came to be built in the late twentieth century.

Notes

1   *AR* February 1960, pp. 93–4.
2   Reyner Banham, *Theory and Design in the First Machine Age*, London: Architectural Press, 1960.
3   *Pioneers of Modern Design*, London: Thames & Hudson, 1960, was the revised title of Pevsner's book, formerly *Pioneers of the Modern Movement from William Morris to Walter Gropius*, London: Faber, 1936.
4   At the University of East London, June 1995.
5   Banham, op. cit., p. 99.
6   Ibid., p. 326.
7   Ibid., p. 330.
8   Pevsner wrote in *Pioneers of Modern Design* (1960) that his narrative had been shaken, but not completely demolished, presumably by Banham's study.
9   Alan Colquhoun, 'The Modern Movement in Architecture', (1962) reprinted in A. Colquhoun, *Essays in Historical Criticism*, Cambridge, MA: MIT Press, 1981, pp. 21–5.
10 Banham had joined the *AR* staff in 1953, see p. 89.
11 A selective anthology of his writing is *A Critic Writes*, eds Mary Banham et al., Berkeley: University of California Press, 1996. A full account and evaluation of his work as a whole can be found in Nigel Whiteley, *Reyner Banham: Historian of the Immediate Future*, Cambridge, MA: MIT Press, 2002.
12 For a full account of the social housing programme in general, see M. Glendinning and S. Muthesius, *Tower Block*, New Haven: Yale University Press, 1994.
13 See R. Banham, *Megastructures: Urban Futures of the Recent Past*, London: Thames & Hudson, 1976.
14 *Archigram* 1, London, 1961.
15 On Price, see *Cedric Price: Works*, London: Architectural Association, 1984, and H. Obrist (ed.), *Re: CP*, Basel: Birkhauser, 2003.
16 The first full critical study on the work of Archigram is Simon Sadler, *Archigram: Architecture without Architecture*, Cambridge, MA: MIT Press, 2005; it was published after this chapter was written.
17 *Archigram* 3, 1963.
18 Peter Cook, 'Some Notes on the Archigram Syndrome', *Perspecta* 11, Yale 1967; quoted in *A Guide to Archigram*, London: Academy, 1994, p. 27.
19 *Archigram* 4, Summer 1964, p. 3.

20 Ibid., p. 17.
21 *Archigram 6*, 1965.
22 *Archigram 7*, 1966.
23 *Archigram 8*, 1968.
24 *Archigram 9*, 1970.
25 D. Greene, 'Architecture and the Rain', *Journal of Architecture*, Summer 2001, p. 197.
26 Joseph Kosuth, 'Art after Philosophy', *Studio International*, October 1969, pp. 13–17; November 1969, pp. 160–1; December 1969, pp. 212–13.
27 Peter Cook, *Living City: Introduction* (1963), quoted in Peter Cook et al. *A Guide to Archigram*, London: Academy, 1994, p. 76.
28 Dennis Crompton, 'City Synthesis' in Peter Cook et al. *A Guide to Archigram*, London: Academy, 1994, p. 88.
29 Warren Chalk, 'Housing as a Consumer Product', quoted in Peter Cook et al. *A Guide to Archigram*, London: Academy, 1994, p. 92.
30 The magazines have become rare: there is a complete set in the British Library. An Archigram archive has now been set up at the University of Westminster.
31 P. Cook et al. (eds) *Archigram*, London: Studio Vista, 1972: reissued by Birkhauser, 1991.
32 The six were originally eight: the announcement of the group in *Archigram* 2 includes also Ben Fether and Peter Taylor.
33 Project MAXX in *Archigram* 7, by Craig Hodgetts and others, was described as 'Archigram American Blend'.
34 Banham, 'A Clip-on Architecture', *Design Quarterly*, 1965: p. 30.
35 Banham in Cook et al., op cit., p. 5.
36 Colin Rowe and Fred Koetter, *Collage City*, Cambridge, MA: MIT Press, 1978, p. 40.
37 Francis Duffy (ed.), 'Some Notes on Archigram', *Arena*, January 1966, pp. 171–2, was the product of a discussion of a group also including Rodney Mace, Peter Eley, Robin Webster and Charles Jencks.
38 Peter Murray's account of *AD* in the 1960s is 'Zoom! Whizz! Pow!' *AD*, April 2002, pp. 100–4.
39 Frampton's account of his time at *AD* is published in 'AD in the 60s: a Memoir', *AD*, March 2000, pp. 98–102.
40 *AD*, June 1964, pp. 304–5.
41 Ibid., pp. 304.
42 See Simon Sadler's, *Situationist City*, Cambridge, MA: MIT Press, 1998.
43 *AD*, October 1966, pp. 483–97.
44 *AR*, January 1965, p. 8 and pp. 74–5.
45 Quoted in *Link*, June–July 1965.
46 *AD*, February 1967, p. 64.
47 Ibid., p. 63.
48 Ibid., p. 95.
49 *AD*, May 1968, p. 207.
50 *AD*, June 1968, edited by Simon Conolly, Mike Davies, Johnny Devas, David Harrison and Dave Martin.
51 *AD*, August 1968 pp. 356–60; see also John Turner et al., *Freedom to Build*, New York: Macmillan, 1972.
52 *AD*, December 1968.
53 Introduction: Letter from the editor, *AD*, February 1972, p. 68.
54 *AD*, May 1970, pp. 235–58.
55 *AD*, March 1970, pp. 140–5.
56 Ibid., pp. 146–9.
57 See Martin Pawley, *Garbage Housing*, London: Architectural Press, 1975.
58 *AD*, March 1972, pp. 145–65.
59 *AD* on Superstudio, December 1971, pp. 737–42.
60 *AD*, June 1971, pp. 348–9.

61 B. Tschumi and M. Pawley, 'The Beaux Arts since 1968', *AD*, September 1971, pp. 533–66.
62 R. Evans, 'Notes towards the Definition Of Wall', *AD*, June 1971, pp. 335–9.
63 Cedric Price, *Supplements* in *AD*, October 1970, January 1971, June 1971, October 1971 and January 1972.
64 A. Boyarsky, 'Summer Session 71' in *AD*, April 1972, p. 220.
65 After leaving *AD*, Middleton became Head of History and Theory (General Studies) at the AA School, and also Librarian at Cambridge School of Architecture.
66 Quoted in *AD*, July 1972, p. 407.
67 Landau, 'British Architecture: a Historiography', *UIA International Architect* 5, 1983, p. 9.

CHAPTER 6
searching for the subject
Alvin Boyarsky and the Architectural Association School

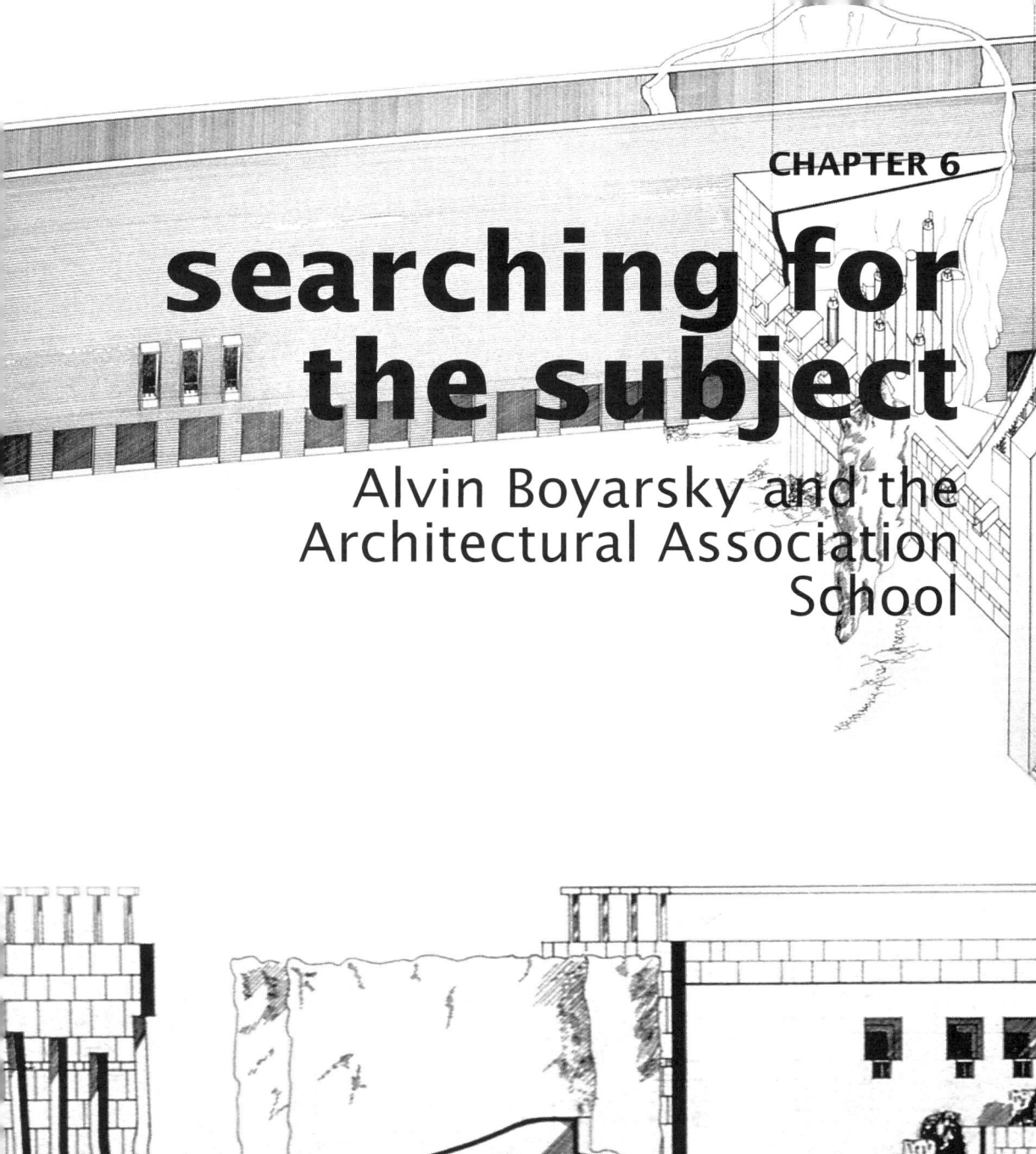

SEARCHING FOR THE SUBJECT

> We create a very rich compost for students to develop and grow from and we fight the battle with the drawings on the wall. We're in pursuit of architecture, we discuss it boldly, we draw it as well as we can and we exhibit it. We are one of the few institutions left in the world that keeps its spirit alive.
>
> (Alvin Boyarsky on the AA School, 1983)[1]

Under Alvin Boyarsky's leadership, which began in 1971, the Architectural Association School took on a role unparalleled both in its own history, and in the intensity of its engagement with renewing the culture of architecture. Architects internationally were seeking alternatives to the hegemony of modernism, but only the AA School,[2] effectively reinforcing Britain's new role in the vanguard, pursued several directions of enquiry and experiment simultaneously, and consistently put forward new theoretical positions. Much of the architectural agenda of the next decades emerged from the highly experimental stances and practices developed within the School through its educational dialogue, made known through an extensive programme of publications. A radical culture of architecture was created within which Rem Koolhaas, Daniel Libeskind, Bernard Tschumi, Zaha Hadid, Nigel Coates, Peter Wilson and Peter Salter were among a much greater number enabled to develop their ideas and practice. The AA of this period also has a further importance: it represented a very particular practice of architectural education and an unparalleled model of an institution, significant in international as well as British terms.

Boyarsky's quotation at the head of this chapter can be seen as the most succinct statement of his strategy and of his attitude, but it begs a number of questions. He uses the analogy of organic growth: students are produced or transformed into architects through being planted in rich soil; how was that growing medium formed and constituted? Fighting the 'battle' with what enemy? The drawings (exhibited) are his main ammunition: the statement reveals a paranoia and belligerence but against whom? And how was the spirit of architecture threatened with extinction? This battle-cry, taken from an interview twelve years after he had assumed leadership of the School, can be contrasted with what he envisaged in his statement when standing for election to the AA chairmanship in 1971:

> An independent academic institution with a long history of radical activity ... can aspire to the creation of an ambience where the unique style, experiment and valuable local conversations can be elevated, amplified and counterpointed by

SEARCHING FOR THE SUBJECT

6.1
Alvin Boyarsky pictured on the cover of *Architectural Design*, April 1972, seven months after starting as AA Chairman.

an overlay of the everyday concerns of those charged with building the environment and polemical, special interest and research groups ... In this way the diversity of enquiries and assumed polemical positions of the 1960s can be monitored and horizontally linked, to provide a forum for the 1970s, and incidentally increasingly shift the burden of financial survival from entirely local sources to international foundations.[3]

However different in tone, these statements have in common the ambition to synthesise new positions in architecture, and to do so in a profoundly transformed educational institution.

There are several ways in which the subject of this chapter – the work produced over two decades by and in the AA School –

155

SEARCHING FOR THE SUBJECT

differs from the others. First, as (merely) a School of Architecture, it has neither the obvious significance of a journal influential in a national or international arena, nor of a momentous book; nor, is it an influential architectural practice whose ideas and innovation have resonated. Nevertheless it has, as will be seen, elements of each of these. Second, it is very evidently a discourse in the sense of a debate, however heterogeneous it might have appeared, with obvious limits of space and also of time – the years of the 1970s and 1980s. It is also, palpably, the product of the controlling influence of one individual, who, without evident model or precedent, re-made the School completely. Alvin Boyarsky was aware that his programme involved nothing less ambitious than the revival of architecture, and initiated a strategy of restructuring the working of the School, which was finally fulfilled after a decade's determined effort. However he also had a second strategy, which scarcely wavered over the nearly twenty years he was in office: that was to change the role of the AA from being a British institution with local concerns, to one that located itself firmly in the global arena. This was to mirror the renewed international role of British architectural practice in the 1980s and beyond.

The theme of this chapter also differs from others in that I was there as a minor participant[4] in the AA's activities during most of this time but able, particularly in retrospect, to draw out its narrative. One important part of Boyarsky's strategy was the creation of a highly professional publishing programme, so memory and anecdote have corroboration in the publications which directly or indirectly came out of the School's development. This account is largely based on the AA's own contemporary publications, which comprise in particular the School's *Prospectus*, published annually from 1974, which gave a full account of its programme and projected activities, and from 1975 the *Projects Review*, which on a unit-by-unit and subject area basis, published the student work which the year had produced.

A twenty-first century generation is aware of the leading architects who were educated by the Boyarsky-led AA: some might also be aware of the huge influence its teaching strategy has had on other schools of architecture, so that, paradoxically, the current AA has to reassert its distinctiveness. But even without these two evident outcomes, the AA of the 1970s and 1980s would be the most important sustained cultural construct in the architecture of that period. Alvin Boyarsky was appointed Chairman in June 1971 and took up his position in September of that year: he was there uninterruptedly until his death in office in August 1990. His identification with the role, and

SEARCHING FOR THE SUBJECT

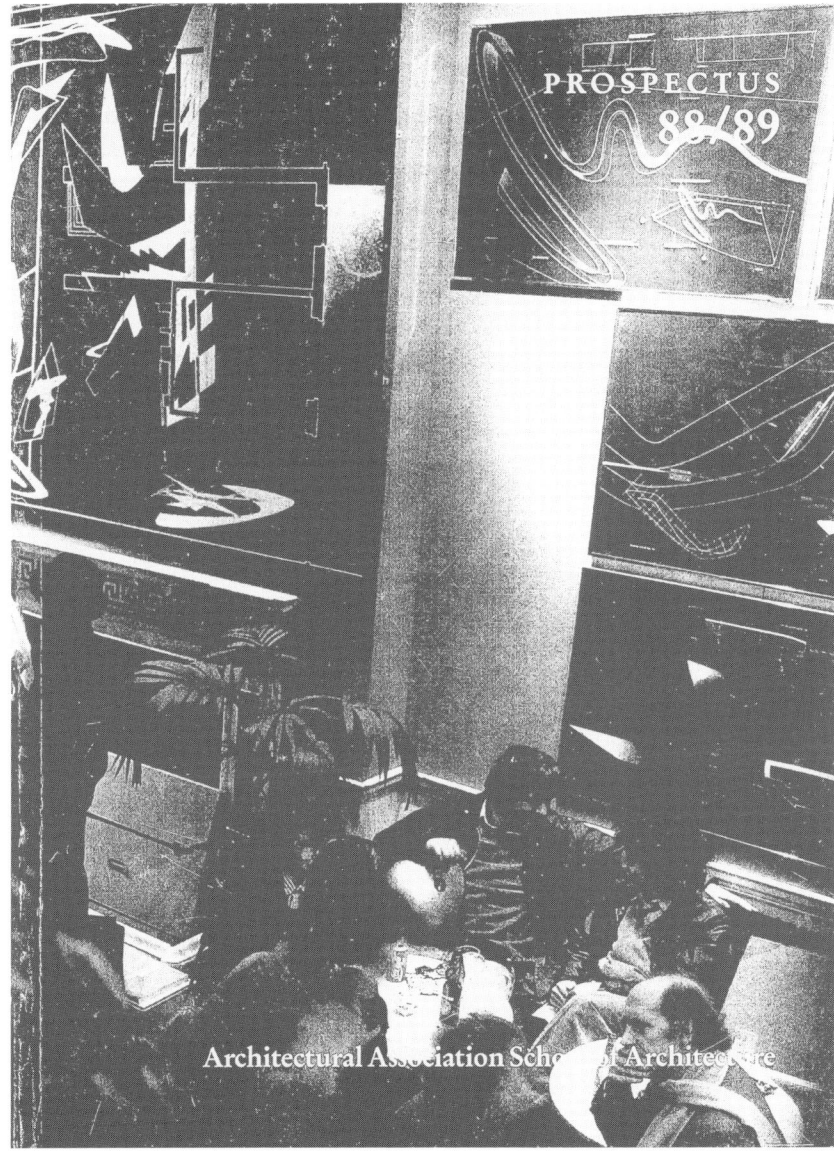

6.2
AA Prospectus, 1988–9: cover photograph by Paul Barnett showing students in AA bar and exhibition of Zaha Hadid drawings.

even with the institution was total: to say that he wanted control over everything that took place would be both an understatement but also wide of the mark. Fred Scott's description written in 1981 evokes the paradox of his character:

> Never has a head of the School inhabited the Bedford Square premises as intensely as the present incumbent. To paraphrase a fellow Canadian, the buildings seem at times to be an extension of his central nervous system, and at other times he of

theirs.[5] Never a man to leave his mind uncluttered for higher things, he can appear as upset by an unemptied ashtray in a formally set room as he is by an unfavourable letter from some government body. Always open to propositions, the Chairman's own tastes and prejudices rarely colour the appointments he makes, or the best work done in the School. The depth of his pragma allows him an ambivalence towards even the most acclaimed work.[6]

Scott's comments capture well who he was, but comments written after his death by Peter Cook are highly apposite in terms of what he actually achieved:

Over the nineteen years of his Chairmanship, the AA became the most talked-about architectural centre in the world. Technically he not only spent fourteen hours a day living the AA, but he became uncannily expert in knowing the names and track-records, the networks and foibles of almost every student in the School. He was able to sniff out talent, turn it over, give it a rough time and then flatter it. He was able to turn it over once again, offer it a teaching job and maybe an exhibition, and not be in the least surprised when its work was turning up all over the world in the magazines and exhibition galleries, and, eventually, out of the ground.[7]

There was little in Boyarsky's own background to suggest the success that was to come. Born in Montreal, he trained as an architect there and was later a graduate student at Cornell where he was taught by Colin Rowe.[8] As well as working in offices in North America and later Britain, he taught, in particular as Dean at the University of Illinois, and for short period at the AA, where he had been fourth year master. In the immediate past, and the cause of his local renown, he had been convenor of the International Institute of Design Summer School, which he set up in London.

The AA was defined by Boyarsky from the start as an international institution. There were two simultaneous reasons, neither taking precedence over the other. The AA (decades before other, state-supported institutions were faced with this), had to attract fee-paying students in order that the School could survive. These, he correctly deemed, would largely be from overseas. However, he was also explicitly contemptuous of the British architectural culture into which he was parachuted from his former base of Chicago: Britain, he would say, was provincial and complacent. He partly meant it:

indeed, it might well have been true of the leading established offices at the beginning of the 1970s. But he was well aware of the architectural counter-culture, in the shape first of the work of Archigram and Cedric Price, then in the transformed *AD* with its agenda of innovation and internationalism.

Nevertheless (self-described as an 'outsider type') he made a separation between what he saw as the British architectural Establishment, including most of the Architectural Association membership, and the iconoclasm of Archigram and *AD*. This disconnection was reciprocated: very little appeared in the British media about the AA School's work, with the notable exception of an issue of *Architectural Review* in 1983.[9] Even though a partial picture, not least because of its date, this is as yet the fullest account of Boyarsky's enterprise, in addition to the contemporary publication programme of the AA itself. The most candid interview Boyarsky ever gave was not to any of the British press but to an obscure American journal.[10] Thus his leadership of the School drew a wedge between the institution and its British context in favour of an international arena, but was inextricably connected with it, both through the recent dynamic British scene and the institution of the AA itself.

The AA's ambience

The new role of Chairman to which Boyarsky was appointed was more powerful than that of former Principals and Directors of the School, and was formed in the wake of a crisis which had left the AA with the real threat of closure. Its governing Council and former Principal, Michael Lloyd, had attempted and failed to get the School incorporated into the Imperial College of Science and Technology,[11] as in the 1960s it was under considerable pressure to join the state system of educational institutions, and in any case had its own particular crisis with the lease on its Bedford Square building about to expire. The School community, consisting of a vociferous group of current students and staff, took upon itself to safeguard the AA's independence, its radical potential and honourable history. A shortlist of two candidates for the role of Chairman (there was also the third option of 'no Chairman') was put to a vote of the community as a whole, and Boyarsky was appointed to this uncertain future. The other candidate was Kenneth Frampton who as well as being a former AA student, was teaching at Princeton and had already developed a role as a critic. Leon van Schaik, then a student, has recently written about the contest:

Frampton's position was everything that can be known about architecture is already known. All we have to do is devise the proper curriculum and teach it rigorously. Alvin Boyarsky's was that the world is a place to be experienced, and we certainly cannot deal with that through a curriculum system.[12]

Boyarsky's strategy was to set up a situation in which the unexpected would happen; divergent ideas and positions would catalyse each other. This apparent irresponsibility was anathema to most of the educational establishment, even though chiming with the free spirit of the age. His track record, and what in the end ensured him the post, was his running of a 'Summer Session' in July and August 1970, housed at the AA. This Summer School, the International Institute of Design, attracted students from twenty-four countries. He had got together a diverse group of highly articulate speakers who, working with a committed and enquiring group of students, produced a highly successful event and provided him with a template for the future AA.[13] It was as if by putting together widely divergent people, each very committed to their formulation of a position, given the project of rethinking architecture, that something would emerge. And it seems clear that Boyarsky did not know what that would be.

So, Boyarsky's aim was to create an ambience or context which was broadly inclusive and characterised by a diversity of polemics, and to locate this activity within a wide cultural discourse. This strategy is reminiscent of the radical political aims of Guy Debord, who, over the preceding decade, had formed and defined the Situationist International. It was as if Boyarsky was to set up a 'situation' in Debord's terms. As he had written:

> Our central idea is the construction of situations, that is to say, the concrete construction of momentary ambiances of life and their transformation into a superior passional quality. We must develop a systematic intervention based on the complex factors of two components in perpetual interaction: the material environment of life and the behaviours which it gives rise to and which radically transform it.[14]

Accordingly, a radical architectural Situationism was developed at the AA which counterposed material conditions with actions precipitated by crisis.

The AA's own history was already over a century long, and its origins provided a potent myth used both by Boyarsky and by those who preceded him. Its democracy and lack of hierarchy, its advocacy of originality, of architecture as a creative act, have provided a consistency since its 1847 foundation by Robert Kerr and Charles Gray. Without a Director, without paid teachers, these young architectural apprentices started a school based on self-help and mutual criticism: not determined by its usefulness to the profession, but rather (as an early speech to the organisation by John Ruskin expressed it) that architecture was nothing but a fine art. It is certainly possible to develop an argument, as was done in the period of Boyarsky's Chairmanship, that the AA's consistent role had been to reiterate Ruskin's belief, especially necessary in the early 1970s with its twin exigencies of architectural failure and a renascent technological agenda.

Boyarsky's attention concentrated on the restructuring of the institution: as the *AR* said,

> the most important project to be produced in the last decade has been the structure of the AA itself. The organisation is therefore examined here in some detail, not simply as a school of architecture, but as a model urban institution designed to counteract the increasing fragmentation, specialisation and consumerisation of modern life.[15]

Rather than a traditional hierarchy, he set up local autonomy, with each area responsible for itself and dealing with its own budget.[16] The structures put in place by Boyarsky as Chairman seem relatively simple. He extended the existing system of teaching units throughout the School. He created a competitive marketplace in which each unit master had to 'sell' his or her programme to the student body at the beginning of the year. At the end of the year both staff and students faced another public test as each unit put its work on show in an exhibition installation and the pages of an accompanying *Projects Review* publication.

Juries attended by outside critics and by students from other units ensured the frequent open debate of student projects. Boyarsky also instituted a system of cross-unit reviews to assess student work, and strengthened the Summer Diploma Committee. Along with this achievement was the development of an open role for the AA with an unrivalled programme of lectures and exhibitions, and these activities were documented in the review publication, *AA Files*. The public facilities of the building – exhibition gallery, lecture hall, bookshop, bar and restaurant – were newly provided or refitted from the late 1970s.

The unit system of teaching, which had in part preceded him, was extended throughout the School in 1972. This required the unit tutor or tutors to prepare a programme which they would offer to students: a specific position was taken, an ideology adopted, and most likely a brief and given site were provided. Students chose (and were chosen for) the unit they would work with; as if cast adrift with this diverse group of people, it became pretty much the sole focus of the student's life for that year or sometimes two. The dynamic of this group was led and originated by its tutors, with widely differing processes of working. As Boyarsky himself described:

> Each of the Unit Masters had to attract the students with a programme of their own making. Suddenly, people with great intelligence and potential who came through the 1960s in London were faced with the question, 'What do you stand for?' There was an incredible burst of energy, theoretical positions were assumed, enormous rivalry emerged between the teachers, and students could help develop the ongoing propositions.[17]

The teachers thus described included Dalibor Vesely, Michael Gold, Elia Zenghelis, Fred Scott and others who, it will be seen, used their unit teaching as a remarkable arena to elaborate original positions in architectural discourse.

The educational implications of this process were radical. There is the implication underlying the unit system that nothing is 'right' – nothing available provides the one true way that architecture should be pursued. Equally, little is 'wrong': everything is possible to include – the formal, the philosophical, the material, the social and political and so on. Exclusions of course did exist: despite the concerns of the architectural world outside the AA at the time, there was little interest in surface and nothing about the decorative. There were assumptions, too: it was taken for granted that the modernist shift had irrevocably taken place and had constructed a platform for further development. No one engaged with the revival of the Arts and Crafts movement or of the Georgian terraced house for example, although there was a very broad inclusion of reference and allusion to all manner of historical thought and making. What is effectively a lack of intellectual conviction in architectural discourse is very much of its time, echoing the late 1960s when everything was open to question. But it is dialectically opposed to other models of architectural education: however iconoclastic the Bauhaus's teaching for example, one cannot imagine this plurality existing there. The Paris *Beaux-Arts* School, historically the most pervasive model of architectural education and in particular characterised by its rigidity of programme and process and its conventions, represents the opposite polarity of educational methods. And other contemporary schools, such as the Cooper Union in New York led by John Hejduk, by contrast made a virtue of their highly specific approach.

What the AA's inclusiveness led to was the dropping of taboos, beginning to think what had been unthought, expressing what had been suppressed. In Britain, architecture had for more than a generation focused on a narrow version of social responsibility to the exclusion of much else that might shape it. In the world at large, architectural practices of modernism had become established at the same moment that they proved to be impoverished. The Boyarsky strategy of forming an inclusive arena admitted the circumstance that there was no clear direction for architecture to take, but by including so much that was divergent, the situation was created through which new possibilities would emerge. Thus the process of the School was one of almost alchemical experiment, with its results open-ended and astonishing.

Boyarsky's former tutor at Cornell, Colin Rowe, can illuminate this process. As he writes in *Collage City*, there are two forms of modernism, one represented by (say) Gropius, the other by Picasso or Stravinsky. The former is characterised by a restrictive certainty: the other engaged in a far richer process of exploration, underpinned by discernment rather than research. Rowe asks the rhetorical question: 'whether it must indeed be assumed that the serious strivings of honest anonymity (an ideal in the architect's tradition) are so very much more important than the enlightened findings of sensitized intuition.'[19] He articulates at least the possibility that architecture should engage with play, with disbelief, with the composite and the impure. No modernist architect, after all, would turn a bicycle seat into a bull's head, or a urinal into art. But the possibility of wit and imagination may exist in contemporary formulations of an unrestricted architecture that engages with the culture of the modern world as it is.

New programmes

Among a divergent group of tutors dealing with such questions as renewable energy sources, alternative forms of social housing in the UK and the developing world, as well as the continuing agenda of Archigram, Bernard Tschumi was the first to create a distinct and rigorous programme for his unit. Then in his late twenties, he had graduated as an architect from E.T.H. Zurich and spent time in the late 1960s in Paris, before starting teaching at the AA in 1971. His early programme for Diploma Unit 2, published as 'A Chronicle of Urban Politics'[19] took its agenda from outside architectural discourse, combining several distinct contemporary art practices with the spatial-political analysis of Lefebvre.[20] As Nigel Coates, then a student of Tschumi's and later his co-tutor, recalled in 1983:

> It was said from the beginning that architecture lay somewhere between the body and the city, that it was by no means exclusive, but *dependent* on the experience it contained. It therefore had to consider fleeting meanings as well as solid architectural forms, movement as well as the volumes that contained them, the subjective as well as the rational – in fact be an interpretation of structures and life itself.[21]

Tschumi himself made the point more epigrammatically that 'there is no space without event, no architecture without programme.'[22] The implications of this position were that architecture had lost, in his word, a certain 'innocence', in the context of contemporary political upheavals, a radical art culture and, not least, the discovery that architecture was more likely to embody social control than to express socialist values. In Tschumi's exacting practice, the processes of a never-impartial architecture meant that any authentic architectural enquiry had to seriously engage with issues of programme and representation. Primarily, his position stood against architecture being about style, and against students' learning being reduced to the understanding of form: its emphasis on *process* distinguishing it from architecture as it developed outside the AA in the following decade into issues of postmodernism.

What this meant in terms of student projects was that each student engaged with a reinvention not of architectural form but of what architecture would respond to: what aspect of human life, sometimes trivial, sometimes extreme to which an architectural proposition would be the response. The overarching thesis was that each project embodied questions about the nature of architecture: was it to imprison or to liberate? Was it to enhance experience or to acknowledge the impossibility of architecture doing so? The background, unacknowledged in the texts which the unit produced, was a reaction to the failure of modernism's social programme. A different and predominant reaction, for the most part taking place outside the AA, was to change the style of architecture from modernism to that inspired by historical reference. The more perceptive and ultimately wiser response was to examine the limits and problems of a programme for architecture which had aimed to make the world a better

SEARCHING FOR THE SUBJECT

place for all its people. Architecture was never neutral: and life was far more complex, and much richer, than the programmes of CIAM and its ideals of a new city. The healthy, functioning communities which modernism had proposed and which had later been built had left unacknowledged the deficiency of their starting point: that of reducing human experience to a series of ciphers.

Students thus were engaged with process: and second to questions of programme was the issue of representation and spatial notation. One result, baffling to contemporaries, was that the investigation became the outcome: where was the building? Early projects included 'Prison Park' by Nigel Coates (1974): a photographic documentation of a linear walk in Hyde Park which enquired into the nature of the control of space, while 'Embrace' by Chris Macdonald (1978) made a series of images of fleeting events in the city which constitute a reflection on issues of form and programme. Derek Revington's 'Alkahest' (1975) brought together several issues of Tschumi's teaching programme: an event was staged in a derelict Thames-side warehouse which had its origin in a passage of Herman Hesse's novel *The Glass Bead Game*. Besides the notation of the event, which formed the drawing of the project, was the connection with the literary: the narrative of imaginative writing provided exactly the richness denied by architectural convention: architecture's connection with language is not only as a metaphor for form.

6.3
Derek Revington, Alkahest, Diploma Unit 2, 1975, taught by Bernard Tschumi: document of a ritual performance of place, enacted in a warehouse at Butlers Wharf.

And what was enacted in that space was analogous to the ancient ritual of foundation of the city: architecture had engaged in the past, and could engage again, with far more than the making of new housing, parks and highways.[23]

Revington did not present what such an architecture might *look* like, and in later projects of the unit there was a movement towards architectural forms that speculatively practised a modification, reuse, or transformation of the existing forms of the city. Projects in 1978–9 for Soho took that dense and layered urban area and proposed a violent disjunction of architectural programme and context. In James Campbell's project 'Prison Passage', a rough timber screen divided the linear site into two, at the same time as police accommodation was intermixed with the street's clubs and prostitution. What was a constant in the unit's concerns was the paradox of conjunction of the unlike: forms and programmes were subverted by their opposite. In 1977, the impossibility of overlaying James Joyce's linguistic dislocations in *Finnegan's Wake* on to the site of Covent Garden, in the unit's 'Joyce's Garden' project, provided the ground for the coexistence of the fixed narrative of city forms with the always – unexpected nature of its inhabitation. Architecture itself might be a fiction of representation over substance. How, as Nigel Coates enquired, could architecture 'define an anthropomorphic field which constantly parallels and opposes experience itself?'[24] For Coates, this meant the fracture of buildings into elements, each autonomous and wilful, simultaneously assembling and disintegrating the whole: 'every building could become a *city* of parts'.[25] This idea has resonances of dissimilar architectural discourses – Aldo Van Eyck, quoting Alberti, had written of the house as like a small city – but it also forms an early formulation of the position which later came to be called deconstruction.

Nigel Coates became the unit master of what was now Diploma Unit 10 in 1980. While the unit had constantly developed in earlier years as it engaged with avant-garde art practices, issues of literary and filmic narratives and codes of spatial representation, one constant had been to engage with what might be called the *problem* of London. At the time, many at the AA only regretted that London was not New York, or perhaps Paris, which for different reasons appeared far more vital: but Coates's engagement first with the Lansbury Estate, then with the vast and unexplored area (only then beginning to be termed 'docklands') – gave new territories into which architectural intentions might be valuably introduced. Projects in the unit had developed into something closer to building propositions, though generally without the conventional modes of representation. The St Andrew's Exchange project (1980), for example, proposed converting

SEARCHING FOR THE SUBJECT

6.4
Mark Prizeman, Albion street scene, Diploma Unit 10, 1983, taught by Nigel Coates: expressing a programme of radical exaggeration of the life of the inner city, later to shape the NATO group.

a Wren church to an employment exchange, subverting current concerns of building conservation into something more radical, dramatising the act of signing-on with interventions which were far from deferential.

It was, however, in 1983 that a strong group of students presented a wildly energetic, dynamic and vital set of images of London. The 'Albion' project in run-down south east London, centred on Tooley Street, and was the subject of a kind of radical exaggeration: subversive programmes expressed in jagged and chaotic forms conveyed the possibilities of the real city, already 'almost-there', not some tidied-up architectural project. Christina Norton, Catrina Beevor and Robert Mull created memorable images of this, the new urbanism of conjunction and contradiction. Mark Prizeman's 'Zoo Housing' in Rotherhithe provided teetering deck housing with a wolf-run on the roof. What they in their provocative fashion were proposing was the enhancement of London as it was, rather than the unspoken task of the architect to order and control.

It was this that led to one of the most significant quarrels between what had become the architectural Establishment in the shape of external examiners James Stirling and Edward Jones, and the Boyarsky-led AA: Stirling and Jones left the external assessors' meeting, refusing to pass any of Diploma Unit 10. The argument which became a widely publicised row – was over 'drawings, mainly rough perspectives, with dizzy distortions like those of wide-angle photography and tilting high-level viewpoints'[26] addressing contemporary London. In Nigel Coates's account:

> The landscapes of big English cities like London certainly display all the staccatoed contradictions that we are talking about, that is if you bother to look at everything about you – railway tracks, advertising hoardings, scaffolding, old factories, traffic jams.[27]

The unit formed NATO (Narrative Architecture Today) and their work was published by the AA as a kind of avant-garde style magazine, *NATO*.[28]

In a larger reading, this work is part of the shift which formed a common discourse in the School of this period: that of moving away from the model of architecture of a discrete object which embodies explicit principles and plans. An alternative approach, which emerged as common to several units' strategies, was that of architecture which forms the ground of subjective experience. This questioning of architecture was not only a critique of practice, but also made clear a rejection of the mechanistic model – that idea inherent in modernism that architecture, correctly done, could determine an effect as sure as that of the object which an industrial process might produce.

Michael Gold taught in the School from 1973, having been a student there in the early 1960s. Before joining the teaching staff, he had built substantial developments of social housing and evolved a teaching programme at the AA which was effectively a critique of his earlier architectural work. The 'People in Architecture' project, first run by him in Diploma Unit 5 in 1980, utilised the idea of sensibility and, notably, of intuition. Instead of seeing 'people' in architecture as a mass, the project started with the student's choice of an illustration of a human figure. This specific figure had particular qualities, and these qualities, formal, visual and cultural, would provide the basis for the step-by-step creation of a building. Each stage of this ten-week process was autonomous: first, a piece of furniture was added to the image of the figure, then an architectural element, then a room, then an ante-room, then the apartment, then the adjoining apartment, then a typical floor of the block, then the whole building, and – finally – the London site. Each week the student made a drawing or painting, since Gold's approach was that of working with visual, not strategic, means. Neatly reversing the customary architectural process of starting with a site and moving into progressively smaller-scale decisions, the deliberately slow process unlocked an alternative way to develop architectural ideas, starting not with the whole project but a fragment, and not only inhabited space but highly specific embodied space.[29] Ada Wilson's 'Nightclub' (1981), Robert Griffin's 'Twisted Tower' (1981), and Peter St John's 'Staircase' (1982) were among projects which developed divergent ideas of the architectural development from the figure to an architectural form. This exploration of the idiosyncratic provided a welcome enrichment to the understanding of how buildings might, after all, be regarded.

The unit led by Fred Scott and Robin Evans had earlier engaged with the hypothesis of inhabited space. The subject of the house, the project they ran in Diploma Unit 4 in 1975/6, was explicitly intended to lead to the 'reinvention of architecture' by engaging with an understanding of the way life took place in the house and in the city. Their social–spatial interests were more likely to engage with a reading of nineteenth-century plans or a Renaissance palazzo than building of more recent date: projects produced over the three years of the unit created complex and ingenious plans and sections, based on historical understanding. The unit's work might have appeared historicist but on closer analysis, work such as that by Rodney Place (1977) or Bill Greensmith (1978) evolved new and dynamic spatial configurations.

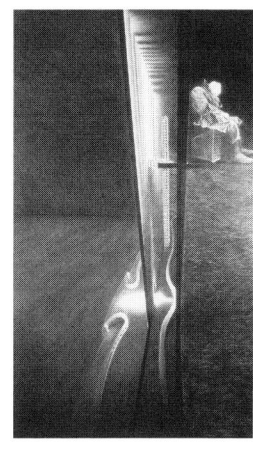

6.5
Ada Wilson, 'Nightclub', *People in Architecture* project, Diploma Unit 5, tutored by Michael Gold 1981: projects were derived, by analogy or opposition, from the qualities of a human figure.

Other units, however, adopted a grander ambition to remedy the problems of modernist practice in the city. As Leon Krier, then teaching an Intermediate School unit, (Years Two and Three) wrote in 1975:

> The art of building cities has been replaced by the one-dimensional and bureaucratic operations of the planner. The city as a complex spatial continuum has been replaced by isolated buildings whose order is solely dictated by arbitrary prescriptions and restrictions . . . We re-propose the study of history.[30]

The model – Rationalism – that Krier proposed was that of the discovery of types; through historical analysis, uncovering the nature of the street, square, public building and so on. Rodrigo Perez and René Davids started to teach in 1978/9, following his example at first with an orthodox Rationalist programme, 'The City Possible'.[31] Unlike Krier, Perez and Davids were to modify their position in later programmes, but what distinguishes these units in their initial form is their didactic approach, which serves to make clear their difference from what had become the strategy common to other units.

With Krier and the approach of Rationalism, projects by students were seen as the illustration of a theory – and students' opportunity was not to react to the given programme but (simply) to illustrate it. Their end-of-year publication thus remained a manifesto of an ideological position: elsewhere at the AA, students engaged with, developed, and modified a unit's position, in what was to a great extent an open-ended dialogue.

Daniel Libeskind taught in the Intermediate School, and later Diploma School, from 1975 at an early stage in his career;[32] his unit programme reflected on the loss of meaning in the city and considered the possibility of the poetic. As he wrote in 1976:

> The following motifs will constitute the fundamental framework of the unit's work: the idea of a city – its anthropological, historic and economic significance; the poetics of urban space ... the interpenetration of values and symbols – collective myths and existential participation.[33]

Work produced was anything but prescribed: the most celebrated project to emerge was nevertheless far from typical: the surreal monuments of 'Travulgar Square' by Ben Nicholson (1977). Libeskind's thought on the city led to the foundation of Diploma Unit 1, taught by Dalibor Vesely and Mohsen Mostafavi[34] for three successive years from 1978, and which provided at that time perhaps the clearest proof that the AA had reached the stage of *achieved* work; resolved, not tentative, not experimental. Vesely had been teaching at the AA from 1968 in different contexts, but with a constant focus on the question of the city.

For Vesely, architecture provided the means to engage with the world. Their initial unit programme in 1978 rejected ideas of urban design in the normative sense: 'To us the city is a vision of culture in its most concrete and contemporary form. The order of the city, as we see it, is both designed and not designed, created by myth and (everyday) life.'[35] The role of architecture was to re-poeticise the city: their programme was to study precedents rather than types in the urban context, to re-engage with tradition, to re-invest the city with meaning. The ongoing project was for a number of buildings – a necropolis, a specialist museum, an urban forum, an apartment building – in the context of the banal inner-London suburb of Kentish Town. Individual student projects were assembled as visually stunning large-scale city plans, and given a highly characteristic style which both evoked and represented a series of carefully wrought buildings; these clearly made a relationship between private and

SEARCHING FOR THE SUBJECT

6.6
Diploma Unit 1, 1980 taught by Dalibor Vesely and Mohsen Mostafavi: composite plan of buildings forming an urban residential block, Kentish Town, with projects by eleven students.

public space in a rich and expressive urban landscape. Their work provided evidence not only of stunning graphic accomplishment, but also of a lyrical sensibility applied to the modern city. There was more individual expression than might at first appear, and the distinctiveness of the projects by, for example, Eric Parry, Athanasios Spanomarides and Kaveh Mehrabani, articulated a particular emphasis and quality of design. The work formed a fitting subject for the first of the series of 'Themes' publications of unit work, entitled *Architecture and Continuity*.[36]

A radical response to the idea of repudiating and re-poeticising the modern city was provided by the contemporary programme of Diploma Unit 9, led by Elia Zenghelis and Rem Koolhaas. Zenghelis, a long-time AA teacher and former student, formed the unit in 1975 with Koolhaas, his ex-student. It was perhaps most evident that their teaching was part of a much larger project; their own Office for Metropolitan Architecture (OMA) was formed in 1975, at first engaging only with competition entries, and followed by Koolhaas's publication in 1978 of *Delirious New York*.[37] For them there was a problem with the modern city, in that it was not modern *enough*: reacting to the architecture of Le Corbusier and the urbanism of CIAM, they developed alternative models of modernism, notably based on that of Russian Constructivism, with the specific formal application of

171

SEARCHING FOR THE SUBJECT

work by Leonidov, El Lissitsky and Malevich. The 'culture of congestion' was the true condition of the modern world, as explored by Koolhaas in *Delirious New York*: but even New York made only a limited model for the possible architecture of an intense urbanism. They wrote in the 1976 *Prospectus*:

> The aim of Unit 9 is to rediscover and develop a form of urbanism appropriate to the final part of the twentieth century – new types of architectural scenarios that exploit the unique cultural possibilities of high densities and result in a critique and rehabilitation of the Metropolitan lifestyle.[38]

What this account could miss is the undoubted irony of their approach: and the strong provocation at this point in the 1970s of celebrating office towers and urban complexes, when the reputation of large urban development was at its lowest. Nevertheless, students including Alex Wall and Stefano de Martino developed powerful proposals for buildings of a new dynamic urbanity; and graduating in 1977 was Zaha Hadid. Her final project was for a 'Museum of the Nineteenth Century' in London, which in Suprematist fashion designed the building as a series of linear volumetric elements – tectonics – emerging from the roof of Charing Cross station and bridging the Thames. It embodied a new optimism in a transformational social programme. Rem Koolhaas reported on Hadid:

6.7
Zaha Hadid, Diploma Unit 9, 1977, taught by Elia Zenghelis and Rem Koolhaas; Malevich *tektonic* over Hungerford Bridge, London.

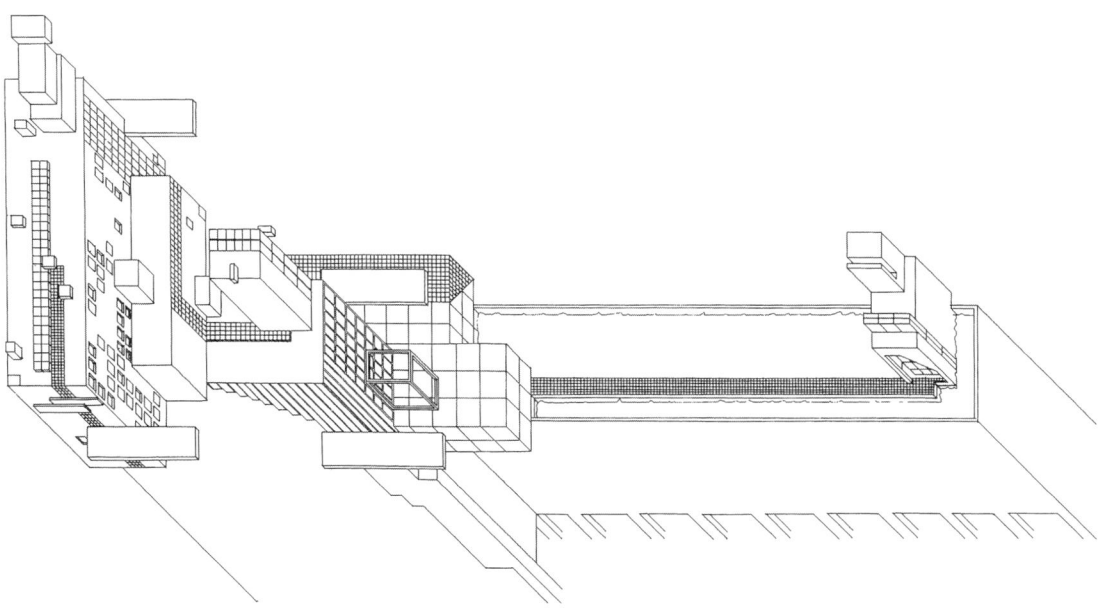

Zaha's performance during the fourth and fifth years was like that of a rocket that took off slowly to describe a constantly accelerating trajectory. Now she is a PLANET in her own inimitable orbit. That status has its own rewards and difficulties: due to the flamboyance and intensity of her work, it will be impossible [for her] to have a conventional career. She owes it to her talent to refine and develop it over the next few years.[39]

This she indeed did: already awarded the Gold Medal in *AD*. British Architecture Awards in 1982, winning the first of an unprecedented set of competitions with the Hong Kong Peak in 1983, and by the twenty-first century, with several major buildings achieved, emerging in popular consciousness as one of the world's leading architects. She began to run the AA unit in 1980 and with a further generation of students produced strong and formally inventive projects, on both a large urban scale – there were projects for the then-undeveloped Royal Docks, and Brian Ma Siy's linear Cultural Strip (1983) – and on the scale of an interior landscape, such as Marian Van der Waals' Open University (1982).

Second Generation

Nigel Coates wrote in the 1979–80 *Prospectus*: 'Gone are the geodesics, fun architecture, technology for its own sake ... gone is the undiluted conceptualism of the mid-70s ... There is a new tide of interest in investing architecture with *significance*.'[40] The end of the 1970s indeed provided a watershed, and those units not concerned with architecture as design but as a process inflected by technical, environmental or political processes had terminally declined; as had also what could be called the high seriousness of intellectual activity which characterised certain units at an earlier stage. The great achievements of inventive design expressing a unit programme, as seen in Unit 1 and Unit 9, became the dominant mode. What the AA School now engaged with in the 1980s was the search for form.

Peter Wilson, like Hadid, was a representative of the second generation of tutors, educated in the AA of the 1970s and beginning to develop a strong profile of his own through years of teaching, in his case with Zenghelis, Gold and others. Despite or because of his sophisticated pedigree, it seemed that when his unit was established in 1981, that the making of architecture was actually uncomplicated; all that was needed was invention, delight, optimism. Buildings like figures, buildings like ships – asked why, the question would remain

SEARCHING FOR THE SUBJECT

6.8
Cornel Naf, Diploma Unit 1, 1982, taught by Peter Wilson: Spider house as Fashion Institute; theatre with 'columns of fame' and communal island elevation.

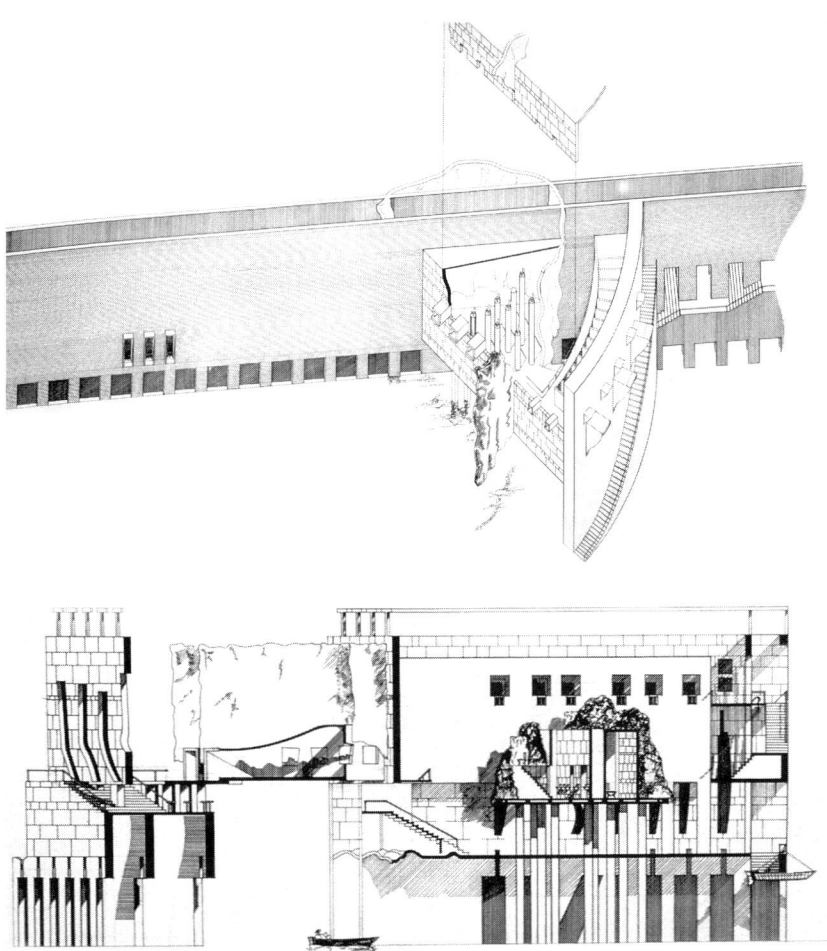

unanswered. The unit's engagement with themes – 1981-2 was *The Press* – involved not responding to any programme on qualities of site or analysis of function, but using the theme as a metaphor or simply as a point of origin. That spirit gave rise to the ingenuity of William Firebrace's 'Column(ist) House' near Fleet Street (1982), and Guy Comely's restaurant both 'like a horse' and parasitic on another building, for Peter Langan, (1984). The project by Cornel Naf, 'Spider House as Fashion Institute' (1982) took the fashion journalist as a 'spider', 'trapping her victims in webs of appearance', and transported her to the (architecturally fashionable) Villa Malaparte on Capri where the 'spider house' is designed in great detail, eroding the Villa and extending on platforms in the sea – surely one of the most surreal and original designs of the whole period.

Inventive form-making had, in fact, never gone away: the second catalogue in the Themes series, *Spirit and Invention*[41] featured the work produced in Unit 6, taught by Peter Cook, Ron Herron and Christine Hawley, thus representing the second generation emerging from the unit. It included projects by strongly individual students of the recent past: Amarjit Kalsi, Peter Salter and Kathryn Findlay. Resolutely anti-theory in a particularly British way, as Cook described other contemporaries with deliberate irony and exaggeration: 'incoherent, uncompromising, culturally-lateral murmurings of foreigners who turn up in London and use its ambience to regather their wits'.[42] Architecture was, rather, to relate to itself: Peter St John's 'Glass Magazine' project of 1984 was one of a number of the unit's highly elegant and inventive projects.

May 1983 saw one of the most extraordinary weeks in the AA's recent history, as the results of two major international competitions were announced. First the *Peak Club* in Hong Kong was won outright by Zaha Hadid, ahead of a large field which included many of the world's best-known architects. Then the Paris *Parc de la Villette* was won jointly by OMA (Rem Koolhaas and Elia Zenghelis) and by Bernard Tschumi, whose scheme was ultimately built. While only Hadid was on the current staff, the programmes of each of those architects had been largely formed while at the AA. It was seen as a great vindication of the experiment and innovation which the AA had been nurturing

6.9
Peter St John: Diploma Unit 6, 1984, taught by Christine Hawley and Peter Cook, Glass Magazine Venice Arsenale, section sketch.

over the previous decade. But it also underlined that architectural discourse, by itself, perhaps needed the validation not just of publication and exhibition but of a public commission. It may well be remarked also that the only substantial notice *Architectural Review* took of the AA immediately followed these professional successes.[43]

An AA-educated generation formed a third wave of unit staff. In Peter Salter can be seen the fruition of work reflecting both his education at the AA (he joined the First Year in 1975) and his work in the Smithsons' office, although his unquestionable individuality remains. When he came to evolve a unit programme, it was after a number of years in the supporting role of a Technical Tutor. But this role had generated work of a particular structural inventiveness which could be seen over many units' work. Called by Peter Cook 'lyrical mechanism', this term could describe much work about this time. According to Salter, muscular steel and tension structures clad in diaphanous envelopes worked towards an 'architecture that was responsive, with cantilevers gently moving from different positions of compression and tension, a set of shapes evolving because of this'.[44] Götz Stockmann's 'Cliff Hotel' project in Diploma Unit 6 in 1982/3 is an accomplished example of the type. In 1985 Salter inaugurated a workshop course that had students tackling a 1:1 drawing and constructing a 1:1 detail, thus working with materials at full size. Among his unit programmes was that of the Weather Register; as he explained, 'the first weather register project we did was a mechanism. We were uneasy about that and felt it should have more to do with poetic qualities than with structure; be something supple, corroded and cracking.'[45]

On an aesthetic level, Salter's own work was much emulated, although he saw issues of style as anathema: on a conceptual level, his concerns with materiality and site permeated the school. Materiality, for him, engaged with issues of time and of use; and the intuitive process formed the basis of his approach, seen also in his developing practice with Chris Macdonald. As the latter introduced a project:

> [S]tudents were asked to anticipate the qualities of site associated with a depositional coastline. The programme required an intuitive piece which, when taken to the site, prompted a critical examination. In the event, many of the touchstones became instruments for developing particular perceptions of the site.[46]

What became established across units at this later stage of the AA's practice in the Boyarsky period was the preoccupation with the dialectic of nature and culture, working both at the level of intellectual enquiry and as intuitive response. Engaged with this were Peter Wilson, William Firebrace, as well as Salter, Macdonald and two former students of Daniel Libeskind's, Don Bates and Raoul Bunschoten[47] who had set up a unit in 1983. Bunschoten, later leading Diploma Unit 2, introduced a project '*Imago Mundi: Imago Naturae*', engaging with a profound understanding of the process of myth-making and its relation to experience: and in 1987 the project of 'Urban Caves' as a 'sac of space' subtending from the skin of the earth. The totemic objects created by the unit remained evocative and obscure. But by the end of the period of Boyarsky Chairmanship, issues of site, building, occupation, and the culture of architecture, however that was expressed, had again become the subject of the School's enquiry.

Publications

The two decades of the Boyarsky AA saw the production of many thousands of architectural hypotheses in the form of student projects: this selection scarcely does justice to their wealth and invention. The continual renewal of architecture which it represented encompassed many architectural philosophies, a number of which had sufficient potential to develop far beyond the context of the AA. The nature of its enquiry, as the contrary example of Krier and a Rationalist programme illustrates, was far from that of expounding a coherent theory and expecting students to comprehend and apply it. The strength of its approach lay rather in the making of fields within which students' propositions could develop. The period was characterised by the development of representational technique into areas not conceived of elsewhere, and a parallel explosion of architectural thought in several divergent directions. But however accomplished drawings may appear, however convincing their underlying ideologies, they provide only glimpses of the wider discourse taking place in those years. Transcending any individual project, however accomplished, however original, is its relationship to the discourse of the continuing development of the culture of the School.

This larger culture of the AA did not solely consist of unit programmes, but was enriched by its theory and history courses, and by a developing programme of publications and exhibitions. Each was an integral part of the Boyarsky strategy: referring to the students' broader education, he remarked that a 'rich table is laid', which consisted of the other offerings, and which provided 'compost' for the students' own developing ideas.[48] Led by Robin Middleton,[49] who was appointed by Boyarsky in 1973, the so-called General Studies programme was anything but that, proving highly specific in its specialisation and academic expertise.

Among lecture courses in that first year, Peter Murray of the Courtauld Institute lectured on 'Renaissance Art' and Charles Jencks on 'Semiology'. During one week in December 1973, Jonathan Miller and Umberto Eco were both guest lecturers. Each year there were something like twenty series of lectures, together with additional evening lectures. A rich programme of lectures in Autumn 1978, for example, included John Dixon Hunt on 'English Garden Design', Robert Harbison on 'Primitivism from Rousseau to Kandinsky', Roselee Goldberg on 'Performance Art', Jasia Reichardt on 'Robots' and Yolanda Sonnabend on 'Baroque Opera and Transformations'. Reflecting a new concern with form, in 1979 there were lecture courses on Lutyens, Palladio, Lequeu and 'Utopias'. In 1987, subjects included Mark Cousins on the 'Locality of Thought', Fenella Crichton on 'Contemporary Sculpture', and Robin Evans on 'The Curve'. Experts in whatever field deemed relevant by Middleton were secured to give courses. Sometimes audiences were tiny, and sometimes their subjects caught the imagination of students and staff, but there is no doubt that this highly ambitious programme, which exceeded that of any other London institution, consolidated the AA's role as a place distinguished by its openness to ideas and intellectual investigation.[50]

The publication programme, from 1980 consistently publishing work of students and staff as monographic studies, underlined an acknowledgement and new confidence in what had been achieved, and invariably reflected the AA itself rather than externally determined issues. The editorial control of these publications was Boyarsky's, and he was undoubtedly responsible for the image of the AA which they produced. He chose the subjects covered, commissioned writers, editors and designers, and paid close attention to texts[51] as well as being aware of their larger cumulative picture of the School. From 1982 a series of more substantial books on the work and thought of certain units was produced, and in the Boyarsky period (this *Themes* series has since been revived) six were published. Other more informal publications of student work were undertaken, and the weekly programme of lectures, seminars, juries and presentations was published in the professionally produced *Events list*. An important stage, in addition to catalogues of the AA's equally ambitious exhibition schedule, was the publication from 1981 of an academic journal, *AA Files*, which reflected the changing work and cultural life of the School.[52]

6.10
Architecture and Continuity 1982: the work of Dalibor Vesely and Mohsen Mostafavi's Diploma Unit 1. The first of the *Themes* series of AA publications documenting the work of a unit, cover drawing by Athanasios Spanomaridis.

The scale and aspiration of this publications programme was evidently far beyond what a single school had ever done before: the only possible model being the range of Bauhaus publications edited by Moholy-Nagy. They asserted that the AA's student projects were of more importance than simply student work; young tutors' work should be made known in publication and, equally, that both gained value from their place in the larger context of the School's endeavour. Perhaps, like James Richards' *Architectural Review*, these publications embodied rather than simply represented new architectural ideas: the School's work as a whole could be seen to repudiate the positivism and the collectivism of other current architecture. There was a necessity for the work to be taken seriously – it needed to be given a heightened status through the means of publication.

Boyarsky's production standards were high[53] and the books often inventive in form and content, for him extending the discourse of architecture already expressed in its literature. He was an avid collector of classic architectural texts and the shape and quality of the more extravagant books aimed to extend the tradition of

SEARCHING FOR THE SUBJECT

architectural publishing. Among them were the loose-leaf box set *Folio* series begun in 1983, the first two being devoted to work by Libeskind and Hadid (in both cases their first substantial publication): the large format *Mega* series was produced to a particularly high quality and included figures of recent history as well as the work of current AA culture. *AA Files*, of which Boyarsky wrote that it was 'motivated by a desire to portray the spirit and ambience of the place; the preoccupations of staff and student . . . the propositions

6.11
***AA Files 16*, 1987, layout showing Blackburn House, Hampstead, by Peter Wilson: innovative architecture with relatively conservative layout.**

SEARCHING FOR THE SUBJECT

and images produced, the formally spoken word',[54] in its first decade it did exactly that. But it did so in far from experimental form, its conservative layout and image sometimes belying its contents. Since the argument of this book is that architecture is invariably shaped by ideas, and that such ideas are formed and transmitted through their cultural expression in publication, the achievement of the AA at this time was unprecedented in Britain: publications confidently expressed its role.

Adding to the established regular programme of the *Projects Review*, *Prospectus* and *Events list*, and later *AA Files*, among the first to be given the chance to publish were OMA, Peter Wilson, Michael Gold and Ron Herron. There were also historical studies[55] and comprehensive monographs – *Works* – forming a series on key modern British practices, notably Cedric Price and Ernö Goldfinger.[56] Most books would not have been considered feasible by another publisher, and they served to consolidate the sense of achievement of a specific culture of architecture. Indeed, they underlined what was surely Boyarsky's position: that the culture of architecture can be located in what is published. Thus the existence of the AA School in the form which he had carefully constructed was materialised by its publications, which as material objects as well as their embodied content, expressed its value. As he said in an interview:

> A relatively small group of people at one point on the map, working hard and intensely, and with a comprehensive view of what's going on in the rest of the world, can actually make a great difference to the history of ideas, I suppose that's what we're doing.[57]

The AA's new gallery opened in November 1978, a key part of the re-ordering of the public spaces of the building (designed by Rick Mather), which was undertaken by Boyarsky. It provided for the first time an opportunity for large and three-dimensional exhibitions at the School as well as other spaces in the Bedford Square building, many exhibitions having the counterpart of a publication. Most memorable are the exhibitions which also had an installation in the Square outside the gallery, including the constructions for John Hejduk's *Collapse of Time* in 1987 and Co-op Himmelblau's *Open House* in 1988.

However distinct unit programmes were, there was cross-influence and connections were made, not least by the students themselves. There was an interrelation and interdependence between many projects: students learned from each other within the School. Peter Salter provides an example: his technological ingenuity was

6.12
Zaha Hadid: furniture for an early project for the Bitar apartment, exhibited at the AA in 1988.

SEARCHING FOR THE SUBJECT

6.13
Peter Salter and Chris Macdonald: Osaka Folly plan and section. Built for the 1989–90 Garden exhibition at Osaka, Japan, which with eight 'folly' buildings designed by current or former AA tutors became a live exhibition of the Boyarsky AA.

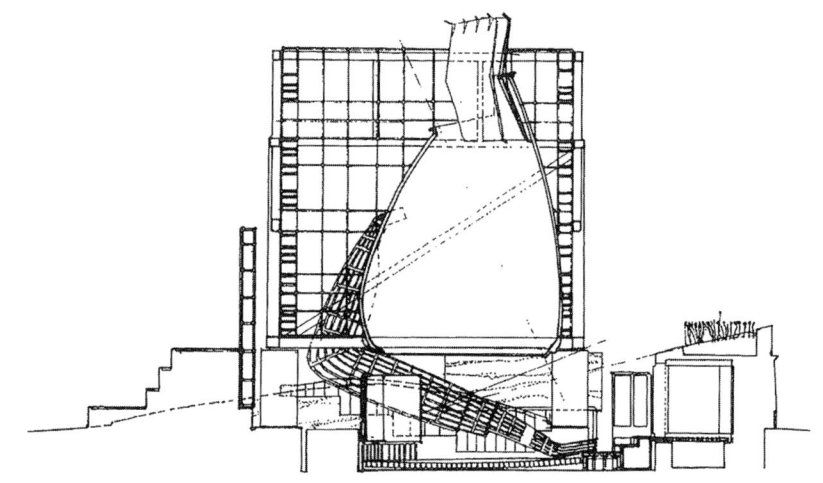

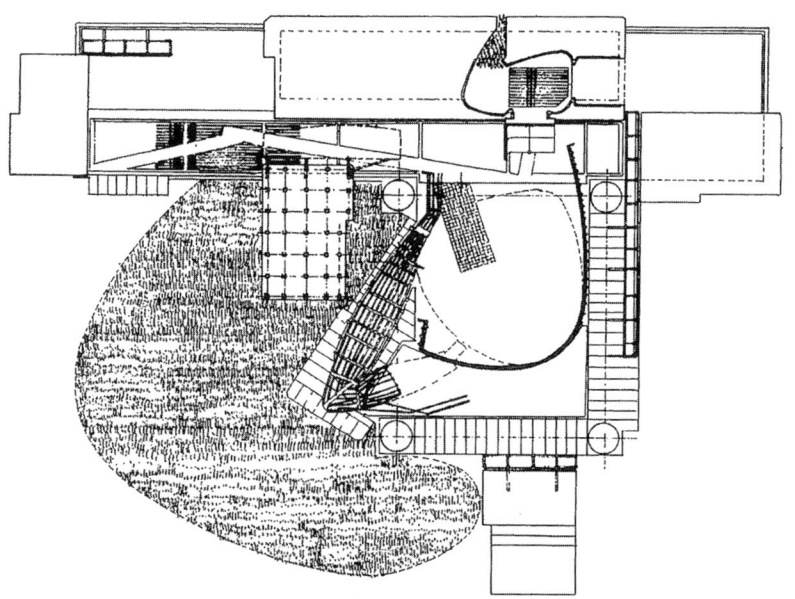

inflected through the poetic sensibility of fellow student Chris Macdonald, and this conjunction also provided the basis for them to later develop their own practice which was, in turn, acknowledged by publication and exhibition at the AA.[58] Uniquely, the AA provided a culture of architecture rather than the more usual educational fare; attitudes to work almost always developed from conversations generated by tutor and student. This discourse was surprisingly self-referential (despite the occasional presence of such figures as Coop

SEARCHING FOR THE SUBJECT

Himmelblau and John Hejduk), rather than looking to any outside architectural influence: the important visitors to the AA were more likely to be artists or philosophers or other experts in their particular fields rather than successful practising architects. Architecture was imagined as a field of forces, making clear that the idea of architecture as object was not enough. The relationship of architecture to its own subject, architecture and the subjective experience of it, and an appraisal of the pragmatic limits of practice led to the AA School's search for the subject.

But for those to whom reinventing architecture was a stage too far, the AA of this period was a bewildering and frustrating experience: for all its successes, there was an at least equal number of failures. The unit system by definition sets up a high-risk experiment and there undoubtedly were unit teachers, even those surviving for a number of years, whose architectural programmes and teaching methods were less than inspired and sometimes little more than a

6.14
Taxim Nightpark nightclub Istanbul, Branson Coates, 1991: an extensive practice developed post-AA continued to engage with issues of the body and dynamic space.

cover for pretension (or worse) – antithetical to the more committed tutor. It was easy for the profession at large to dismiss the work produced at the AA as irrelevant to the actual business of designing buildings. However, as the other subjects of this study have shown, ideas at first dismissed as frivolous and absurd have later transformed to become part of the mainstream. The strangeness of the intellectual basis for enquiry by tutors such as Tschumi, Libeskind and Bunschoten in particular made their activity appear pointless to some, who felt that architecture was, finally, about the pragmatic – a particularly British response.

A historical judgement must however be made, even for those who considered its architectural content as somewhat questionable, that the AA represents a momentous achievement, which would not have been possible without the extraordinary talent and commitment of Boyarsky. He shifted the focus of architecture in Britain to a global arena, and by creating a new model of education akin to that of a free market, empowered the individual student and teaching staff member. If its architectural enquiry is seen to be extraordinarily innovative and consistent, establishing lines of investigation which were to prove fruitful in the programme of rethinking modernism after its moment of crisis, then Boyarsky's achievement should also be seen as the most critical in the whole development of modernist architectural culture in Britain.

The story of British architecture in the following decades is to some extent the working out of issues first raised at the Boyarsky AA: it ensured that for many, Britain was to remain among the leaders in architectural culture. Without doubt, teaching methods were transformed: indeed, a number of leading schools throughout the world, including many in the UK, are led by AA graduates of this period. Architecture *as* discourse, the subject of the following chapter, began in this period of the AA, with its emphasis on the production of worked-through and materialised ideas. The distinction Tschumi drew in a 1976 lecture – on 'the utter mediocrity of the built environment'[59] – drew a line between the exigencies of practice and the art of architecture, which the following generation at the same time continued and tried to resolve. Architecture as an autonomous cultural practice, that is to say as an art, was nurtured by its removal from a direct relationship to issues of practice, its universality in any case referring to possible modes of practice far beyond British codes. The question of art was, after all, the subject of architecture.

SEARCHING FOR THE SUBJECT

Notes

1 From 'Ambience and Alchemy: Alvin Boyarsky interviewed', *AR*, October 1983, p. 28.
2 The Architectural Association was founded in 1847 by two young office apprentices as a forum for self-education, without teachers or prescribed programme. It became a more formalised school in 1890 and developed in the earlier twentieth century as the school that educated the majority of leading British architects. Its role as an elite school was moderated in the years after 1938 by its adoption of a socially committed role for architecture, and later as an arena for members of Archigram. See John Summerson, *The Architectural Association*, London: Pleiades Books, 1947, for its early history; also James Gowan, *A Continuing Experiment*, London: Architectural Press, 1975, for a series of articles covering the pre-Boyarsky AA.
3 From Alvin Boyarsky's election statement, 1971.
4 I ran the AA Slide Library (later Photo Library) from 1975 to 1989, was a student in the Graduate School from 1982 to 1984, and began to teach the history and theory of architecture in the AA General Studies unit in 1988.
5 Scott is referring to Marshall McLuhan's idea of the media becoming an extension of the human central nervous system.
6 Fred Scott, AA School of Architecture, *Prospectus*, 1981, p. 4.
7 Peter Cook, Alvin Boyarsky obituary, *Architects Journal*, 15 August 1990, p. 16.
8 Colin Rowe was an English-born professor at Cornell, influential through his teaching and publication in particular of a series of articles collected later as *The Mathematics of the Ideal Villa*, Cambridge, MA: MIT Press, 1976, and *Collage City*, Cambridge, MA: MIT Press, 1978.
9 *AR reviews AA*, guest-edited by Peter Buchanan and Colin Davies, *Architectural Review*, October 1983.
10 *Design Book Review*, Winter 1987, no. 11.
11 Michael Lloyd, also known as John Lloyd, was Principal of the AA from 1966. His account of this period can be read in 'Reply' in J. Gowan (ed.), *A Continuing Experiment: Learning and Teaching at the Architectural Association*, London: Architectural Press, 1975, pp. 163–5, which also has contrasting accounts from Charles Jencks '125 Years of Quasi Democracy', and Fred Scott 'Myth, Misses and Mr Architecture'.
12 Leon van Schaik, quoted in Diane Baird, *Constructing a Learning Environment: An Interview with Leon van Schaik*. <http://ultibase.rmit.edu.au/Articles/june97/schai1.htm> accessed 11.9.05.
13 For an account of the International Institute of Design 1970 Summer Session, see *Architectural Design*, April 1971, pp. 219–40. It was followed by a 1971 Summer Session after Boyarsky had been appointed as AA Chairman.
14 Guy Debord, 'Report on the Construction of Situations and on the International Situationist Tendency's Conditions of Organization and Action' (1957) in K. Knabb (ed.), *A Situationist Anthology*, Berkeley, CA: Bureau of Public Secrets, 1981.
15 *Architectural Review*, October 1983, p. 23.
16 The restaurant and bookshop were privatised before Thatcher had started the privatisation of government services.
17 *Design Book Review*, Winter 1987, no. 11 p. 10.
18 *A Chronicle of Urban Politics* was published by the AA in 1974.
19 Colin Rowe and Fred Koetter, *Collage City*, Cambridge, MA: MIT Press, 1978, p. 137.
20 While Lefebvre's work became influential in British architectural discourse at a later date, as for example in the writing of Iain Borden and others, this was in the wake of the translation of *The Production of Space* in 1991. Tschumi as a French native speaker had read the original texts as well as being exposed to these ideas in late 1960s Paris.
21 Nigel Coates, 'Narrative Break-up' in *The Discourse of Events*, in series Themes 3, London: Architectural Association, 1983, p. 13.

SEARCHING FOR THE SUBJECT

22 Bernard Tschumi, 'Spaces and Events' in *The Discourse of Events*, in series Themes 3, London: Architectural Association, 1983, p. 6.
23 See *The Discourse of Events*, in Themes 3, London: Architectural Association, 1983, pp. 30–1.
24 Coates, op.cit., p. 15.
25 Ibid.
26 See Nigel Coates, 'Ghetto and Globe' in *NATO* 1, London: Architectural Association, 1983, p. 9.
27 Ibid.
28 *NATO* 1, London: Architectural Association, 1983: there were also two subsequent issues.
29 Michael Gold's text in the publication of this project in *People in Architecture*, in series Themes 4, London: Architectural Association, 1983, is particularly illuminating on its evolution.
30 Leon Krier, *Projects Review 1975*, London: Architectural Association, Intermediate Unit 10, n.p.
31 Rationalism, or more correctly Neo-Rationalism, originated with texts by Giorgio Grassi and in particular Aldo Rossi, *The Architecture of the City*, 1966. Krier had earlier worked in James Stirling's office in London.
32 Libeskind had earlier studied at Cooper Union, New York and on the MA led by Joseph Rykwert at the University of Essex. His later career developed a distinctive teaching programme at Cranbrook Academy of Art and his architectural office was established with the construction of the Jewish Museum, Berlin, won in competition in1990.
33 Daniel Libeskind in Architectural Association School of Architecture *Prospectus*, 1976/7, p. 39.
34 Vesely later taught at Cambridge School of Architecture, and published the long-awaited *Architecture in the Age of Divided Representation* in 2004 (Cambridge, MA: MIT Press). After teaching at the University of Pennsylvania and Yale, Mostafavi returned as AA Chairman from 1995 to 2004.
35 Architectural Association School of Architecture *Prospectus*, 1978/9, p. 29.
36 *Architecture and Continuity*; in series Themes 1, London: Architectural Association, 1982.
37 Rem Koolhaas, *Delirious New York*, London: Thames & Hudson, 1978.
38 Architectural Association School of Architecture, *Prospectus*, 1976/7, p. 49.
39 Rem Koolhaas, *Zaha M Hadid*, quoted in *GA Architect* 5, 1986, p. 9.
40 Nigel Coates in Architectural Association School of Architecture, *Prospectus*, 1979/80, p. 11.
41 *Spirit and Invention*; in series Themes 2, London: Architectural Association, 1982.
42 Cook's 'Grand Tour' in *AR*, October 1983, p. 32.
43 See *Architectural Review*, October 1983, pp. 68–75.
44 Peter Salter in conversation with the author, 6 July 2005.
45 *TS Intuition and Process*; in series Themes 6, London: Architectural Association, 1989, p. 9.
46 Architectural Association, *Prospectus*, October 1987, p. 36.
47 Both had studied with Daniel Libeskind at Cranbrook Academy of Art, Michigan.
48 See *Architectural Review*, October 1983, p. 29.
49 Middleton was formerly Technical Editor of *Architectural Design* (see p. 135) and at the same time Librarian at Cambridge School of Architecture and Art History.
50 One success was the *Beaux-Arts* week, a conference held in May 1978, accompanied by an exhibition of original drawings from the Paris School. A particular enthusiasm of Middleton's, it related directly to the concern of certain units as well as showing extraordinarily accomplished draughtsmanship. In 1979 a course of lectures, 'Engineers on Engineering', had to be cancelled because of lack of support.
51 For example, my own writing of a history of the AA, in various versions starting with

the 1983 edition of the *Prospectus*, was subject to his editorial revision of the names and projects that were included.
52 This replaced *AA Quarterly*, edited by Dennis Sharp, which had in turn replaced the *AA Journal*.
53 The production, apart from printing, was done in the Print Studio at the AA, led by Dennis Crompton.
54 'Introduction', *AA Files*, vol. 1, no. 2, July 1982, p. 3.
55 Historical studies exposed and re-evaluated new subjects: for example, S. de Martino and Alex Wall, *Cities of Childhood: Italian Colonie of the 1930s*, London: Architectural Association, 1988; and St John Wilson *et al.*, *Sigurd Lewerentz: the Dilemma of Classicism*, London: Architectural Association, 1989, both on subjects otherwise little known in Britain.
56 A full list of AA publications of the Boyarsky period can be found in Robin Middleton (ed.), *Architectural Associations: The Idea of the City*, London: Architectural Association, 1996, pp. 232–8. The book is a *florilegium* of contributions by former colleagues, friends and students in memory of Boyarsky.
57 *Design Book Review* 18, spring 1990, reprinted in Middleton, 1996, op. cit., pp. 225–31.
58 *Macdonald and Salter Building Projects 1982–86*, Mega 3, London: Architectural Association, 1987.
59 Bernard Tschumi lecture at Art Net, London 1976.

CHAPTER 7

architecture *as* discourse

rethinking the culture of architecture

ARCHITECTURE *AS* DISCOURSE

> In architecture, architects themselves do much of the talking and writing – which indeed constitutes a major component of their 'production'; one of the features of the architecture system ... is the contest between architects and the press for control over the verbal element.
>
> (Adrian Forty, *Words and Buildings*, 2000)[1]

John Ruskin wrote that the identity of the nation was the origin of architectural practice,[2] but a century and a half later the location of architecture was for most, rather than in any country, to be found in the pages of a journal. It became apparent, in a kind of fulfilment of a process begun at the start of modernism, that architecture was created and validated in the media, whether the sumptuously photographed magazine or the theoretical text. A second transformation can be seen in the history of modernist polemic, which had begun with the Sant'Elia's battle-cry 'we must invent and rebuild the futurist city',[3] echoing in Britain three decades later. The end of the century patently had no such appetite for action, and instead architecture became engaged with a dialectic of reconsidering the processes of its production. Forty, Professor in the History of Architecture at the Bartlett School, University College London, is here discussing the fundamental role of language in creating interpretation, in defining what the culture of architecture is, taking Roland Barthes' essay on the *Fashion System*[4] as a basis for understanding, and he points out the conflict which may occur between the architect and the critic's role in articulating it. Further to Barthes' ideas of the construction of meaning, Foucault's notion of 'discourse' effectively removed the distinction between architecture and representations of architecture. As he wrote of the work of an individual: '[T]here must be a level ... at which the *oeuvre* emerges, in all its fragments, even the smallest ones ... as the expression of the thought, the experience, the imagination, or the unconscious of the author'. The unity of interpretation includes the notebooks, the 'jumble of laundry bills and sketches'[5] to make sense of what is behind one particular position.

Significant in the recent past is the production of key texts that have effectively deconstructed the practice of architecture. Forty's *Words and Buildings* has emphasised and enlarged on the issue that there is nothing 'natural' about the way architects talk about their practice, and instead the process is one of their engaging with the existing condition of architectural language. Robin Evans[6] and Beatriz Colomina[7] have illustrated that there is nothing straightforward and seamless about the relationship of architecture and its representations – for Evans in the practices of drawing; for Colomina in the creation of the architectural publication.

The subject of this chapter, which deals with the architectural culture of the 1990s and beyond, rather than emphasising one key book, chooses to survey an extensive body of recent literature. The major change in the field in the past decade or so has been an explosion in architectural publishing, both books and journals. Many have indeed had a relationship to the debate about the properties of architecture, including opening to question the basis of architectural practice itself. It has often appeared that books that reflect the separation of theory and practice (in favour of the former) have formed the bulk of those published within the discipline in recent times. The literature engaging with this includes the publication of books by Forty and Evans, by Dalibor Vesely,[8] and by Jonathan Hill and Iain Borden,[9] among others, and the publication of a revived *Architectural Design*.[10] A further illustration is the book *Rethinking Architecture* published in 1997,[11] an edited selection of texts from philosophy and cultural theory, which has sold far more copies than most monographs on well-known contemporary architects.

What this genre of books effectively does is question the fundamental basis of practice – so it draws a line between the literal and physical praxis of building on one side, and the nature of the thinking and framing of architecture on the other. The intention is by no means to assert that there is a crisis of meaning underlying all current practice, but to maintain that a culture of architecture has grown up which has no obvious relation to the pragmatic business of building. This discourse, reflected in a number of publications, journals and exhibitions, is not restricted simply to a small section of academia. The RIBA, for example, has chosen for its Annual Discourse Jennifer Bloomer and Anthony Vidler,[12] both theoreticians, over the discussion of practitioners. Beyond, architectural education, as seen at the Bartlett and AA, has been at the forefront of development of this new concern, which it might be remarked has been the case with the majority of the significant discourses outlined earlier in this book.

Just as art, over recent decades, has become engaged with the *processes* of art, its institutions, its traditions, its modes of representation, so architecture has begun belatedly to examine its practice in a fundamental way. Who is the 'architect'? What might he or she be making? How can the process of design become more autonomous? If 'space' is essentially defined politically, how might the architect subvert political structures? If architecture is a culture, what does that culture represent? This questioning process repudiates the former grand narrative of 'progress' in modernism – and is also a rejection of the necessity of 'originality' which the progressive drive of that narrative set up. But, beyond this process of questioning, *culture* in the broadest sense has become central to a new platform upon which architecture has begun to re-create itself. It is necessary, in approaching the making of architecture, to be aware of a range of issues around the inhabitation of space, and of architecture's representational function as well as a developed understanding of site and context, its relationship to the city. The informing process of thought within this intricate condition becomes all the more necessary to avoid the trap of reducing architecture solely to the creation of an image: a real engagement with the complexities of culture should preclude the easy solution.

The assumptions of the modernist position have thus been mediated by a far more complex position, informed by a far richer range of conditions.[13] The nature of architecture involves, implicitly or explicitly, conceptual frameworks. Writing inevitably explores cultural norms and values which the writer is both writing within and departing from; while in its relationship to language, writing is always engaged with issues of representation, whether in describing, evoking or creating architecture. There have been times in the recent past when it has seemed that the act of writing on architecture was privileged over the act of building: that writing was somehow more important than the development of a building project. It is as if the integrity of thought is far less compromised than the messy business of making. And further, that the basis of the act of making architecture was so flawed that anything more than an empty gesture was an impossibility. As Manfredo Tafuri had earlier expressed this dilemma: 'The inconsistency and elusiveness of so much current production makes it obvious that one is facing a tacit and perhaps unconscious effort to state ... the ineffective nature of architecture.'[14]

The philosopher Jean-François Lyotard characterised postmodernism as 'witnessing the death of centres' and of displaying 'incredulity towards metanarratives':[15] all existing principles of organisation are opened to question, are no longer seen as natural, or necessarily legitimate. Thus he announced the end of the notion of progress leading to social improvement. The implication was of a greater inclusivity, so what had been marginal could be valued: judgements did not have to be validated by history or so-called common sense. So for him it was a process of opening up rather than retrenchment; he wrote that: 'under the name of postmodernism, architects are getting rid of the Bauhaus project, throwing out the baby of experimentation with the bathwater of functionalism'.[16] Lyotard's assertion leads to the question of the particular use in architectural discourse of the term 'postmodern': rather than (fundamentally, but also simply) meaning the condition that follows on from the structured narrative of modernism, it has come to mean the kind of architecture that is conditioned by the language of the past.

Charles Jencks's appropriation of the term in the 1977 book *The Language of Post-Modern Architecture*[17] became its definition in architectural discussion. Rather than an acknowledgement of the loss of the doctrine of social progress matched by architectural positivism, Jencks's 'postmodernism' became a retreat, an abrupt move to a different set of architectural forms, those validated by history. What this also implied was an end to architectural evolution, rather than the possibility which Lyotard and others had revealed, of release from the restriction of architectural determinism into new territories of investigation.

For Jonathan Hill, the fundamental question is that of the nature of the architect. He develops a theory of the relationship of the architect to the building's users as its powerful critique: that 'architecture' is limited to what the architect does, excluding the daily making of architecture by those, not so professionally empowered, who effectively create the spaces they occupy. As he says, 'the presence of the user is perceived as a direct threat to the authority of the architect'.[18] His book *Occupying Architecture: between Architect and the User* has a counterpart in the polemic project for an 'alternative' RIBA; the 'Institute of Illegal Architects'.[19] In this work, Hill follows Barthes in his questioning of the roles of the writer, reader and text.

A profound influence in British architectural culture has been that of the philosopher Henri Lefebvre; his *Production of Space*[20] was translated into English in 1991. For him, 'space' is neither a neutral nor an abstract concept, nor as architecture would have it, 'a container without content'. Space is essentially *social*, gaining its meanings from use, but also essentially formed in relation to the political structures that control it. Lefebvre develops a critique of architectural practice as an instrument of social control and develops the idea of 'spatial practice', an inclusive term far beyond the actions of architecture, as the material expression of social relations in space. The *Strangely Familiar* exhibition and conference held at the RIBA in 1996[21] was an attempt by a group of architectural historians, designers and urbanists to articulate issues of identity, the body, and memory in a Lefebvrian context of the interpretation of cities as the ground of experience. Iain Borden, a founder member of that group, was to develop this reading in a number of other contexts, notably *Skateboarding Space and the City*,[22] in which the transgressive nature of the skateboarder is interpreted as an extreme model for

ARCHITECTURE *AS* DISCOURSE

7.1
Occupying Architecture: between Architecture and the User, edited by Jonathan Hill, 1998. According to Hill's questioning of architectural practice, 'the presence of the user is perceived as a direct threat to the authority of the architect'.

understanding the use a city's dwellers may make of its spaces: a fuller use, enriched by its own culture and practices.

The hierarchy of the importance and strength of conventional narratives of course has been more generally rejected, and has led to a number of publications relating to gender. One British example of the this was Francesca Hughes', *The Architect: Reconstructing her Practice*,[23] and the collective project, *Desiring Practices*,[24] which radically engaged with issues of gender and led to a number of events at the RIBA and elsewhere, with a particularly rich group of contributors. Issues of cultural identity, a major preoccupation in discourses outside architecture, have been given voice in Lesley Lokko's *White Papers Black Marks*.[25]

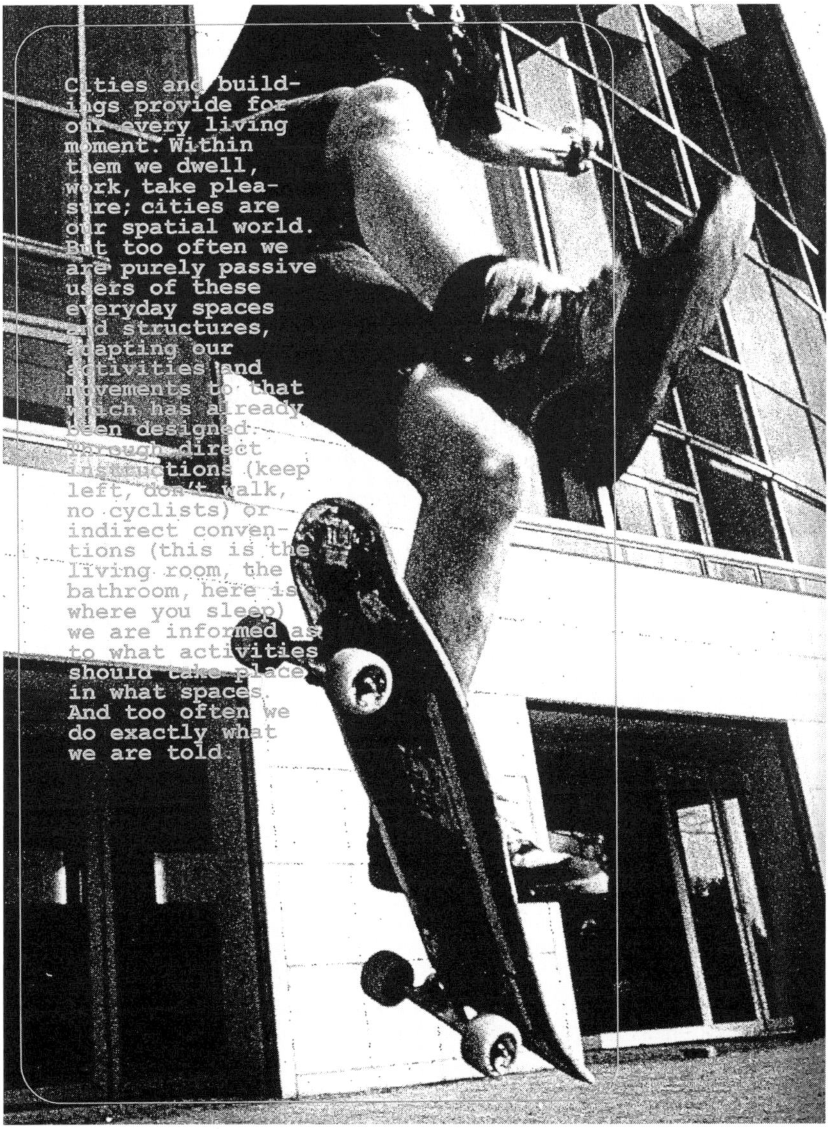

ARCHITECTURE *AS* DISCOURSE

7.2
Layout from *Strangely Familiar: Narratives of Architecture in the City*, 1996: Iain Borden argues here that skateboarders in their antagonism to the built environment 'produce an overtly political space, a pleasure ground carved out of the city'.

7.3
This Is Not Architecture: Media Constructions, edited by Kester Rattenbury; 2002, one of a number of texts which has examined the role of the published media and photographic image in creating architecture.

Anthony Vidler gave the RIBA Annual Discourse in 1996 and entitled it: 'Architecture after History: Nostalgia and Modernity at the End of the Century'.[26] He commented:

> In this moment of paradigm ambiguity, there is no doubt that, even as we experienced a severe nostalgia for time and history at the beginning of the modern period ... we are now in the throes of an equally strong nostalgia for space, in both theory

and practice ... what is spatial about an endless string of 0's and 1's, a string that for the purposes of display has to be looped around screen; an endless line, without direction, displayed on a screen without depth?[27]

Vidler's sense of loss faced with the development of the digital in architecture has been inverted by others, including the work Neil Spiller has developed at the Bartlett School and articulated in *Digital Dreams: Architecture and the New Alchemic Technologies*. Starting with the assertion that 'Our spaceshape is changing. Our flesh and its inert environment currently imprison us ... The pseudo-dynamics of architectural modernism have left us ill-prepared for the physical and spatial changes that are daily rocketing towards us',[28] Spiller envisages an architecture developed from the basis of the cell, encompassing technologies as yet unrealised, fundamentally shifting the relationship of man and universe and disempowering the architect. Brett Steele has dated the beginning of the digital period in architecture to the *Complexity and Architecture* conference held at the AA in May 1994, and the easier access to spatial software opened up by 1997.[29] Optimistic about the possibilities it may harness, the Design Research Lab at the AA formed in 1996 has developed rapidly alongside the technological changes of the decade. The experimental model adopted has been to develop new forms as the result of a consciously new dynamic of working

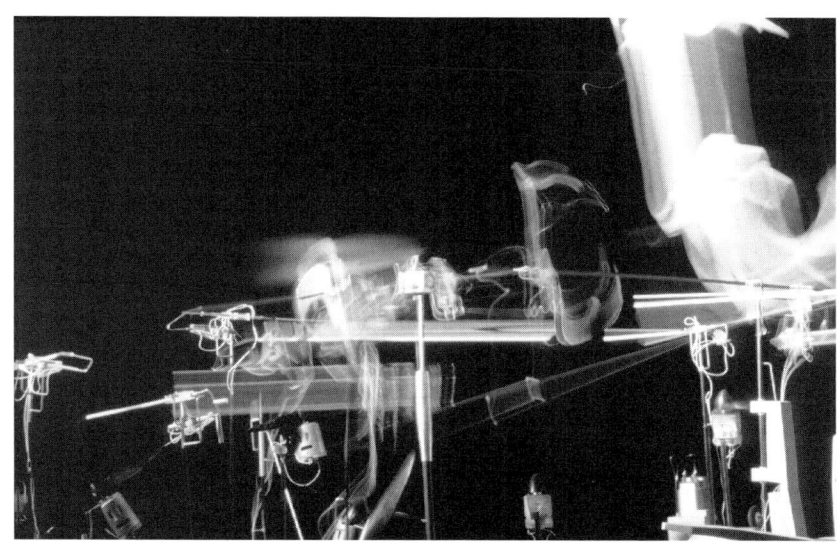

7.4
Mark Smout: Edge Assemblage: kite flocks in motion, project at the Bartlett School tutored by Christine Hawley and C.J. Lim 1997, published in the *Bartlett Book of Ideas*, 2000. The Bartlett, led by Peter Cook from 1990 to 2005, was transformed into a school characterised by new ideas and inventiveness.

ARCHITECTURE *AS* DISCOURSE

which adopts and utilises networks and technologies to develop and self-reflect.

Processes of building

Recent building projects represent and illustrate moments of the discourse of a reconsidered and revived modern architecture. What this has effectively meant is that buildings, or at least those buildings that aspire to contribute to the extension of the parameters of architectural practice, have had a didactic role which is quite distinct from the built work of the immediate past. In a sense it has resonances of the relationship of ideas to building seen in the period of 'high' modernism. Just as in the 1930s James Richards could write: 'the new architecture that we are calling "modern" . . . is something that is needed in the world today', knowing exactly what that would mean in terms of consequent building,[30] so likewise Rem Koolhaas could say in 1994: 'Liberated from its former obligations, architecture's last function will be the creation of symbolic spaces that accommodate the persistent desire for collectivity.'[31] In other words, the confident assertion of architecture's purpose results in building that illustrates the aspiration of that specific programme.

The fundamental shift of architecture in the 1990s and beyond is certainly expressed in an expansion of practice, supported initially through lottery-funded projects,[32] and later through a renascent economy, providing opportunities to build that had been lacking for two decades after the decline of the public commission. Apart from the huge field of opportunities currently presented, the difference between the practice of the 1990s and 1930s is one of plurality. Two buildings completed in 2000 would consider themselves at the cutting edge of contemporary practice: although both are museums (and both lottery-funded), they adopt opposing principles. The British Museum Great Court by Foster and Partners is predicated on advanced design technology: the adoption and development of technique. Caruso St John's Walsall Art Gallery instead considers the contextual, the material and the scale of inhabitation. While Foster has for more than a decade adopted the assured position of being the architectural norm, it has become necessary for those taking other views to set up a resistance to the limitations of so-called high-tech. Faced with the perfected forms of Norman Foster's work, the artist Richard Wentworth observed:

7.5
Great Court, British Museum: Foster and Partners, 2000: one of a large number of public buildings in London and elsewhere built or modified by Foster's practice at this time; the complex roof form was the subject of highly complex form generation.

ARCHITECTURE *AS* DISCOURSE

7.6
Walsall New Art Gallery, Caruso St John, 2000: entrance and main stairs. Douglas fir boards were used to form shuttering, and also used as lining panels mounted on concrete: Caruso writes of 'the ontology of construction'.

there's a classic disjuncture between the world inside the architect's head and the world people live in. It's between Descartean idealism, the abstract world of the head, and the medieval, mercantile reality we actually live in. We're still essentially medieval. We have bad breath, we fart.[33]

Will Alsop represents one polarity in his text *Towards an Architecture of Practical Delight*, which outlines his rejection of the rational, of the explanation and justification of an architectural decision. Describing the way his processes often start by painting, he explains:

> The paint has a life of its own, beyond your control. It is possible to see what you cannot think. The paintings do not have the authority of traditional scaled drawings and as such can be used in discussions. This act is an invitation to misinterpret, extend and corrupt.[34]

The same dilemma of allowing unconscious and unfiltered expression is identified by Jeffrey Kipnis, an American theorist who was highly influential in his teaching at the AA from 1994 to 1997:

198

> If the growing irrelevance of architecture is the result of systematic repression, then it seems that the principal vector for the persistence and dissemination of that repression has been rational design theory. This is true even when theory in that form has taken upon itself the self-reflexive problem ... rational discourse cannot give form to the necessary question 'what is (the form of) irrationality?'[35]

After all, Kipnis argues, no practice has in the past been true to rational discourse, and cannot be expected to be. The solution he proposes is a surprising one: given the inevitable incursion of the ego into the design process, its interventions should be delayed, and in the instant of design no authority, 'no ethical or moral imperative, no priority or precedent, no cultural or aesthetic responsibility rightfully restrains the exploration into possibilities of occupying material form.' If the aim is the unrestrained expression of authentic design, then the question remains of what this unfettered form might be: might it demonstrate plasticity, might it be painterly, might it be the effect of materiality? Each of these and others has been part of recent British discourse. The idea of the fold, of which Kipnis himself was a key originator, is one which has generated new spatial and formal principles. He introduced the idea in the essay 'Towards a New Architecture: Folding' in the first *AD* issue on the fold.

> Neither pure figure nor pure organisation, folds link the two; they are monolithic and often non-representational, replete with interstitial and residual spaces, and intrinsic to non-developable surfaces. As a process exercised in a matrix such as an urban site, folding holds out the possibility of generating field organisations.[36]

As a new model of space, this discourse became established at the same time that its forms could, relatively easily, be digitally rendered: it was to generate numerous striking projects, even if their content did not necessarily touch on the radical democratisation which its philosophical underpinning by Deleuze[37] might have evoked.

There is a specific architecture of resistance which has developed in the recent past, defined in part by what it opposes; the dominance of high-tech design strategies emerging from former members of the Foster and Rogers offices, the brash modernities of Koolhaas, and the conscious formal invention found elsewhere. The *Architectural Review* under the long editorship of Peter Davey, which ended in 2005, championed an organicist tendency: the influence of a new kind of work from continental Europe, including Herzog de Meuron, Siza, and Diener and Diener was first exposed only in the academic publication *9H* and exhibited in its gallery.[38] Tony Fretton's first major building, the London Lisson Gallery, voiced a relationship to this new sensibility and as he described created an 'elevation empty and scaleless, rhyming with the surrounding highrises, voids and small objects to point out that in an industrialised society nothing can be ignored as merely a by-product.'[39]

This reading of the qualities of site with an inclusive attitude to urban phenomena, an indifference to style and avoidance of novelty, has led to the making of buildings that are both sensitive and mute. Surprisingly, the Smithsons have provided a model for a new generation of how to be an architect, and in this, to make distinct that their thinking – and writing – was an integral part of their practice. Caruso St John, who with the Walsall Art Gallery, produced the most achieved work of this discourse, have spoken of their building's relationship to the vernacular, which relates to the Smithsons' concerns with the specificity of site: '[T]he vernacular is not about appearance but about presence. It is a physical artefact that contains within itself the continuously evolving social technological situation in which it was built.'[40] This engagement with the familiar and the everyday has provided a new theoretical basis for a practice both modest, and at its best, powerful which represents a revival of the Loosian interpretation of modernism.

The echoes of the AA's work of the 1980s have continued: at the same time the dominance of a global economy has made the notion of a British architecture less clearly defined than in any previous period. Instant mass communications have been joined by the export of British architecture. Foster's office has become the most admired worldwide, according to some reports, and the profile of Hadid's practice widely recognised as a world leader. But something like a dozen other British practices have achieved substantial work in other countries over the past decade or so. A counterpart in British popular culture has been a new interest in architecture on the part of the mass media, reflected in newspaper critiques of new buildings and a variety of television programmes. The annual award of the Stirling Prize for best building of the year, begun in 1995, with a much-hyped awards ceremony broadcast live, is one event that has given current architecture a profile far beyond what the earlier popularisers of modernism could have imagined.

Francis Fukuyama wrote in 1992 of the end of history – not that this was literally what he meant. But perhaps the beginning of the

ARCHITECTURE *AS* DISCOURSE

7.7
Hotel Puerta America, Madrid by Plasma Studio, 2005. Eva Castro, graduate of the AA's Graduate Design Programme and Holger Kehne, graduate of the University of East London School formed their practice in 1999, won the award Architect of the Year in 2002, and have been internationally published with this built project, in the vanguard of digital practice.

new millennium sees the end of Britishness with the definitive realisation of McLuhan's 'Global Village' of the mass media. This most porous of cultures, both in an inward and outward direction, with its location between the USA and continental Europe but, effectively, the affect of neither, has continued to prove itself the focus of the world culture of architecture. Zaha Hadid, Iraqi born but a British citizen, Foreign Office Architects with Iranian and Spanish partners, as well as Plasma Studio, a German-Argentinian partnership show that Britain has become a culture where the discourse of modern architecture continues to be re-created. The mediation of modernity has developed to fulfil certain of the original aspirations of modernism, while casting others aside. If there is a golden age of British modern architecture, it might just possibly be now.

Notes

1. Adrian Forty, *Words and Buildings: a Vocabulary of Modern Architecture*, London: Thames & Hudson, 2000, p. 14.
2. John Ruskin, *Seven Lamps of Architecture* [1849] London: George Allen, 1901, pp. 368–9.
3. Sant'Elia, 'Futurist Manifesto' in Ulrich Conrad, *Programmes and Manifestos in 20c Architecture*, London: Lund Humpries, 1970, p. 34.
4. See Forty, op. cit., pp. 13–14.
5. Michel Foucault, *The Archaeology of Knowledge*, London: Tavistock, 1972, p. 24.
6. Robin Evans, *Translations from Drawing to Building and Other Essays*, London: Architectural Association, 1997; *The Projective Cast*, Cambridge, MA: MIT Press, 1995.
7. Beatriz Colomina, *Privacy and Publicity: Modern Architecture as Mass Media*, Cambridge, MA: MIT Press, 1994.
8. Dalibor Vesely, *Architecture in the Age of Divided Representation*, Cambridge, MA: MIT Press, 2004.
9. Jonathan Hill's publications include his editing of *Occupying Architecture: between the Architect and the User*, London: Routledge, 1998, and *The Illegal Architect*, London: Black Dog, 2001. Iain Borden's publications include, co-edited with Jane Rendell, *Intersections: Architectural Histories and Critical Theories*, London: Routledge, 2000, and *Skateboarding Space and the City*, Oxford: Berg, 2001.
10. *Architectural Design* was edited by Maggie Toy from 1993, replacing Andreas Papadakis, with an extensive list of guest editors.
11. Neil Leach (ed.), *Rethinking Architecture*, London: Routledge, 1997.
12. Jennifer Bloomer (1992) and Anthony Vidler (1996) among others.
13. The clarity of the *spirit of the age* outlined in the historical narratives of Pevsner or Richards is now seen as a crude suppression of ideas and work which did not appear to fit, a repudiation of which Banham and Venturi, and later Colin Rowe, began in the 1960s.
14. Manfredo Tafuri, *Theories and History of Architecture*, trans. G. Verrecchia, London: Granada, 1980, p. 4. (First Italian edn 1968.).
15. J.-F. Lyotard, *The Postmodern Condition*, trans. G. Bennington and B. Massumi, Manchester: Manchester University Press, 1986, p. xxiv.
16. Lyotard, op. cit., p. 71.
17. Charles Jencks, *The Language of Post-Modern Architecture*, London: Academy,1977; see also p. 18.
18. Jonathan Hill, *Occupying Architecture: between the Architect and the User*, London: Routledge, 1998, p. 3.
19. Jonathan Hill, *The Illegal Architect*, London: Black Dog, 1998.
20. H. Lefebvre, *The Production of Space*, Oxford: Blackwell, 1991.
21. The group, founded in 1994, included Iain Borden, Jane Rendell, Joe Kerr and Alicia Pivaro. See I. Borden *et al.* (eds), *Strangely Familiar*, London: Routledge, 1996; and *The Unknown City*, Cambridge, MA: MIT Press, 2001.
22. Iain Borden, *Skateboarding Space and the City: Architecture and the Body*, Oxford: Berg, 2001.
23. Francesca Hughes, *The Architect: Reconstructing her Practice*, Cambridge, MA: MIT Press, 1996.
24. D. McCorquodale, S. Wigglesworth and K. Ruedi, *Desiring Practices: Architecture, Gender and the Interdisciplinary*, London: Black Dog, 1996.
25. Lesley Lokko, *White Papers Black Marks*, London: Athlone Press, 2000.
26. Anthony Vidler, RIBA Annual Discourse 1996, 'Architecture after History: Nostalgia and Modernity at the End of the Century', in *The Journal of Architecture*, vol. 1, Autumn 1997, pp. 177–87.
27. Ibid., p. 184.

28 Neil Spiller, *Digital Dreams: Architecture and the New Alchemic Technologies*, London: Ellipsis, 1998.
29 Conversation with the author, 25 October 2005. See Brett Steele, 'Designing the DRL' in *Corporate Fields*, London: Architectural Association, 2005.
30 J.M. Richards, *Modern Architecture*, Harmondsworth: Penguin, 1940, p. 9.
31 Rem Koolhaas on 1989 Paris Library competition entry: Koolhaas and Mau, *S M L XL*, Rotterdam 010, 1995, p. 604.
32 The National Lottery supported major public building projects from 1994, including the Tate Modern competition, the Millennium Dome, the Lowry Salford, Walsall Gallery, British Museum Great Court and Duxford Museum.
33 Richard Wentworth in *I Shot Norman Foster*. Exhibition catalogue, London: Architecture Foundation, 2005, p. 15.
34 Will Alsop, *Towards an Architecture of Practical Delight*, AD Architectural monographs no. 33, 1993, p. 15.
35 Jeffrey Kipnis, 'Forms of Irrationality', in J. Whiteman, J. Kipnis and R. Burdett (eds), *Strategies in Architectural Thinking*, Cambridge, MA: MIT Press, 1992, p. 160.
36 Jeffrey Kipnis, 'Folding in Architecture', *AD*, nos 3–4, 1993, p. 47.
37 Gilles Deleuze, *Fold: Leibniz and the Baroque*, London: Athlone Press, 1993.
38 *9H* Magazine 1979–95; 9H Gallery 1985–90.
39 Tony Fretton, 'The Lisson Gallery London', *AA Files* 23, Summer 1992, p. 20.
40 Quoted by Peter Allison in 'The Presence of Construction', *AA Files* 35, Spring 1998, p. 70.

Select bibliography

The primary sources on which each chapter concentrates are the books and journals themselves which are the subject of each study. The most significant journals over the whole period are, as can be seen, the *Architectural Review* published continually through the twentieth century, and *Architectural Design* published from the 1950s, but with several abrupt shifts of direction. The Architectural Association journals, successively *AA Journal, AA Quarterly* and *AA Files* have included much useful primary as well as critical material. Other journals of contemporary practice, pre-eminently *Archigram,* also include *Uppercase* (c. 1960, ed. Theo Crosby) and NATO (c.1983, ed. Nigel Coates). Professional journals, significant at particular times, include *Architect and Building News, Architects Journal, Blueprint, Building Design* and *RIBA Journal.* The critical journal *9H* (1979–) should be mentioned, and since 1994, the Twentieth Century Society has produced an annual journal which is the best source of historical studies of twentieth-century British architecture.

Abercrombie, Patrick, *The Greater London Plan*, London: HMSO, 1944.
Abercrombie, Patrick and Jackson, H., *West Midlands Plan*, London: Ministry of Town Planning, 1948.
Ackroyd, Peter, *London: the Biography*, London: Chatto & Windus, 2000.
Alexander, Christopher, 'A City Is Not a Tree' in *Design*, February 1966, pp. 46–55.
Allan, John, *Lubetkin: Architecture and the Tradition of Progress*, London: RIBA Publications, 1992.
Amery, Colin and Cruikshank, Dan, *The Rape of Britain*, London: Paul Elek, 1975.
Appleyard, Brian, *The Pleasures of Peace*, London: Faber & Faber, 1989.
Architectural Association: For a full bibliography of publications during Boyarsky's chairmanship *see* Middleton, Robin (ed.) *Architectural Associations: The Idea of the City*, 1996. pp. 232–8.
Architectural Association, *Architecture and Continuity*, Themes 1, London: Architectural Association, 1982.
—— *Spirit and Invention*, Themes 2, London: Architectural Association, 1982.

SELECT BIBLIOGRAPHY

—— *The Discourse of Events*, Themes 3, London: Architectural Association, 1983.
—— *People in Architecture*, Themes 4, London: Architectural Association, 1983.
—— *Informing the Object*, Themes 5, London: Architectural Association, 1986.
—— *TS Intuition and Process*, Themes 6, London: Architectural Association, 1989.
—— *Architecture Is Not Made with the Brain: the Labour of Alison and Peter Smithson*, London: Architectural Association, 2005.
Banham, Mary and Hillier, B. (eds), *A Tonic to the Nation: the Festival of Britain 1951*, London: Thames & Hudson, 1976.
Banham, Mary et al. (eds), *A Critic Writes*, Berkeley: University of California Press, 1996.
Banham, Reyner, 'The New Brutalism', *AR*, December 1955, pp. 355–61.
—— *Theory and Design in the First Machine Age*, London: Architectural Press, 1960.
—— *The New Brutalism: Ethic or Aesthetic?*, London: Architectural Press, 1966.
—— 'Revenge of the Picturesque: English Architectural Polemics 1945–65', in J. Summerson (ed.), *Concerning Architecture*, London: Allen Lane, The Penguin Press, 1968, pp. 265–73.
—— *Megastructures: Urban Futures of the Recent Past*, London: Thames & Hudson, 1976.
Barthes, Roland, *The Eiffel Tower and Other Mythologies*, New York: Hill & Wang, 1979.
Blomfield, Reginald, *Modernismus*, London: Macmillan, 1934.
Borden, Iain, *Skateboarding, Space and the City: Architecture and the Body,* Oxford: Berg, 2001.
Borden, Iain and Rendell, J. (eds), *Intersections: Architectural Histories and Critical Theories*, London: Routledge, 2000.
Borden, Iain et al. (eds), *Strangely Familiar: Narratives of Architecture in the City*, London: Routledge, 1996.
Buchanan, Peter and Davies, Colin, *AR reviews AA:* Architectural Review, October 1983.
Bullock, Nicholas, *Building the Post-war World: Modern Architecture and Reconstruction in Britain*, London: Routledge, 2002.
Campbell, Louise (ed.), *Twentieth Century Architecture and its Histories,* Society of Architectural Historians of Great Britain, 2000.
Cantacuzino, S., *Wells Coates,* London: Gordon Fraser, 1978.
Carter, E.J. and Goldfinger, Ernö, *The County of London Plan Explained*, Harmondsworth: Penguin Books, 1945.
Casson, H., 'The Elusive H de C', *RIBA Journal,* February 1971, pp. 58–9.
Central Housing Advisory Committee's Sub Committee on housing standards, chaired by Sir Parker Morris, *Homes for Today and Tomorrow*, London: HMSO, 1961.

Cherry, Gordon E. (ed.), *Pioneers in British Planning*, London: Architectural Press, 1981.
Coates, Nigel, *Guide to Ecstacity*, London: Booth-Clibborn, 2002.
Colomina, Beatriz, *Privacy and Publicity: Modern Architecture as Mass Media*, Cambridge, MA: MIT Press, 1994.
Colquhoun, Alan, *Essays in Historical Criticism*, Cambridge, MA: MIT Press, 1981.
Cook, Peter, 'Some Notes on the Archigram Syndrome', *Perspecta* 11, New Haven: Yale University Press, 1967.
—— *The Bartlett Book of Ideas*, London: Bartlett, 2000.
Cook, Peter *et al.* (eds.), *Archigram*, London: Studio Vista, 1972: republished by Birkhauser (1991).
—— *A Guide to Archigram*, London: Academy, 1994.
Crysler, Greig, *Writing Spaces: Discourses of Architecture, Urbanism and the Built Environment*, London: Routledge, 2002.
Cullen, Gordon, *Townscape*, London: Architectural Press, 1961.
Deleuze, Gilles, *Fold: Leibniz and the Baroque*, London: Athlone Press, 1993.
Diefendorf, Jeffry N., *Rebuilding Europe's Bombed Cities*, London: Macmillan, 1990.
Elwall, Robert, *Photography Takes Command: The Camera and British Architecture 1890–1939*, London: RIBA, 1994.
Eric de Maré Photographer: Builder with Light, London: Architectural Association, 1990.
Esher, Lionel, *A Broken Wave*, London: Allen Lane, 1981.
Evans, Robin, *The Projective Cast*, Cambridge, MA: MIT Press, 1995.
—— *Translations from Drawing to Building and Other Essays*, London: Architectural Association, 1997.
Forshaw, J.H. and Abercrombie, P., *The County of London Plan*, London: Macmillan, 1943.
Forty, Adrian, 'Being and Nothingness: Experience and Public Architecture in Post-War Britain', *Architectural History* 58, 1995, pp. 25–35.
—— *Words and Buildings: a Vocabulary of Modern Architecture*, London: Thames & Hudson, 2000.
Foucault, Michel, *Archaeology of Knowledge*, London: Tavistock, 1972.
Frampton, Kenneth, *Modern Architecture: A Critical History*, London: Thames & Hudson, 1992.
Girouard, M., *Big Jim: the Life and Work of James Stirling*, London: Chatto & Windus, 1998.
Glendinning, M. and Muthesius, S., *Tower Block: Modern Public Housing in England, Scotland, Wales, and Northern Ireland*, New Haven: Yale University Press, 1994.
Gold, John R., *The Experience of Modernism*, London: Spon, 1997.
—— London MARS plan, in Thomas Deckker (ed.), *The Modern City Revisited*, London: Spon, 2000, pp. 80–99.
Goldhagen, S.W., Freedom's Domiciles: Three projects by Alison and Peter

SELECT BIBLIOGRAPHY

Smithson, in S.W. Goldhagen and R. Legault (eds), *Anxious Modernisms*, Cambridge, MA: MIT Press, 2000.

Gosling, David, *Gordon Cullen: Visions of Urban Design*, London: Academy Editions, 1996.

Gowan, James (ed.), *A Continuing Experiment: Learning and Teaching at the Architectural Association*, London: Architectural Press, 1975.

Greene, D., 'Architecture and the Rain', *Journal of Architecture*, Summer 2001.

Gropius, Walter, *The New Architecture and the Bauhaus*, London: Faber & Faber, 1935.

Harrison, C. and Wood, P., *Art in Theory 1900–2000*, Oxford: Blackwell, 2002.

Harwood, Elain and Powers, Alan (eds), *Festival of Britain*, London: Twentieth Century Society, 2001.

—— 'The Heroic Period of Conservation', Twentieth Century Architecture 7, London: The Twentieth Century Society, 2004.

Higgott, Andrew (ed.), *Travels in Modern Architecture*, London: Architectural Association, 1989.

—— 'Eric de Maré and the Functional Tradition', in *Eric de Maré*, London: Architectural Association, 1990.

—— 'Birmingham: Building the Modern City', in Thomas Deckker (ed.), *The Modern City Revisited*, London: Spon, 2000, pp. 150–66.

—— 'Frank Yerbury and the search for the new', in *F.R. Yerbury: Itinerant Cameraman*, London: Architectural Association, 1987.

Hill, Jonathan (ed.), *Occupying Architecture: between the Architect and the User*, London: Routledge, 1998.

—— *The Illegal Architect*, London: Black Dog, 2001.

Hughes, Francesca, *The Architect: Reconstructing her Practice*, Cambridge, MA: MIT Press, 1996.

Jackson, Anthony, *The Politics of Architecture*, London: Architectural Press, 1970.

Jackson, Frank, *Raymond Unwin*, London: Zwemmer, 1985.

Jencks, Charles, 'The Rise of Post Modern Architecture', *AA Quarterly*, October/December 1975, pp. 3–14.

—— *The Language of Post-Modern Architecture*, London: Academy, 1977.

Kipnis, Jeffrey, 'Folding in Architecture', *AD*, 3–4, 1993.

Koolhaas, Rem, *Delirious New York*, London: Thames & Hudson, 1978.

Koolhaus Rem and Mau, Bruce, *S M L XL*, Rotterdam: 010, 1995.

Landau, Royston, *New Directions in British Architecture*, London: Studio Vista, 1968.

—— 'Notes on the Concept of an Architectural Position', *AA Files* 1, 1981–2, pp. 111–14.

—— 'British Architecture: a Historiography', *UIA International Architect* 5, 1983, pp. 6–9.

Le Corbusier, *Vers une architecture*, Paris: Cres et Cie, 1923; *Towards a New Architecture*, trans F. Etchells, London: Rodker, 1927.

—— *Radiant City (La Ville radieuse)*, London: Architectural Press, 1967.

SELECT BIBLIOGRAPHY

Leach, Neil (ed.), *Rethinking Architecture*, London: Routledge, 1997.
Lefebvre, Henri, *The Production of Space*, Oxford: Blackwell, 1991.
Lokko, Lesley, *White Papers Black Marks*, London: Athlone Press, 2000.
Lyotard, J-F., *The Postmodern Condition: a Report on Knowledge*, Manchester: Manchester University Press, 1986.
McCorquodale, D., Wigglesworth, S. and Ruedi, K., *Desiring Practices: Architecture, Gender and the Interdisciplinary*, London: Black Dog, 1996.
McLuhan, Marshall, *The Gutenberg Galaxy*, London: Routledge, 1962.
—— *Understanding Media*, London: Routledge, 1964.
McLuhan, Marshall, and Fiore, Quentin, *The Medium is the Massage*, Harmondsworth: Penguin, 1967.
Middleton, Robin (ed.), *Architectural Associations: The Idea of the City*, London: Architectural Association, 1996.
Obrist, H. (ed.), *Re: CP*, Basel: Birkhauser, 2003
Pevsner, Nikolaus, *Pioneers of the Modern Movement from William Morris to Walter Gropius*, London: Faber & Faber, 1936.
—— *The Englishness of English Art*, London: Architectural Press, 1956.
——*Pioneers of Modern Design*, London: Thames & Hudson, 1960.
Price, Cedric, *Works*, London: Architectural Association, 1984.
Purdom, C.B., *How Should We Rebuild London?*, London: J.M. Dent, 1945.
Rasmussen, S.E., *London: the Unique City*, London: Penguin, 1960.
Rattenbury, Kester (ed.), *This Is Not Architecture: Media Constructions*, London: Routledge, 2002.
Read, Herbert, *Art and Industry*, London: Faber & Faber, 1956.
Report of the Royal Commission on the Distribution of the Industrial Population, (chair Montague Barlow) London: HMSO, 1940.
Richards, J.M., *Modern Architecture*, Harmondsworth: Penguin, 1940.
—— *Castles on the Ground*, London: Architectural Press, 1946.
—— (ed.), *The Functional Tradition in Early Industrial Buildings*, photographs by Eric de Maré, London: Architectural Press, 1958.
—— *Memoirs of an Unjust Fella*, London: Weidenfeld & Nicolson, 1980.
Richards, J.M.: see J. Mordaunt Crook, 'Sir James Richards (1907–92): a Bibliographical Tribute', in *Architectural History*, vol. 42, 1999, pp. 354–74 for a full bibliography.
Robbins, D. (ed.), *The Independent Group: Postwar Britain and the Aesthetics of Plenty*, Cambridge, MA: MIT Press, 1990.
Robertson, Howard, *The Principles of Architectural Composition*, London: Architectural Press, 1924.
—— 'Some Recent French Developments in Domestic Architecture', *AR*, January 1927, pp. 2–7.
—— *Modern Architectural Design*, London: Architectural Press, 1932.
Robertson, Howard: see Higgott, *Travels in Modern Architecture,* pp. 122–8, for a full bibliography of his and Yerbury's articles.
Rowe, Colin, *The Mathematics of the Ideal Villa*, Cambridge, MA: MIT Press, 1976.
Rowe, Colin and Koetter, Fred, *Collage City*, Cambridge, MA: MIT Press, 1978.

SELECT BIBLIOGRAPHY

—— *The Architecture of Good Intentions*, London: Academy Editions, 1994.
Russell, Barry, *Building Systems, Industrialisation and Architecture*, London: John Wiley, 1981.
Rykwert, Joseph, 'Review of a Review', *Zodiac* 4, 1959, pp. 12–15.
Sadler, Simon, *Situationist City*, Cambridge, MA: MIT Press, 1998.
—— *Archigram: Architecture without Architecture*, Cambridge, MA: MIT Press, 2005.
Saint, Andrew, *Towards a Social Architecture: the Role of School Building in Post-war England*, New Haven: Yale University Press, 1987.
St John Wilson, Colin, *The Other Tradition of Modern Architecture: the Uncompleted Project*, London: Academy, 1995.
Salter, Peter, *4+1 Building Projects*, London: Black Dog, 2000.
Schregenburger, T. *et al.*, *As Found*, Baden: Lars Müller, 2001.
Sennett, Richard, *The Uses of Disorder*, London: Penguin, 1971.
Shonfield, Katherine, *Walls Have Feelings: Architecture, Film and the City*, London: Routledge, 2000.
Silver, Nathan and Boys, Jos (eds), *Why Is British Architecture So Lousy?*, London: Newman Publications, 1980.
Sjaasted, M., 'From Mind to Matter', in *AA Files* 1, Winter 1981–2, vol. 1, no. 1, pp. 64–7.
Smithson, Alison, *Without Rhetoric*, London: Latimer New Dimensions, 1973.
Smithson, Alison and Smithson, Peter, *Ordinariness and Light*, London: Faber, 1970.
—— *Italian Thoughts*, London (privately published), 1993.
—— *The Charged Void: Architecture*, New York: Monacelli, 2001.
Sontag, Susan (ed.), *A Barthes Reader*, London: Vintage, 1993.
Spiller, Neil, *Digital Dreams: Architecture and the New Alchemic Technologies*, London: Ellipsis, 1998.
Steele, Brett, 'Designing the DRL' in *Corporate Fields*, London: Architectural Association, 2005.
Stirling, James, 'The "Functional Tradition" and Expression', *Perspecta* 6, 1960, pp. 88–97.
Summerson, J., *The Architectural Association*, London: Pleiades Books, 1947.
—— *45–55 Ten years of British Architecture*, London: Arts Council, 1956.
—— 'The Case for a Theory of Modern Architecture', *RIBA Journal*, June 1957, pp. 307–10.
—— (ed.), *Concerning Architecture: Essays on Architectural Writers and Writing*, London: Allen Lane, The Penguin Press, 1968.
Tafuri, M. and Dal Co, F., *Modern Architecture*, London: Academy, 1980.
Tönnies, F., *Community and Civil Society*, Cambridge: Cambridge University Press, 2001.
Tournikiotis, P., *The Historiography of Modern Architecture*, Cambridge, MA: MIT Press, 1999.
Tripp, H. Alker, *Town Planning and Road Traffic*, London: Edward Arnold, 1942.

SELECT BIBLIOGRAPHY

Tschumi, Bernard, *Manhattan Transcripts*, London: Academy, 1981.
—— *Questions of Space*, London: Architectural Association, 1990.
Tubbs, Ralph, *Living in Cities*, Harmondsworth: Penguin, 1942.
—— *The Englishman Builds*, Harmondsworth: Penguin, 1945.
Uthwatt Report, *Report of the Expert Committee on Compensation and Betterment*, London: HMSO, 1942.
Vesely, Dalibor, *Architecture in the Age of Divided Representation*, Cambridge, MA: MIT Press, 2004.
Waller, Maureen, *London 1945*, London: John Murray, 2005.
Walsh, Victoria, *Nigel Henderson: Parallel of Life and Art*, London: Thames & Hudson, 2001.
Warburton, Nigel, *Ernö Goldfinger: the Life of an Architect*, London: Routledge, 2004.
Watkin, David, *Architecture and Morality*, Oxford: Clarendon, 1977.
Webster, Helena (ed.), *Modernism without Rhetoric*, London: Academy, 1997.
Whitechapel Art Gallery, *This is Tomorrow*, London: 1956.
Whiteley, Nigel, *Reyner Banham: Historian of the Immediate Future*, Cambridge, MA: MIT Press, 2002.
Williams, Raymond, *Keywords*, London: Fontana, 1976.
Williams-Ellis, Clough (ed.), *Britain and the Beast*, London: Dent, 1937.
Wittkower, R., *Architectural Principles in the Age of Humanism*, London: Warburg Institute, 1949.
Yerbury, F.R. and Robertson, Howard, *Examples of Modern French Architecture*, London: Ernest Benn, 1928.
—— *Modern European Buildings*, London: Gollancz, 1928.
—— *Modern Dutch Buildings*, London: Ernest Benn, 1931.
Yorke, F.R.S., *The Modern House*, London: Architectural Press, 1934.
—— *The Modern House in England*, London: Architectural Press, 1937.
—— *The Modern Flat*, London: Architectural Press, 1937.

Index

9H 200, 203

Abercrombie, Patrick 59, 62
Abercrombie Plan (County of London Plan) (1943) 58–82; central London 72–5; *see also* Greater London Plan (1944) (Abercrombie)
aesthetic of modernism (*AR*) 42–51
Albert Dock, Liverpool *105*
'Albion' project, London 167
Alexander, Christopher 79
'Alkahest', London 165–6
Alsop, Will 198
anti-modernist movement 18
Archigram 13, 14–15, 121–33
Archigram (journal) *7*, 13, 121–9, 131–3, 147, 159
Architect and Building News 20–30
Architectural Association (AA) School 14, 21, 25, 39, 96–7, 103, 112, 125–6, 185, 196, 200; ambience 159–63; Alvin Boyarsky as Chairman 146, 154–62, 167–8, 176–81, 184; and MARS group 37; new programmes 163–77, 196; *Prospectus* 156, *157*, 172, 173; publications 177–84; Howard Robertson as Principal 21; Frank Yerbury as Secretary 21–2
Architectural Design (*AD*) 18–19, 89, 92–3, 120, *155*, 199, 202; 1960s 133–44; 1970s 144–7; and *Architectural Review* (*AR*) 120, 133–4, 137; 'Cosmorama' (*AD*) 135, 144, *145*, 146

Architectural Press 38, 39–40
Architectural Review (*AR*) *25*, *29*, 30, 34–55, 159, 161, 176; aesthetic of modernism 42–51; and *Architectural Design* (*AD*) 120, 133–4, 137; campaigns 107–9; Reyner Banham and 89, 92; Peter Davey as editor 199–200; 'functional tradition' 99–105, 110; layout and graphics 42–6; organicist tendency 199–200; James Richards as editor (1930s) 34–55, 100, 104, 106, 133–4, 197; role in 1930s 37–41; 'shift to the specific' 111–12, 113; and Alison and Peter Smithson 86, 89, 92, 110–11
architecture as discourse 5–6, 14–20, 190–7
Arts and Crafts movement 20, 26, 36, 97, 98; *see also* Morris, William; Ruskin, John

Bancroft, John 112
Banham, Reyner 21, 28, 87, 89, 92, 96, 98, 110–11, 118–20, 132
Barbican Estate, London *9*, 15, *113*, 149
Barlow Commission 67, 68–9
Barlow, Sir Montague 61–2, 63
Barthes, Roland 10, 11–12, 190
Bartlett School 17–18, 191, 196
Bauhaus 48, 179
Beaux-Arts School, Paris 21, 39, 107, 128, 162–3
Bentley Wood, Sussex 45–6
Betjeman, John 40, 42

212

INDEX

Beveridge Report (1942) 50, 60, 67
Birmingham *15*, 77
Bjerke, Arvid 22
Blackburn House, Hampstead, London *180*
Blomfield, Reginald 4, 14–15, 18, 21, 30, 37, 41
Bloomsbury 'university precinct', London 72, *73*
Blueprint (journal) 19–20
Borden, Iain 193–4, *195*
Boyarsky, Alvin 128, 146, 154–9, *155*, 160–84
Branson Coates *183*
British Museum, London 197
Brutalism 91–9, 112, 121
The Builder (journal) 26
Bunschoten, Raoul 177

Capsule Tower *124*
Caruso St John 112, 197, *198*, 200
Casson, Hugh 40, 46, *47*
Castro, Eva *201*
Chalk, Warren 122–3, *124*
Chamberlin Powell and Bon 9, *113*, 135
Chermayeff, Serge 45–6, 51
Churchill Gardens, Pimlico, London *75*
CIAM (Congrés Internationaux d'Architecture Moderne) 37, 38, 41, 61, 64, 91, 93
Circle (journal) 41
Coates, Nigel 164, 165, 166–8, 173
Cobb, Lyme Regis 102, *103*
Colomina, Beatriz 11, 30
Connell, Amyas 44
Connell, Ward and Lucas 53
Constant: 'New Babylon' 134–5
Cook, Peter 7, 121–33, *128*, 149, 158, 174–5, *176*, *196*; 'Plug-In City' *122*, 124
Copcutt, Geoffrey 15
'Cosmorama' (*AD*) 135, 144, *145*, 146
County of London Plan (1943) see Abercrombie Plan (County of London Plan) (1943)
Crompton, Dennis 122–33, 187
Crosby, Theo 89, 129, 133, 134
Cullen, Gordon *35*, 107–9, *110*
Cumbernauld Town Centre 15, 121
'Cushicle' 126–7, 141

Davey, Peter 109, 199–200
Davies, Mike 15
Debord, Guy 160
de Maré, Eric 101–6, 112
Dell, M. and Wainwright, H.L. 45, 48, 50
digital technology 195–7, *201*
discourse, architecture as 5–6, 10, 14–20, 190–7
Dubuffet, Jean 99
Dutch architecture 21–2, 26
Dymaxion House 119

Economist Building, St James's, London *98*
Electricity showrooms, Regent Street, London *44*
Eliot, T.S. 9
Empiricism 149
Entertainment Centre, Leicester Square, London 123, 134
Esher, Lionel 72
L'esprit nouveau 8
European architecture 21–9, 38, 39
Evans, Robin 169, 190
existentialism 99, 111

Festival of Britain, London 86–8
Firebrace, William 174, 177
Forshaw, J.H. *66*, 67
Forty, Adrian 11–12, 82, 190
Foster, Norman 144, 197–8, *199*, 200
Foucault, Michel 10, 11, 190
Frampton, Kenneth 133, 151, 159–60
French architecture 10, 24, *25*, 26, *27*, *28*, 46
Fretton, Tony 200
Frognal, Hampstead, London *53*
Fry, Maxwell *44*, 45, *52*, 63
Fuller, Buckminster 119, 120, 139, 140
'Fun Palace' 137–9, 150
'functional tradition' 99–107
Futurism 118–19, 120, 124

Garage Marbeuf, Paris *25*
Garches villa, France 26, *27*, *28*
'Garden City' tradition 63–4, 66, 72, 78, 89, 90
German architecture 24–5, 72
Gibberd, Frederick *78*, 87
Glasgow *81*

213

INDEX

Gold, Michael 168–9, 181
Grayswood, Sussex 44
Greater London Plan (1944) (Abercrombie) 67, 77–8
Greene, David 121–2, 126–7, 129
Grimshaw, Nick 126
Gropius, Walter 40, 41, 47–8, 63, 105–6

Hackney, London *13*, 72
Hadid, Zaha 172–3, 175, *181*, 200, 201
Harlow *78*
Hastings, Hubert de Cronin 38, 40, 44, 45, 51, 92, 100, 103, 107, 109, 133–4
Helicon office development, Moorgate, London *149*
Henderson, Nigel 88, 92, 93–4, *95*
Herron, Ron 122–7, *128*, 174–5, 181
Highpoint, Highgate, London 49–50
Hill, Jonathan 193, *194*
Hotel Puerta America, Madrid *201*
housing 25, 26, 135–6, 141; projects 112, *113*, 123; social 18, 140; villas 26, *27*, *28*, 46
Hughes, Francesca 194
Hunstanton, Norfolk 88

Independent Group 88–9, 92, 98
Inns of Court, London 72, 74
Instant City 127, *128*
International Style 21, 32, 38
Isozaki, Arata 34–5

Jackson, Anthony 87, 89–90
James and Pierce *29*
Jencks, Charles 18, 193
Jenkins, Gilbert 25

Kahn, Louis 106–7
Kehne, Holger *201*
Kensal House, Ladbroke Grove, London 52
Kipnis, Jeffrey 198–9
Koolhaas, Rem *19*, 171–3, 175, 197
Korn, A. and Samuely, F. 65
Krier, Leon 169, 170

Landau, Royston 11, 142, 149
Lasdun, Denys 46, *47*; Lasdun and Partners 5, 15
Le Corbusier 8, 11, 15, 24, 49–50, 64, 66, 78, 80, 106, 132; critics 25, 41; *Complete Works* 11; villas 26, *27*, *28*, 46
Lefebvre, Henri 185, 193
Libeskind, Daniel 170
Limbour, Georges 99
Ling, Arthur 67
Lisson Gallery, London 200
Living City exhibition (ICA) 129–31, 150
'Living Pod' 126–7
Llewelyn Davies, Richard 17–18, 31
Lloyd, Michael 159, 185
Lokko, Lesley 194
London: AA student projects 165–8; Abercrombie Plan (County of London Plan) (1943) 58–82; Albion Project 167; Barbican Estate 9, 15, *113*, 149; Blackburn House, Hampstead *180*; Bloomsbury 'university precinct' 72, *73*; British Museum 197; Churchill Gardens, Pimlico *75*; East End 93–4, 123; Economist Building, St James's *98*; Entertainment Centre, Leicester Square 123, 134; Frognal, Hampstead *53*; Greater London Plan (1944) 67, 77–8; Hackney *13*, 72; Harlow *78*; Helicon office development, Moorgate *149*; Highpoint, Highgate 49–50; Inns of Court 72, 74; Kensal House, Ladbroke Grove 52; Kentish Town project 171; Lisson Gallery 200; MARS Plan 65, 66; Millennium Dome 15–16; Mount Royal Flats, Oxford Street 47–8; National Theatre 5, 15, 149; Newton Road, Bayswater 46, *47*; Pimlico School 112; Pioneer Health Centre, Peckham 48–9, 53, 63; post-war 70–2, *74*, *76*; Regent Street *4*, 21, *44*; Shoreditch 70, *71*, 72, *76*; Soho House 92–3; South Bank 74–5, *76*–7, 88, 112; Stepney 69; wartime 58–9; Whitehall 72
Loos, Adolf 16, 98
Lubetkin, Berthold 49, 50, 55, 87

214

INDEX

Lynn, J. and Smith, I. 112, *113*
Lyme Regis 108; Cobb 102, *103*
Lyotard, Jean-François 192–3

Macdonald, Chris 165, 176, 181–2
McHale, John 139
McLuhan, Marshall 12–13, 200–1
MacQuedy, James (pseudonym of James Richards) 52, 55
MARS group 37, 38, 48, 61
MARS Plan for London 65, 66
mass production 18, 47–8
Mendelsohn, Erich *23*, 24, 25, 47–8
Middleton, Robin 135, 139, 144, 146, 147, 152, 177–8, 186
Millennium Dome, London 15–16
Miller, Jonathan 141
Moholy-Nagy, Laszlo *42*, 43, 179
Montreal exhibition 139–40
moral improvement and urban planning 64, 66
Morris, William 63, 66
Mostafavi, Mohsen 170, *179*
Mount Royal Flats, Oxford Street, London 47–8
Murray, Peter 19, 132, 133, 135, 178

Naf, Cornel 174
Nairn, Ian 82
National Theatre, London *5*, 15, 149
'neighbourhood units' 65–6, 69, 72
'New Empiricism' 92, 103
Newman, Barnett 98
Newton Road, Bayswater, London 46, *47*
New Towns 77–8, *78*
Norwich City Hall 27, *29*

Osaka Garden Exhibition, Japan *182*
Ostberg, Ragnar 22
'Outrage' campaign (*AR*) 107–8

Paolozzi, Eduardo 88–9, 93, 94, *95*
Papadakis, Andreas 18–19, 31
Paris 10, *25*, 147–9
Park Hill housing estate, Sheffield 112, *113*
'Patio and Pavilion', Whitechapel Gallery, London 93, 94–6
Pepler, George 77
Perez, Rodrigo 169
Pevsner, Nikolaus 20, 36, 118–19, 120

Piano, Renzo 147–8
Picturesque 87, 110
Pimlico School, London 112
Pioneer Health Centre, Peckham, London 48–9, 53, 63
Piper, John 51–2, 100–1, 106
Plasma Studio 201
'Plug-in City' 124–5, 135–6
Pompidou Centre, Paris 147–9
postmodernism 18, 192–3
'Potteries Thinkbelt' project 136–7, *138*, 141
Powell and Moya 75
precinct planning 72–5
Price, Cedric 122–3, 132–42, 150, 159, 181; 'Potteries Thinkbelt' project 136–7, *138*, 141
Prizeman, Mark 167
Prospectus (AA School) 156, *157*, 172, 173
publications 6–8, 190–7; AA School 177–84; *Archigram* 7, 13, 121–9, 131–3, 147, 159; *Architect and Building News* 20, 21, 23, 26, *27*; *Blueprint* 19–20; *The Builder* 26; *Circle* 41; *see also Architectural Design* (*AD*); *Architectural Review* (*AR*)
Pugin, A.W.N. 63
Purdom, C.B. 63–4

Rattenbury, Kester 12, *195*
Read, Herbert 87
reconstruction areas, post-war London 70–2, *74*, *76*
Reeve, Geoff *125*, 126
Regent Street, London *4*, 21, *44*
Reith, Lord 66–7, 75
Revington, Derek 165–6
Richards, James 34–7, 39–41, 48–56
Robertson, Howard 20–2, 24–6, *27*, 28–30, 32
Rogers, Richard (and Partners) 15, 144, 147–8, 199
Rowe, Colin 34, 60, 87, 111–12, 132, 163
Ruskin, John 63, 190
Rykwert, Joseph 109

St John, Peter 169, 175
St John Wilson, Colin 17
Salter, Peter 176, 181–2

215

INDEX

Sansom, Adrian 123
Sartre, Jean-Paul 99, 111
Saussure, Ferdinand de 9, 10
Schocken Shop, Stuttgart 23
Schools Building Programme, Hertfordshire CC 97
science, influence of 17–18, 82
Scott, Fred 157–8, 169
Scott, Giles 62, 68–9
Scott, Kenneth 93
Seaside, Architectural Review (AR) *42*, 43
Sennett, Richard 82
Shand, P. Morton 37, 55
Sheffield 96, 112
'shift to the specific' 111–12, 113
Shoreditch, London 70, *71*, 72, 76
skateboarders 193–4, *195*
Smithson, Alison and Peter 15, 16, 86, 87–97, 109–10, 112, 113, 133, 145, 200
Smout, Mark *196*
Soho House, London 92–3
South Bank, London 74–5, 76–7, 88, 112
Spiller, Neil 196
Stanley textile mill, Stroud Valley, Gloucester *104*
Steele, Brett 196–7
Stepney, London *69*
Stirling, James 88, 106, 111, 112, 141, 167–8
Stirling Prize 200
Stockholm Town Hall, Sweden 22
Structuralism 9
Sugden House, Watford 97
Summerson, John 86–7
Swedish architecture 22, 23, 26–8, *29*, 41

Tafuri, M. 192; and F. Dal Co 36, 81

Tatton Brown, William 61, 65
Taxim Nightpark, Istanbul *183*
technology 120–1, 139, 140–1; digital 195–7, *201*; tradition and 118
Tecton 49, 50, 51; *see also* Lubetkin, Berthold
Tönnies, F. 65–6
Townscape 107–9, 110
Trelawney Estate, Hackney, London *13*
Tripp, H. Alker 73–4
Tschumi, Bernard 163–4, 175, 184
Tubbs, Ralph 59, *60*
Turner, John 141

Unwin, Raymond 77
urban planning 58–66, 124–42, 150
Uthwatt Report 62, 68–9

van Schaik, Leon 159–60
Vesely, Dalibor 170, *171*, *179*
Vidler, Anthony 195–6
Villa Cook, Boulogne-sur-Seine, France 46

Walsall New Art Gallery 197, *198*, 200
Watkin, David 18
Webb, Mike 123, 126–7, 134, 141
Weissenhof Siedlung, Stuttgart 24
Wentworth, Richard 197–8
Williams, Owen 48, 63
Wilson, Ada 169
Wilson, Peter 173, *180*, 181
Wittkower, Rudolf 17

Yerbury, Frank 20–3, 24–6, *27*, 28–30, 41
Yorke, F.R.S. 36, *43*, *46*

Zenghelis, Elia 171–2